FOUR ESSAYS ON
LIBERTY

Sir Isaiah Berlin, OM, died in 1997. He was born in Riga, capital of Latvia, in 1909. When he was six, his family moved to Russia; there in 1917, in Petrograd, he witnessed both the Social-Democratic and the Bolshevik Revolutions.

In 1921 his family moved to England, and he was educated at St Paul's School and Corpus Christi College, Oxford. At Oxford he was a Fellow of All Souls, a Fellow of New College, Professor of Social and Political Theory, and founding President of Wolfson College. He also held the Presidency of the British Academy.

From the reviews:

'These famous essays . . . are informed by that radical humanism, in the truest sense of that impoverished word, which has attached Sir Isaiah so closely to such nineteenth-century figures as Herzen and Mill, and which has enabled him to find the same spirit lurking behind even the gruff beard and encrusted reputation of Karl Marx.'

Observer

'*Historical Inevitability* is the finest thing Mr Berlin has produced so far . . . a magnificent assertion of the reality of human freedom, of the role of free choice in history.'

The Economist

ISAIAH BERLIN

FOUR ESSAYS ON
LIBERTY

Oxford New York

OXFORD UNIVERSITY PRESS

Oxford University Press, Great Clarendon Street, Oxford OX2 6DP

Oxford New York

Athens Auckland Bangkok Bogota Bombay
Buenos Aires Calcutta Cape Town Dar es Salaam
Delhi Florence Hong Kong Istanbul Karachi
Kuala Lumpur Madras Madrid Melbourne
Mexico City Nairobi Paris Singapore
Taipei Tokyo Toronto Warsaw

and associated companies in
Berlin Ibadan

Oxford is a registered trade mark of Oxford University Press

Published in the United States
by Oxford University Press Inc., New York

First issued as an
Oxford University Press paperback 1969

British Library Cataloguing in Publication Data

Data available

Library of Congress Cataloging in Publication Data
Berlin, Sir Isaiah.
Four essays on liberty.
1. Liberty.
I. Title
123   JC585
ISBN 0-19-281034-0

Printed in Great Britain by
Cox & Wyman Ltd,
Reading, Berkshire

To Stephen Spender

CONTENTS

INTRODUCTION

'L'on immole à l'être abstrait les êtres réels: et l'on offre au peuple en masse l'holocauste du peuple en détail.'

BENJAMIN CONSTANT, *De l'esprit de conquête.*

I

THE first of the four essays in this book appeared in the mid-century number of the New York periodical *Foreign Affairs*; the remaining three originated in lectures.[1] They deal with various aspects of individual liberty. They are concerned in the first place with the vicissitudes of this notion during the ideological struggles of our century; secondly, with the meaning it is given in the writings of historians, social scientists, and writers who examine the presuppositions and methods of history or sociology; thirdly, with the importance of two major conceptions of liberty in the history of ideas; and, finally, with the part played by the ideal of individual liberty in the outlook of one of its most devoted champions, John Stuart Mill.

The first and last of these essays evoked little comment. The second and third stimulated wide and, as it seems to me, fruitful controversy. Since some of my opponents have advanced objections that seem to me both relevant and just, I propose to make it clear where I think that I stand convicted of mistakes or obscurities; other strictures (as I hope to show) seem to me mistaken. Some of my severest critics attack my views without adducing either facts or arguments, or else impute to me opinions that I do not hold; and even though this may at times be due to my own lack of clarity, I do not feel obliged to discuss, still less to defend, positions which, in some cases, appear to me as absurd as they do to those who assail them.[2]

[1] My thanks are due to the institutions at whose invitations the lectures were delivered, and to the respective publishers of the essays for granting permission for their republication.

[2] While I have not altered the text in any radical fashion, I have made a number of changes intended to clarify some of the central points which have been misunderstood

The main issues between my serious critics and myself may be reduced to four heads: firstly, determinism and its relevance to our notions of men and their history; secondly, the place of value judgments, and, in particular, of moral judgments, in historical and social thinking; thirdly, the possibility and desirability of distinguishing, in the realm of political theory, what modern writers have called 'positive' liberty from 'negative' liberty, and the relevance of this distinction to the further difference between liberty and the conditions of liberty, as well as the question of what it is that makes liberty, of either sort, intrinsically worth pursuing or possessing; and finally, the issue of monism, of the unity or harmony of human ends. It seems to me that the unfavourable contrast sometimes drawn between 'negative' liberty and other, more obviously positive, social and political ends sought by men—such as unity, harmony, peace, rational self-direction, justice, self-government, order, co-operation in the pursuit of common purposes—has its roots, in some cases, in an ancient doctrine according to which all truly good things are linked to one another in a single, perfect whole; or, at the very least, cannot be incompatible with one another. This entails the corollary that the realization of the pattern formed by them is the one true end of all rational activity, both public and private. If this belief should turn out to be false or incoherent, this might destroy or weaken the basis of much past and present thought and activity; and, at the very least, affect conceptions of, and the value placed on, personal and social liberty. This issue, too, is therefore both relevant and fundamental.

Let me begin with the most celebrated question of all as it affects human nature: that of determinism, whether causal or teleological. My thesis is not, as has been maintained by some of my most vehement critics, that it is certain (still less that I can show) that determinism is false; only that the arguments in favour of it are not conclusive; and that if it ever becomes a widely accepted belief and enters the texture of general thought

by critics and reviewers. I am most grateful to Professors S. N. Hampshire, H. L. A. Hart, and Thomas Nagel and Mr. Patrick Gardiner for drawing my attention to errors and obscurities. I have done my best to remedy these, without, I feel sure, fully satisfying these distinguished and helpful critics.

and conduct, the meaning and use of certain concepts and words central to human thought would become obsolete or else have to be drastically altered. This entails the corollary that the existing use of these basic words and concepts constitutes some evidence, not, indeed, for the proposition that determinism is false, but for the hypothesis that many of those who profess this doctrine seldom, if ever, practise what they preach, and (if my thesis is valid) seem curiously unaware of what seems, prima facie, a lack of correspondence between their theory and their real convictions, as these are expressed in what they do and say. The fact that the problem of free will is at least as old as the Stoics; that it has tormented ordinary men as well as professional philosophers; that it is exceptionally difficult to formulate clearly; that medieval and modern discussions of it, while they have achieved a finer analysis of the vast cluster of the concepts involved, have not in essentials brought us any nearer a definitive solution; that while some men seem naturally puzzled by it, others look upon such perplexity as mere confusion, to be cleared away by some single powerful philosophical solvent, all this gives determinism a peculiar status among philosophical questions. I have, in these essays, made no systematic attempt to discuss the problem of free will as such, but principally its relevance to the idea of causality in history. Here I can only restate my original thesis that it seems to me patently inconsistent to assert, on the one hand, that all events are wholly determined to be what they are by other events (whatever the status of this proposition[1]), and, on the other, that men are free to choose between at least two possible courses of action—free not merely in the sense of being able to do what they choose to do (and because they choose to do it), but in the sense of not being determined to choose what they choose by causes outside their control. If it is held that every act of will or choice is fully determined by its respective antecedents, then (despite all that has been said against this) it still seems to me that this belief is incompatible with the notion of choice held by ordinary men and by

[1] It has the appearance of a universal statement about the nature of things. But it can scarcely be straightforwardly empirical, for what item of experience would count as evidence against it?

philosophers when they are not consciously defending a determinist position. More particularly, I see no way round the fact that the habit of giving moral praise and blame, of congratulating and condemning men for their actions, with the implication that they are morally responsible for them, since they could have behaved differently, that is to say, need not have acted as they did (in some sense of 'could' and 'need' which is not purely logical or legal, but in which these terms are used in ordinary empirical discourse by both men in the street and historians), would be undermined by belief in determinism. No doubt the same words could still be used by determinists to express admiration or contempt for human characteristics or acts; or to encourage or deter; and such functions may be traceable to the early years of human society. However that may be, without the assumption of freedom of choice and responsibility in the sense in which Kant used these terms, one, at least, of the ways in which they are now normally used is, as it were, annihilated. Determinism clearly takes the life out of a whole range of moral expressions. Very few defenders of determinism have addressed themselves to the question of what this range embraces and (whether or not this is desirable) what the effect of its elimination on our thought and language would be. Hence I believe that those historians or philosophers of history who maintain that responsibility and determinism are never incompatible with one another are mistaken whether or not some form of determinism is true;[1] and again, whether or not some form of belief in the reality of moral responsibility is justified, what seems clear is that these possibilities are mutually exclusive: both beliefs may be groundless, but both cannot be true. I have not attempted to adjudicate between these alternatives; only to maintain that men have, at all times, taken freedom of choice for granted in their ordinary discourse. And I further argue that if men became truly convinced that this belief was mistaken, the revision and transformation

[1] What kind of incompatibility this is, logical, conceptual, psychological, or of some other kind, is a question to which I do not volunteer an answer. The relations of factual beliefs to moral attitudes (or beliefs)—both the logic and psychology of this— seem to me to need further philosophical investigation. The thesis that no relevant logical relationship exists, e.g. the division between fact and value often attributed to Hume, seems to me to be implausible, and to point to a problem, not to its solution.

of the basic terms and ideas that this realization would call for would be greater and more upsetting than the majority of contemporary determinists seem to realize. Beyond this I did not go, and do not propose to go now.

The belief that I undertook to demonstrate that determinism is false—on which much criticism of my argument has been based—is unfounded. I am obliged to say this with some emphasis, since some of my critics (notably Mr. E. H. Carr) persist in attributing to me a claim to have refuted determinism. But this, like another odd view ascribed to me, namely that historians have a positive duty to moralize, is a position that I have never defended or held; this is a point to which I shall have occasion to revert later. More specifically, I have been charged with confusing determinism with fatalism.[1] But this, too, is a complete misunderstanding. I assume that what is meant or implied by fatalism is the view that human decisions are mere by-products, epiphenomena, incapable of influencing events which take their inscrutable course independently of human wishes. I have never attributed this implausible position to any of my opponents. The majority of them cling to 'self-determinism'—the doctrine according to which men's characters and 'personality structures' and the emotions, attitudes, choices, decisions, and acts that flow from them do indeed play a full part in what occurs, but are themselves results of causes, psychical and physical, social and individual, which in turn are effects of other causes, and so on, in unbreakable sequence. According to the best-known version of this doctrine, I am free if I can do what I wish and, perhaps, choose which of two courses of action I shall take. But my choice is itself causally determined; for if it were not, it would be a random event; and these alternatives exhaust the possibilities; so that to describe choice as free in some further sense, as neither caused nor random, is to attempt to say something meaningless. This classical view, which to most philosophers appears to dispose of the problem of free will, seems to me simply a variant of the general determinist thesis, and to rule out responsibility no less than its 'stronger' variant. Such

[1] See A. K. Sen, 'Determinism and Historical Predictions', *Inquiry*, no. 2, New Delhi, 1959, pp. 99-115. Also Gordon Leff in *The Tyranny of Concepts*, pp. 146-9.

'self-determinism' or 'weak determinism', in which, since its original formulation by the Stoic sage Chrysippus, many thinkers have come to rest, was described by Kant as 'a miserable subterfuge'. William James labelled it 'soft determinism', and called it, perhaps too harshly, 'a quagmire of evasion'.

I cannot see how one can say of Helen not only that hers was the face that launched a thousand ships but, in addition, that she was responsible for (and did not merely cause) the Trojan War, if the war was due solely to something that was the result not of a free choice—to elope with Paris—which Helen need not have made, but only of her irresistible beauty. Mr. Sen, in his clear and moderately worded criticism, concedes what some of his allies do not—that there is an inconsistency between, at any rate, some meanings attached to the contents of ordinary moral judgment on the one hand, and determinism on the other. He denies, however, that belief in determinism need eliminate the possibility of rational moral judgment, on the ground that such judgments could still be used to influence men's conduct, by acting as stimuli or deterrents. In somewhat similar terms, Professor Ernest Nagel, in the course of a characteristically scrupulous and lucid argument,[1] says that, even on the assumption of determinism, praise, blame, and assumption of responsibility generally could affect human behaviour—e.g. by having an effect on discipline, effort, and the like, whereas they would (presumably) not in this way affect a man's digestive processes or the circulation of his blood. This may be true but it does not affect the central issue. Our value judgments—eulogies or condemnations of the acts or characters of men dead and gone—are not intended solely, or even primarily, to act as utilitarian devices, to encourage or warn our contemporaries, or as beacons to posterity. When we speak in this way we are not attempting merely to influence future action (though we may, in fact, be doing this too) or solely to formulate quasi-aesthetic judgments—as when we testify to the beauty or ugliness, intelligence or stupidity, generosity or meanness of others (or ourselves)—attributes

BUT IT DOES

---

[1] *The Structure of Science*, New York, 1961, pp. 599-604. Also, by the same author, 'Determinism in History', *Philosophy and Phenomenological Research*, vol. xx, no. 3, March 1960, pp. 311-17.

which we are then simply attempting to grade according to some scale of values. If someone praises or condemns me for choosing as I did, I do not always say either 'this is how I am made; I cannot help behaving so', or 'please go on saying this, it is having an excellent effect on me: it strengthens (or weakens) my resolution to go to war, or to join the Communist Party'. It may be that such words, like the prospect of rewards and punishments, do affect conduct in important ways, and that this makes them useful or dangerous. But this is not the point at issue. It is whether such praise, blame, and so on, are merited, morally appropriate, or not. One can easily imagine a case where we think that a man deserves blame, but consider that to utter it may have a bad effect, and therefore say nothing. But this does not alter the man's desert, which, whatever its analysis, entails that the agent could have chosen, and not merely acted, otherwise. If I judge that a man's conduct was in fact determined, that he could not have behaved (felt, thought, desired, chosen) otherwise, I should regard this kind of praise or blame as inappropriate to his case. If determinism is true, the concept of merit or desert, as these are usually understood, has no application. If all things and events and persons are determined, then praise and blame do indeed become purely pedagogical devices—hortatory and minatory; or else they are quasi-descriptive—they grade in terms of distance from some ideal. They comment on the quality of men, what men are and can be and do, and may themselves alter it and, indeed, be used as deliberate means towards it, as when we reward or punish an animal; save that in the case of men we assume the possibility of communication with them, which we cannot do in the case of animals. This is the heart of the 'soft' determinism—the so-called Hobbes-Hume-Schlick doctrine. If, however, the notions of desert, merit, responsibility, etc., rested on the notion of choices not themselves fully caused, they would, on this view, turn out to be irrational or incoherent; and would be abandoned by rational men. The majority of Spinoza's interpreters suppose him to have maintained precisely this, and a good many of them think that he was right. But whether or not Spinoza did in fact hold this view, and whether or not he was right in this respect, my thesis is that, however it may be with

Spinoza, most men and most philosophers and historians do not speak or act as if they believe this. For if the determinist thesis is genuinely accepted, it should, at any rate to men who desire to be rational and consistent, make a radical difference. Mr. Sen with admirable consistency and candour does indeed explain that, when determinists use the language of moral praise and blame, they are like atheists who still mention God, or lovers who speak of being faithful 'to the end of time';[1] such talk is hyperbolic and not meant to be taken literally. This does at least concede (as most determinists do not) that if these words were taken literally something would be amiss. For my part I see no reason for supposing that most of those who use such language, with its implication of free choice among alternatives, whether in the future or in the past, mean this not literally, but in some Pickwickian or metaphorical or rhetorical way. Professor Ernest Nagel points out that determinists, who, like Bossuet, believed in the omnipotence and omniscience of Providence and its control over every human step, nevertheless freely attributed moral responsibility to individuals; and that adherents of determinist faiths—Moslems, Calvinists, etc.—have not refrained from attribution of responsibility and a generous use of praise and blame.[2] Like much that Professor Ernest Nagel says, this is perfectly true.[3] But it is nothing to the issue: the fact that not all human beliefs are coherent is not novel. These examples merely point to the fact that men evidently find it perfectly possible to

---

[1] Op. cit.

[2] *The Structure of Science*, pp. 603-4.

[3] See also a similar but equally unconvincing argument in the inaugural lecture by Professor Sydney Pollard at Sheffield University (*Past and Present*, no. 30, April 1965, pp. 3-22). Much of what Professor Pollard says seems to me valid and worth saying, but his view, supported by an appeal to history, that men's professions must be consistent with their practice is to say the least oddly surprising in a historian. Professor Nagel (op. cit., p. 602) suggests that belief in free will may relate to determinism much as the conviction that a table has a hard surface relates to the hypothesis that it consists of whirling electrons; the two descriptions answer questions at different levels, and therefore do not clash. This does not seem to me an apt parallel. To believe that the table is hard, solid, at rest, etc., entails no beliefs about electrons; and is, in principle, compatible with any doctrine about them: the levels do not touch. But if I supposed a man to have acted freely, and am later told that he acted as he did because he was 'made that way', and could not have acted differently, I certainly suppose that something that I believed is being denied.

subscribe to determinism in the study and disregard it in their lives. Fatalism has not bred passivity in Moslems, nor has determinism sapped the vigour of Calvinists or Marxists, although some Marxists feared that it might. Practice sometimes belies profession, no matter how sincerely held.

Mr. E. H. Carr goes a good deal further. He declares: 'The fact is that all human actions are both free and determined, according to the point of view from which one considers them.' And again: 'Adult human beings are responsible for their own personality.'[1] This seems to me to present the reader with an insoluble puzzle. If Mr. Carr means that human beings can transform the nature of their personality, while all antecedents remain the same, then he denies causality; if they cannot, and acts can be fully accounted for by character, then talk of responsibility (in the ordinary sense of this word in which it implies moral blame) does not make sense. There are no doubt many senses of 'can'; and much light has been shed on this by important distinctions made by acute modern philosophers. Nevertheless, if I literally cannot make my character or behaviour other than it is by an act of choice (or a whole pattern of such acts) which is itself not fully determined by causal antecedents, then I do not see in what normal sense a rational person could hold me morally responsible either for my character or for my conduct. Indeed the notion of a morally responsible being becomes, at best, mythological; this fabulous creature joins the ranks of nymphs and centaurs. The horns of this dilemma have been with us for over two millennia, and it is useless to try to escape or soften them by the comfortable assertion that it all depends on the point of view from which we regard the question. This problem which preoccupied Mill (and to which, in the end, he returned so confused an answer) and from the torment of which William James escaped only as a result of reading Renouvier, and which is still well to the forefront of philosophical attention, cannot be brushed aside by saying that the questions to which scientific determinism is the answer are different from those which are answered by the doctrine of voluntarism and freedom of choice between alternatives; or that the two types of question arise at

[1] *What is History?* London, 1964, p. 95.

different 'levels', so that a pseudo-problem has arisen from the confusion of these 'levels' (or the corresponding categories). The question to which determinism and indeterminism, whatever their obscurities, are the rival answers is one and not two. What kind of question it is—empirical, conceptual, metaphysical, pragmatic, linguistic—and what schema or model of man and nature is implicit in the terms used are major philosophical issues; but it would be out of place to discuss them here.

Nevertheless, if only because some of the sharpest criticisms of my thesis come from philosophers concerned with this central issue, it cannot be entirely ignored. Thus Professor J. A. Passmore[1] urges two considerations against me: (a) that the concept of Laplace's observer who can infallibly predict the future, since he has all the relevant knowledge of antecedent conditions and laws that he needs, cannot in principle be formulated, because the notion of an exhaustive list of all the antecedents of an event is not coherent; we can never say of any state of affairs 'these are all the antecedents there are; the inventory is complete'. This is clearly true. Nevertheless, even if determinism were offered as no more than a pragmatic policy: 'I intend to act and think on the assumption that every event has an identifiable sufficient cause or causes', this would satisfy the determinist's demand. Yet such a resolve would make a radical difference, for it would effectively take the life out of any morality that works with such notions as responsibility, moral worth, and freedom in Kant's sense, and do so in ways and with logical consequences which determinists as a rule either forbear to examine, or else play down. (b) That the more we find out about a prima facie morally culpable act, the more we are likely to realize that the agent, given the particular circumstances, characters, antecedent causes involved, was prevented from taking the various courses which we think he should have adopted; we condemn him too easily for failing to do or be what he could not have done or been. Ignorance, insensitiveness, haste, lack of imagination darken counsel and blind us to the true facts; our judgments are often shallow, dogmatic, complacent, irresponsible, unjust, barbarous. I sympathize with the humane and civilized considerations which

[1] *Philosophical Review*, vol. 68, 1959, pp. 93-102.

inspire Professor Passmore's verdict. Much injustice and cruelty has sprung from avoidable ignorance, prejudice, dogma, and lack of understanding. Nevertheless to generalize this—as Professor Passmore seems to me to do—is to fall into the old *tout comprendre* fallacy in disarmingly modern dress. If (as happens to those who are capable of genuine self-criticism) the more we discover about ourselves the less we are inclined to forgive ourselves, why should we assume that the opposite is valid for others, that we alone are free, while others are determined? To expose the deleterious consequences of ignorance or irrationality is one thing; to assume that these are the sole sources of moral indignation is an illicit extrapolation; it would follow from Spinozist premises, but not necessarily from others. Because our judgments about others are often superficial or unfair, it does not follow that one must never judge at all; or, indeed, that one can avoid doing so. As well forbid all men to count, because some cannot add correctly.

Professor Morton White attacks my contentions from a somewhat different angle.[1] He concedes that one may not, as a rule, condemn (as being 'wrong') acts which the agent could not help perpetrating (e.g. Booth's killing of Lincoln, on the assumption that he was caused to choose to do this, or anyway to do it whether or not he so chose). Or at least Mr. White thinks that it is unkind to blame a man for a causally determined action; unkind, unfair, but not inconsistent with determinist beliefs. We could, he supposes, conceive of a culture in which such moral verdicts would be normal. Hence it may be mere parochialism on our part to assume that the discomfort we may feel in calling causally determined acts right or wrong is universal, and springs from some basic category which governs the experience of all possible societies. Professor White discusses what is implied by calling an act 'wrong'. I am concerned with such expressions as 'blameworthy', 'something you should not have done', 'deserving to be condemned'—none of which is equivalent to 'wrong' or,

---

[1] *Foundations of Historical Knowledge*, New York, 1965, pp. 276 ff.). I cannot pretend to be able to do justice here to the complex and interesting thesis which Professor White's luminous book expounds. I hope to do so elsewhere and ask him to forgive me for the summary character of this brief rejoinder.

necessarily, to each other. But even so, I wonder whether Professor White, if he met a kleptomaniac, would think it reasonable to say to him: 'You cannot, it is true, help choosing to steal, even though you may think it wrong to do so. Nevertheless you must not do it. Indeed, you should choose to refrain from it. If you go on, we shall judge you not only to be a wrongdoer, but to deserve moral blame. Whether this deters you or not, you will deserve it equally in either case.' Would Professor White not feel that something was seriously amiss about such an approach, and that not merely in our own society, but in any world in which such moral terminology made sense? Or would he think this very question to be evidence of insufficient moral imagination in the questioner? Is it merely unkind or unfair to reproach men with what they cannot avoid doing, or, like much cruelty and injustice, irrational too? If you said to a man who betrayed his friends under torture that he should not have done this, that his act was morally wrong, even though you are convinced that, being what he is, he could not help choosing to act as he did, could you, if pressed, give reasons for your verdict? What could they be? That you wished to alter his (or others') behaviour in the future? Or that you wished to ventilate your revulsion? If this were all, questions of doing him justice would not enter at all. Yet if you were told that in blaming a man you were being unfair or wickedly blind, because you had not troubled to examine the difficulties under which the man laboured, the pressures upon him, and so on, this kind of reproach rests on the assumption that in some cases, if not in all, the man could have avoided the choice that you condemn, only a good deal less easily than you realize, at the price of martyrdom, or the sacrifice of the innocent, or at some cost which your critic believes that you, the moralizer, have no right to demand. Hence the critic rightly reproaches you for culpable ignorance or inhumanity. But if you really thought that it was (causally) impossible for the man to have chosen what you would have preferred him to choose, is it reasonable to say that he should nevertheless have chosen it? What reasons can you, in principle, adduce for attributing responsibility or applying moral rules to him (e.g. Kant's maxims which we understand whether or not we accept them) which you would not think it reasonable to apply in the case of compulsive choosers—kleptomaniacs, dipsomaniacs, and the like? Where would you draw the line, and why? If the choices in all these cases are causally determined, however different the causes, in some cases being compatible (or, according to some views, identical) with the use of reason, in others not, why is it rational to blame in one case and not in the other? I exclude the utilitarian argument for praise or blame or threats or other incentives, since Mr. White, rightly in my view, ignores it too, to concentrate on the moral quality of blame. I cannot see why it is less unreasonable (and not merely less futile) to blame a man psychologically unable to refrain from it for acting cruelly than a physical cripple for possessing a deformed limb. To condemn a murderer is no more or less rational than to blame his dagger; so reasoned Godwin. At least he was consistent in his fanatical way. Although his best-known book is called *Political Justice*, it is not easy to tell what justice, as a moral concept, would mean to a convinced determinist. I could grade just and unjust acts, like legal and illegal ones, like ripe and unripe peaches. But if a man could not help acting as he did, how much would it mean to say that something 'served him right'? The notion of poetic justice, of just deserts, of moral desert as such, would, if this were the case, not merely have no application, but become scarcely intelligíble. When Samuel Butler in *Erewhon* makes crimes objects of sympathy and pity, but ill health an offence which leads to sanctions, he is set on emphasizing not the relativity of moral values, but their irrationality in his own society—the irrationality of blame directed at moral or mental aberrations, but not to physical or physiological ones. I know of no more vivid way of bringing out how different our moral terminology and conduct would be if we were the really consistent scientific determinists that some suppose that we ought to be. The more rigorous sociological determinists do indeed say precisely this, and consider that not only retribution or revenge, but justice too—outside its strictly legal sense—conceived as a moral standard or canon not determined by alterable rules, is a prescientific notion grounded in psychological immaturity and error. As against this Spinoza and Mr. Sen seem to me to be right. There are some terms which, if we took determinism seriously, we should no longer use, or use only in some peculiar sense, as we speak of witches or the Olympian Gods. Such notions as justice, equity, desert, fairness would certainly have to be re-examined if they were to be kept alive at all and not relegated to the role of discarded figments—fancies rendered harmless by the march of reason, myths potent in our irrational youth, exploded, or at any rate rendered innocuous, by the progress of scientific knowledge. If determinism is valid, this is a price that we must pay. Whether or not we are ready to do so, let this prospect at least be faced.

If our moral concepts belong only to our own culture and society, then what we should be called upon to say to a member of Mr. White's unfamiliar culture is not that he was logically contradicting himself in professing determinism and yet continuing to utter or imply moral judgments of Kantian sort, but that he was being incoherent, that we could not see what reasons he could have for using such terms, that his language, if it was intended to apply to the real world, was no longer sufficiently intelligible to us. Of course the fact that there have been, and no doubt may still be, plenty of thinkers, even in our own culture, who at one and the same time profess belief in determinism, and yet do not feel in the least inhibited from dispensing this kind of moral praise and blame freely, and pointing out to others how they should have chosen, shows only, if I am right, that some normally lucid and self-critical thinkers are at times liable to confusion. My case, in other words, amounts to making explicit what most men do not doubt—namely that it is not rational both to believe that choices are caused, and to consider men as deserving of reproach or indignation (or their opposites) for choosing to act or refrain as they do.

The supposition that, if determinism were shown to be valid, ethical language would have to be drastically revised is not a psychological or a physiological, still less an ethical, hypothesis. It is an assertion about what any system of thought that employs the basic concepts of our normal morality would permit or exclude. The proposition that it is unreasonable to condemn men whose choices are not free rests not on a particular set of moral values (which another culture might reject) but on the particular nexus between descriptive and evaluative concepts which governs the language we use and the thoughts we think. To say that you might as well morally blame a table as an ignorant barbarian or an incurable addict is not an ethical proposition, but one which emphasizes the conceptual truth that this kind of praise and blame makes sense only among persons capable of free choice. This is what Kant appeals to; it is this fact that puzzled the early Stoics; before them freedom of choice seems to have been taken for granted; it is presupposed equally in Aristotle's discussion of voluntary and involuntary acts and in the thinking of unphilosophical persons to this day.

One of the motives for clinging to determinism seems to be the fear on the part of the friends of reason that it is presupposed by scientific method as such. Thus Professor S. N. Hampshire tells us that:

In the study of human behaviour, philosophical superstition might now easily take over the role of traditional religious superstitions as an obstruction to progress. In this context superstition is a confusion of the belief that human beings ought not to be treated as if they were natural objects with the belief that they are not in reality natural objects: one may so easily move from the moral proposition that persons ought not to be manipulated and controlled, like any other natural objects, to the different, and quasi-philosophical, proposition that they cannot be manipulated and controlled like any other natural objects. In the present climate of opinion a very natural fear of planning and social technology is apt to be dignified as a philosophy of indeterminism.[1]

This strongly worded cautionary statement seems to me characteristic of the widespread and influential feeling I have mentioned that science and rationality are in danger if determinism is rejected or even doubted. This fear appears to me to be groundless; to do one's best to find quantitative correlations and explanations is not to assume that everything is quantifiable; to proclaim that science is the search for causes (whether this is true or false) is not to say that all events have them. Indeed the

[1] *The Listener*, 7 September 1967, p. 291.

passage that I have quoted seems to me to contain at least three puzzling elements:

(*a*) We are told that to confuse 'the belief that human beings ought not to be treated as if they were natural objects with the belief that they are not in reality natural objects' is superstitious. But what other reason have I for not treating human beings 'as if they were natural objects' than my belief that they differ from natural objects in some particular respects—those in virtue of which they are human—and that this fact is the basis of my moral conviction that I should not treat them as objects, i.e. solely as means to my ends, and that it is in virtue of this difference that I consider it wrong freely to manipulate, coerce, brainwash them, etc.? If I am told not to treat something as a chair, the reason for this may be the fact that the object in question possesses some attribute which ordinary chairs do not, or has some special association for me or others which distinguishes it from ordinary chairs, a characteristic which might be overlooked or denied. Unless men are held to possess some attribute over and above those which they have in common with other natural objects— animals, plants, things, etc.—(whether this difference is itself called natural or not), the moral command not to treat men as animals or things has no rational foundation. I conclude that, so far from being a confusion of two different kinds of proposition, this connexion between them cannot be severed without making at least one of them groundless; and this is certainly unlikely to forward the progress of which the author speaks.

(*b*) As for the warning not to move from the proposition that 'persons ought not to be manipulated and controlled' to the proposition that 'they cannot be manipulated or controlled like any other natural object', it is surely more reasonable to suppose that if I tell you not to do it, that is not because I think persons cannot be so treated, but because I believe that it is all too likely that they can. If I order you not to control and manipulate human beings, it is not because I think that, since you cannot succeed, this will be a sad waste of your time and effort; but on the contrary, because I fear that you may succeed all too well, and that this will deprive men of their freedom, a freedom which, if they can only escape from too much control and manipulation, I believe they may be able to preserve.

(c) 'Fear of planning and social technology' may well be most acutely felt by those who believe that these forces are not irresistible; and that if men are not too much interfered with they will have opportunities of choosing freely between possible courses of action, not merely (as determinists believe) of, at best, implementing choices themselves determined and predictable. The latter may in fact be our actual condition. But if one prefers the former state—however difficult it may be to formulate—is this is a superstition, or some other case of 'false consciousness'? It is such only if determinism is true. But this is a viciously circular argument. Could it not be maintained that determinism itself is a superstition generated by a false belief that science will be compromised unless it is accepted, and is therefore itself a case of 'false consciousness' generated by a mistake about the nature of science? Any doctrine could be turned into a super-stition, but I do not myself see any reason for holding that either determinism or indeterminism is, or need turn into, one.[1]

To return to non-philosophical writers. The writings of those who have stressed the inadequacy of the categories of the natural sciences when applied to human action have so far transformed the question as to discredit the crude solutions of the nineteenth- and twentieth-century materialists and positivists. Hence all serious discussion of the issues must now begin by taking some account of the world-wide discussion of the subject during the last quarter of the century. When Mr. E. H. Carr maintains that to attribute historical events to the acts of individuals ('bio-graphical bias') is childish, or at any rate child-like, and that the more impersonal we make our historical writing the more scientific, and therefore mature and valid, it will be, he shows himself a faithful—too faithful—follower of the eighteenth-century dogmatic materialists.[2] This doctrine no longer seemed

[1] Hampshire replies: 'The injunction not to treat men as merely natural objects defines the moral point of view precisely because, being studied from the scientific point of view, men can be so treated. Sir Isaiah Berlin disagrees with me (and with Kant) in regarding the question "Are men only natural objects?" as an empirical issue, while I hold that, since no one *can* treat himself as merely a natural object, no one *ought* to treat another as merely a natural object.   [2] *The Listener*, 7 September 1967, p. 291.

altogether plausible even in the day of Comte and his followers, or, for that matter, of the father of Russian Marxism, Plekhanov, who, for all his brilliance, in his philosophy of history owed more to eighteenth-century materialism and nineteenth-century positivism than to Hegel or the Hegelian elements in Marx. Let me give Mr. Carr his due. When he maintains that animism or anthropomorphism—the attribution of human properties to inanimate entities—is a symptom of a primitive mentality, I have no wish to controvert this. But to compound one fallacy with another seldom advances the cause of truth. Anthropomorphism is the fallacy of applying human categories to the non-human world. But then there presumably exists a region where human categories do apply: namely the world of human beings. To suppose that only what works in the description and prediction of non-human nature must necessarily apply to human beings too, and that the categories in terms of which we distinguish the human from the non-human must therefore be delusive—to be explained away as aberrations of our early years —is the opposite error, the animist or anthropomorphic fallacy stood on its head. What scientific method can achieve, it must, of course, be used to achieve. Anything that statistical methods or computers or any other instrument or method fruitful in the natural sciences can do to classify, analyse, predict, or 'retrodict' human behaviour should, of course, be welcomed; to refrain from using these methods for some doctrinaire reason would be mere obscurantism. However, it is a far cry from this to the dogmatic assurance that the more the subject-matter of an inquiry can be assimilated to that of a natural science the nearer the truth we shall come. This doctrine, in Mr. Carr's version, amounts to saying that the more impersonal and general, the more valid; the more generic, the more grown up; the more attention to individuals, their idiosyncrasies and their role in history, the more fanciful, the remoter from objective truth and reality. This seems to me no more and no less dogmatic than the opposite fallacy— that history is reducible to the biographies of great men and their deeds. To assert that the truth lies somewhere between these extremes, between the equally fanatical positions of Comte and Carlyle, is a dull thing to say, but may nevertheless be closer to the truth. As an eminent philosopher of our time once drily observed, there is no *a priori* reason for supposing that the truth, when it is discovered, will prove interesting. Certainly it need not prove startling or upsetting; it may or may not; we cannot tell. This is not the place to examine Mr. Carr's historiographical views,[1] which seem to me to breathe the last enchantments of the Age of Reason, more rationalist than rational, with all the enviable simplicity, lucidity, and freedom from doubt or self-questioning which characterized this field of thought in its unclouded beginnings, when Voltaire and Helvétius were on their thrones; before the Germans, with their passion for excavating everything, ruined the smooth lawns and symmetrical gardens. Mr. Carr is a vigorous and enjoyable writer, touched by historical materialism, but essentially a late positivist, in the tradition of Auguste Comte, Herbert Spencer, and H. G. Wells; what Montesquieu called *un grand simplificateur*, untroubled by the problems and difficulties which have bedevilled the subject since Herder and Hegel, Marx and Max Weber. He is respectful towards Marx, but remote from his complex vision; a master of short ways and final answers to the great unanswered questions.

But if I cannot here attempt to deal with Mr. Carr's position with the care that it deserves, I can at least try to reply to some of his severest strictures on my own opinions. His gravest charges against me are threefold: (*a*) that I believe determinism to be false and reject the axiom that everything has a cause, 'which', according to Mr. Carr, 'is a condition of our capacity to understand what is going on around us'; (*b*) that I 'insist with great vehemence that it is the duty of the historian to judge Charlemagne, Napoleon, etc., for their massacres', i.e. to award marks for moral conduct to historically important individuals; (*c*) that I believe that explanation in history is an account in terms of human intentions, to which Mr. Carr opposes the alternative concept of 'social forces'.

To all this I can only say once again: (*a*) that I have never denied (nor considered) the logical possibility that some version of determinism may, in principle (although, perhaps, only in principle), be a valid theory of human conduct; still less do I hold

[1] I hope to do this on another occasion.

myself to have refuted it. My sole contention has been that belief in it is not compatible with beliefs deeply embedded in the normal speech and thought either of ordinary men or historians, at any rate in the Western world; and therefore that to take determinism seriously would entail a drastic revision of these central notions—an upheaval of which neither Mr. Carr's nor any other historian's practice has, as yet, provided any conspicuous examples. I know of no conclusive argument in favour of determinism. But that is not my point; it is that the actual practice of its supporters, and their reluctance to face what unity of theory and practice in this case would cost them, indicate that such theoretical support is not at present to be taken too seriously, whoever may claim to provide it. (*b*) I am accused of inviting historians to moralize. I do nothing of the kind. I merely maintain that historians, like other men, use language which is inevitably shot through with words of evaluative force, and that to invite them to purge their language of it is to ask them to perform an abnormally difficult and self-stultifying task. To be objective, unbiased, dispassionate is no doubt a virtue in historians, as in anyone who wishes to establish truth in any field. But historians are men, and are not obliged to attempt to dehumanize themselves to a greater degree than other men; the topics they choose for discussion, their distribution of attention and emphasis, are guided by their own scale of values, which, if they are either to understand human conduct or to communicate their vision to their readers, must not diverge too sharply from the common values of men. To understand the motives and outlook of others it is not, of course, necessary to share them; insight does not entail approval; the most gifted historians (and novelists) are the least partisan; some distance from the subject is required. But while comprehension of motives, moral or social codes, entire civilizations does not require acceptance of, or even sympathy with them, it does presuppose a view of what matters to individuals or groups, even if such values are found repulsive. And this rests on a conception of human nature, human ends, which enters into the historian's own ethical or religious or aesthetic outlook. These values, particularly the moral values which govern their selection of facts, the light in which they exhibit them, are conveyed, and cannot but be conveyed, by their language as much and as little as are those of anyone else who seeks to understand and describe men. The criteria which we use in judging the work of historians are not, and need not, in principle, be different from those by which we judge specialists in other fields of learning and imagination. In criticizing the achievements of those who deal with human affairs we cannot sharply divorce 'facts' from their significance. 'Values enter into the facts, and are an essential part of them. Our values are an essential part of our equipment as human beings.' These words are not mine. They are the words of none other (the reader will surely be astonished to learn) than Mr. Carr himself.[1] I might have chosen to formulate this proposition differently. But Mr. Carr's words are quite sufficient for me; on them I am content to rest my case against his charges. There is clearly no need for historians formally to pronounce moral judgments, as Mr. Carr mistakenly thinks that I wish them to do. They are under no obligation as historians to inform their readers that Hitler did harm to mankind, whereas Pasteur did good (or whatever they may think to be the case). The very use of normal language cannot avoid conveying what the author regards as commonplace or monstrous, decisive or trivial, exhilarating or depressing. In describing what occurred I can say that so many million men were brutally done to death; or alternatively, that they perished; laid down their lives; were massacred; or simply, that the population of Europe was reduced, or that its average age was lowered; or that many men lost their lives. None of these descriptions of what took place is wholly neutral: all carry moral implications. What the historian says will, however careful he may be to use purely descriptive language, sooner or later convey his attitude. Detachment is itself a moral position. The use of neutral language ('Himmler caused many persons to be asphyxiated') conveys its own ethical tone. I do not mean to say that severely neutral language about human beings is unattainable. Statisticians, compilers of intelligence reports, research departments, sociologists and economists of certain kinds, official reporters, compilers whose task it is to provide data for historians or politicians, can and are expected to approach it.

[1] Op. cit., p. 131.

But this is so because these activities are not autonomous but are designed to provide the raw material for those whose work is intended to be an end in itself—historians, men of action. The research assistant is not called upon to select and emphasize what counts for much, and play down what counts for little, in human life. The historian cannot avoid this; otherwise what he writes, detached as it will be from what he, or his society, or some other culture regards as central or peripheral, will not be history. If history is what historians do, then the central issue which no historian can evade, whether he knows this or not, is how we (and other societies) came to be as we are or were. This, *eo facto*, entails a particular vision of society, of men's nature, of the springs of human action, of men's values and scales of value—something that physicists, physiologists, physical anthropologists, grammarians, econometricians, or certain sorts of psychologists (like the providers of data for others to interpret) may be able to avoid. History is not an ancillary activity; it seeks to provide as complete an account as it can of what men do and suffer; to call them men is to ascribe to them values that we must be able to recognize as such, otherwise they are not men for us. Historians cannot therefore (whether they moralize or not) escape from having to adopt some position about what matters and how much (even if they do not ask why it matters). This alone is enough to render the notion of a 'value-free' history, of the historian as a transcriber *rebus ipsis dictantibus*, an illusion.

Perhaps this is all that Acton urged against Creighton: not simply that Creighton used artificially non-moral terms, but that in using them to describe the Borgias and their acts he was, in effect, going some way towards exonerating them; that, whether he was right or wrong to do it, he was doing it; that neutrality is also a moral attitude, and that it is as well to recognize it for what it is. Acton had no doubt that Creighton was wrong. We may agree with Acton or with Creighton. But in either case we are judging, conveying, even when we prefer not to state, a moral attitude. To invite historians to describe men's lives but not the significance of their lives in terms of what Mill called the permanent interests of mankind, however conceived, is not to describe their lives. To demand of historians that they try to enter imaginatively into the experience of others and forbid them to display moral understanding is to invite them to tell too small a part of what they know, and to deprive their work of human significance. This is in effect all that I have to say against Mr. Carr's moral sermon against the bad habit of delivering moral sermons.

No doubt the view that there exist objective moral or social values, eternal and universal, untouched by historical change, and accessible to the mind of any rational man if only he chooses to direct his gaze at them, is open to every sort of question. Yet the possibility of understanding men in one's own or any other time, indeed of communication between human beings, depends upon the existence of some common values, and not on a common 'factual' world alone. The latter is a necessary but not a sufficient condition of human intercourse. Those who are out of touch with the external world are described as abnormal, and in extreme cases, insane. But so also—and this is the point—are those who wander too far from the common public world of values. A man who declares that he once knew the difference between right and wrong, but has forgotten it, will scarcely be believed; if he is believed, he is rightly considered deranged. But so too is a man who does not merely approve or enjoy or condone, but literally cannot grasp what conceivable objection anyone could have to, let us suppose, a rule permitting the killing of any man with blue eyes, with no reason given. He would be considered about as normal a specimen of the human race as one who cannot count beyond six, or thinks it probable that he is Julius Caesar. What such normative (non-descriptive) tests for insanity rest on is what gives such plausibility as they have to doctrines of natural law, particularly in versions which refuse them any *a priori* status. Acceptance of common values (at any rate some irreducible minimum of them) enters our conception of a normal human being. This serves to distinguish such notions as the foundations of human morality from such other notions as custom, or tradition, or law, or manners, or fashion, or etiquette—all those regions in which the occurrence of wide social and historical, national and local, differences and change are not regarded as rare or abnormal, or evidence of extreme eccentricity or insanity, or indeed as undesirable at all; least of all as philosophically problematic.

No historical writing which rises above a bare chronicler's narrative, and involves selection and the unequal distribution of emphasis, can be wholly *wertfrei*. What then distinguishes moralizing that is justly condemned from that which seems inescapable from any degree of reflection on human affairs? Not its overtness: mere choice of apparently neutral language can well seem, to those who do not sympathize with an author's views, even more insidious. I have attempted to deal with what is meant by bias and partiality in the essay on Historical Inevitability. I can only repeat that we seem to distinguish subjective from objective appraisal by the degree to which the central values conveyed are those which are common to human beings as such, that is, for practical purposes, to the great majority of men in most places and times. This is clearly not an absolute or rigid criterion; there is variation, there are virtually unnoticeable (as well as glaring) national, local, and historical peculiarities, prejudices, superstitions, rationalizations and their irrational influence. But neither is this criterion wholly relative or subjective, otherwise the concept of man would become too indeterminate, and men or societies, divided by unbridgeable normative differences, would be wholly unable to communicate across great distances in space and time and culture. Objectivity of moral judgment seems to depend on (almost to consist in) the degree of constancy in human responses. This notion cannot in principle be made sharp and unalterable. Its edges remain blurred. Moral categories—and categories of value in general—are nothing like as firm and ineradicable as those of, say, the perception of the material world, but neither are they as relative or as fluid as some writers have too easily, in their reaction against the dogmatism of the classical objectivists, tended to assume. A minimum of common moral ground—interrelated concepts and categories —is intrinsic to human communication. What they are, how flexible, how far liable to change under the impact of what 'forces'—these are empirical questions, in a region claimed by moral psychology and historical and social anthropology, fascinating, important, and insufficiently explored. To demand more than this seems to me to wish to move beyond the frontiers of communicable human knowledge.

(c) I am accused of supposing that history deals with human motives and intentions, for which Mr. Carr wishes to substitute the action of 'social forces'. To this charge I plead guilty. I am obliged to say once more that anyone concerned with human beings is committed to consideration of motives, purposes, choices, the specifically human experience that belongs to human beings uniquely, and not merely with what happened to them as animate or sentient bodies. To ignore the play of non-human factors; or the effect of the unintended consequences of human acts; or the fact that men often do not correctly understand their own individual behaviour or its sources; to stop searching for causes, in the most literal and mechanical sense, in accounting for what happened and how—all this would be absurdly childish or obscurantist, and I did not suggest anything of this kind. But to ignore motives and the context in which they arose, the range of possibilities as they stretched before the actors, of most which never were, and some never could have been, realized; to ignore the spectrum of human thought and imagination—how the world and they themselves appear to men whose vision and values (illusions and all) we can grasp in the end only in terms of our own—would be to cease to write history. One may argue about the degree of difference that the influence of this or that individual made in shaping events. But to try to reduce the behaviour of individuals to that of impersonal 'social forces' not further analysable into the conduct of the men who, even according to Marx, make history is 'reification' of statistics, a form of the 'false consciousness' of bureaucrats and administrators who close their eyes to all that proves incapable of quantification, and thereby perpetrate absurdities in theory and dehumanization in practice. There are remedies that breed new diseases, whether or not they cure those to which they are applied. To frighten human beings by suggesting to them that they are in the grip of impersonal forces over which they have little or no control is to breed myths, ostensibly in order to kill other figments—the notion of supernatural forces, or of all-powerful individuals, or of the hidden hand. It is to invent entities, to propagate faith in unalterable patterns of events for which the empirical evidence is, to say the least, insufficient, and which by relieving individuals of the burdens of personal responsibility breeds irrational passivity in some, and no less irrational fanatical activity in others; for nothing is more inspiring than the certainty that the stars in their courses are fighting for one's cause, that 'History', or 'social forces', or 'the wave of the future' are with one, bearing one aloft and forward. This way of thinking and speaking is one which it is the great merit of modern empiricism to have exposed. If my essay has any polemical thrust, it is to discredit metaphysical constructions of this kind. If to speak of men solely in terms of statistical probabilities—ignoring too much of what is specifically human in men—evaluations, choices, differing visions of life, is an exaggerated application of scientific method, a gratuitous behaviourism, it is no less misleading to appeal to imaginary forces. The former has its place; it describes, classifies, predicts, even if it does not explain. The latter explains indeed, but in occult, what I can only call neo-animistic, terms. I suspect that Mr. Carr does not feel anxious to defend either of these methods. But in his reaction against naïveté, smugness, the vanities of nationalistic or class or personal moralizing, he has permitted himself to be driven to the other extreme—the night of impersonality, in which human beings are dissolved into abstract forces. The fact that I protest against it leads Mr. Carr to think that I embrace the opposite absurdity. His assumption that between them these extremes exhaust the possibilities seems to me to be the basic fallacy from which his (and perhaps others') vehement criticism of my real and imaginary opinions ultimately stems.

At this point I should like to reiterate some commonplaces from which I do not depart: that causal laws are applicable to human history (a proposition which, *pace* Mr. Carr, I should consider it insane to deny); that history is not mainly a 'dramatic conflict' between individual wills;[1] that knowledge, especially of scientifically established laws, tends to render us more effective[2]

---

[1] A view attributed to me by Mr. Christopher Dawson in the *Harvard Law Review*, vol. 70, 1957, pp. 584–8.

[2] My evident failure to state my view sufficiently clearly is brought home to me by the fact that the opposite of this position—a crude and absurd anti-rationalism—is attributed

and extend our liberty, which is liable to be curtailed by ignorance and the illusions, terrors, and prejudices that it breeds;[1]
that there is plenty of empirical evidence for the view that
the frontiers of free choice are a good deal narrower than many
men have in the past supposed, and perhaps still erroneously
believe;[2] and even that objective patterns in history may, for
all I know, be discernible. I must repeat that my concern is
only to assert that unless such laws and patterns are held to leave
some freedom of choice—and not only freedom of action determined by choices that are themselves wholly determined by
antecedent causes—we shall have to reconstruct our view of
reality accordingly; and that this task is far more formidable than
determinists tend to assume. The determinist's world may, at
least in principle, be conceivable: in it all that Professor Ernest
Nagel declares to be the function of human volition will remain
intact; a man's behaviour will still be affected by praise and
blame as his metabolism (at any rate directly) will not;[3] men
will continue to describe persons and things as beautiful or ugly,
evaluate actions as beneficial or harmful, brave or cowardly,
noble or ignoble. But when Kant said that if the laws that
governed the phenomena of the external world turned out to
govern all there was, then morality—in his sense—was annihilated; and when, in consequence, being concerned with the
concept of freedom presupposed by his notion of moral responsibility, he adopted very drastic measures in order to save it,
he seems to me, at the very least to have shown a profound
grasp of what is at stake. His solution is obscure, and perhaps untenable; but although it may have to be rejected, the
problem remains. In a causally determined system the notions
of free choice and moral responsibility, in their usual senses,
vanish, or at least lack application, and the notion of action
would have to be reconsidered.

to me by Mr. Gordon Leff (in *The Tyranny of Concepts*, pp. 146-9), by Prof. J. A. Passmore (in *The Philosophical Review*, loc. cit.), by Mr. Christopher Dawson, op. cit.; and
by half a dozen Marxist writers: some of these in evident good faith.

[1] Though not in all situations: see my article 'From Hope and Fear Set Free', *Proceedings of the Aristotelian Society*, 1959-60.

[2] I state this explicitly on pp. 68, 70-71, 73-75, 84.

[3] See H. P. Rickman's review in *The Hibbert Journal*, January 1958, pp. 169-70.

I recognize the fact that some thinkers seem to feel no intellectual discomfort in interpreting such concepts as responsibility,
culpability, remorse, etc., in strict conformity with causal determination. At most they seek to explain the resistance of those
who dissent from them by attributing to them a confusion of
causality with some sort of compulsion. Compulsion frustrates
my wishes but when I fulfil them I am surely free, even though
my wishes themselves are causally determined; if they are not,
if they are not effects of my general tendencies, or ingredients
in my habits and way of living (which can be described in purely
causal terms), or if these, in their turn, are not what they are
entirely as a result of causes, physical, social, psychological, etc.,
then there is surely an element of pure chance or randomness,
which breaks the causal chain. But is not random behaviour the
very opposite of freedom, rationality, responsibility? And yet
these alternatives seem to exhaust the possibilities. The notion of
uncaused choice as something out of the blue is certainly not
satisfactory. But (I need not argue this again) the only alternative
permitted by such thinkers—a caused choice held to entail
responsibility, desert, etc.—is equally untenable. This dilemma
has now divided thinkers for more than two thousand years.
Some continue to be agonized or at least puzzled by it, as the
earliest Stoics were; others see no problem at all. It may be that
it stems, at least in part, from the use of a mechanical model
applied to human actions; in one case choices are conceived as
links in the kind of causal sequence that is typical of the functioning of a mechanical process; in the other, as a break in this
sequence, still conceived in terms of a complex mechanism.
Neither image seems to fit the case at all well. We seem to need
a new model, a schema which will rescue the evidence of moral
consciousness from the beds of Procrustes provided by the
obsessive frameworks of the traditional discussions. All efforts
to break away from the old obstructive analogies, or (to use a
familiar terminology) the rules of an inappropriate language
game, have so far proved abortive. This needs a philosophical
imagination of the first order, which in this case is still to seek.
Professor White's solution—to attribute the conflicting views to
different scales of value or varieties of moral usage—seems to me

no way out. I cannot help suspecting that his view is part of a wider theory, according to which belief in determinism or any other view of the world is, or depends on, some sort of large-scale pragmatic decision about how to treat this or that field of thought or experience, based on a view of what set of categories would give the best results. Even if one accepted this, it would not be easier to reconcile the notions of causal necessity, avoidability, free choice, responsibility, etc. I do not claim to have refuted the conclusions of determinism; but neither do I see why we need be driven towards them. Neither the idea of historical explanation as such, nor respect for scientific method, seems to me to entail them. This sums up my disagreements with Professor Ernest Nagel, Professor Morton White, Mr. E. H. Carr, the classical determinists, and their modern disciples.

II

Positive versus Negative Liberty

In the case of social and political liberty a problem arises that is not wholly dissimilar from that of social and historical determinism. We assume the need of an area for free choice, the diminution of which is incompatible with the existence of anything that can properly be called political (or social) liberty. Indeterminism does not entail that human beings cannot in fact be treated like animals or things; nor is political liberty, like freedom of choice, intrinsic to the notion of a human being; it is an historical growth, an area bounded by frontiers. The question of its frontiers, indeed whether the concept of frontiers can properly be applied to it, raises issues on which much of the criticism directed upon my theses has concentrated. The main issues may here too be summarized under three heads:

(a) Whether the difference I have drawn between (what I am not the first to have called) positive and negative liberty is specious, or, at any rate, too sharp.

(*b*) Whether the term 'liberty' can be extended as widely as some of my critics appear to wish, without thereby depriving it of so much significance as to render it progressively less useful.

(*c*) Why political liberty should be regarded as being of value.

Before discussing these problems, I wish to correct a genuine error in the original version of *Two Concepts of Liberty*. Although this error does not weaken, or conflict with, the arguments used in the essay (indeed, if anything, it seems to me to strengthen them), it is, nevertheless, a position that I consider to be mistaken.[1] In the original version of *Two Concepts of Liberty* I speak of liberty as the absence of obstacles to the fulfilment of a man's desires. This is a common, perhaps the most common, sense in which the term is used, but it does not represent my position. For if to be free—negatively—is simply not to be prevented by other persons from doing whatever one wishes, then one of the ways of attaining such freedom is by extinguishing one's wishes. I offered criticisms of this definition, and of this entire line of thought in the text, without realizing that it was inconsistent with the formulation with which I began. If degrees of freedom were a function of the satisfaction of desires, I could increase freedom as effectively by eliminating desires as by satisfying them; I could render men (including myself) free by conditioning them into losing the original desires which I have decided not to satisfy. Instead of resisting or removing the pressures that bear down upon me, I can 'internalize' them. This is what Epictetus achieves when he claims that he, a slave, is freer than his master. By ignoring obstacles, forgetting, 'rising above' them, becoming unconscious of them, I can attain peace and serenity, a noble detachment from the fears and hatreds that beset other men—freedom in one sense indeed, but not in the sense in which I wish to speak of it. When (according to Cicero's account) the Stoic sage Posidonius, who was dying of an agonizing disease, said, 'Do your worst, pain; no matter what you do, you cannot make me hate you', thereby accepting, and attaining unity with,

---

[1] The generous and acute anonymous reviewer of my lecture in the *Times Literary Supplement* was the first writer to point out this error; he also made other penetrating and suggestive criticisms by which I have greatly profited.

'Nature', which, being identical with cosmic 'reason', rendered his pain not merely inevitable, but rational, the sense in which he achieved freedom is not that basic meaning of it in which men are said to lose freedom when they are imprisoned or literally enslaved. The Stoic sense of freedom, however sublime, must be distinguished from the freedom or liberty which the oppressor, or the oppressive institutionalized practice, curtails or destroys.[1] For once I am happy to acknowledge the insight of Rousseau: to know one's chains for what they are is better than to deck them with flowers.[2] Spiritual freedom, like moral victory, must be distinguished from a more fundamental sense of freedom, and a more ordinary sense of victory, otherwise there will be a danger of confusion in theory and justification of oppression in practice, in the name of liberty itself. There is a clear sense in which to teach a man that, if he cannot get what he wants, he must learn to want only what he can get may contribute to his happiness or his security; but it will not increase his civil or political freedom. The sense of freedom, in which I use this term, entails not simply the absence of frustration (which may be obtained by killing desires), but the absence of obstacles to possible choices and activities—absence of obstructions on roads along which a man can decide to walk. Such freedom ultimately depends not on whether I wish to walk at all, or how far, but on how many doors are open, how open they are, upon their relative importance in my life, even though it may be impossible literally to measure

[1] There is an admirable discussion of this topic in 'Authoritarianism and Totalitarianism' in *Psychoanalysis and Culture*, by Dr. Robert R. Waelder (New York, n.d., International Universities Press, pp. 185–95). He speaks of the remoulding of the super-ego into 'internalizing' external pressures, and draws an illuminating distinction between authoritarianism, which entails obedience to authority without acceptance of its orders and claims, and totalitarianism, which entails in addition inner conformity to the system imposed by the dictator; hence totalitarian insistence on education and indoctrination as opposed to mere outward obedience, a sinister process with which we have become all too familiar. There is, of course, all the difference in the world between assimilating the rules of reason, as advocated by Stoicism, and those of an irrational movement or arbitrary dictatorship. But the psychological machinery is similar.

[2] This point is well made by one of my critics, Mr. L. J. McFarlane, in 'On Two Concepts of Liberty' (*Political Studies*, vol. 14, February 1966, pp. 77–81). In the course of a very critical but fair and valuable discussion Mr. McFarlane observes that to know one's chains is often the first step to freedom, which may never come about if one either ignores or loves them.

this in any quantitative fashion.[1] The extent of my social or political freedom consists in the absence of obstacles not merely to my actual, but to my potential choices—to my acting in this or that way if I choose to do so. Similarly absence of such freedom is due to the closing of such doors or failure to open them, as a result, intended or unintended, of alterable human practices, of the operation of human agencies; although only if such acts are deliberately intended (or, perhaps, are accompanied by awareness that they may block paths) will they be liable to be called oppression. Unless this is conceded, the Stoic conception of liberty ('true' freedom—the state of the morally autonomous slave), which is compatible with a very high degree of political despotism, will merely confuse the issue.

It is an interesting, but perhaps irrelevant, historical question at what date, and in what circumstances, the notion of individual liberty in this sense first became explicit in the West. I have found no convincing evidence of any clear formulation of it in the ancient world. Some of my critics have doubted this, but apart from pointing to such modern writers as Acton, Jellinek, or Barker, who do profess to find this ideal in ancient Greece, some of them also, more pertinently, cite the proposals of Otanes after the death of pseudo-Smerdis in the account given by Herodotus, the celebrated paean to liberty in the Funeral Oration of Pericles, as well as the speech of Nikias before the final battle with the Syracusans (in Thucydides), as evidence that the Greeks, at any rate, had a clear conception of individual liberty. I must confess that I do not find this conclusive. When Pericles and Nikias compare the freedom of the Athenian citizens with the fate of the subjects of less democratic states, what (it seems to me) they are saying is that the citizens of Athens enjoy freedom in the sense of self-government, that they are not slaves of any master, that they perform their civic duties out of love for their *polis*, without needing to be coerced, and not under the goads and whips of savage laws or taskmasters (as in Sparta or Persia). So might a headmaster say of the boys in his school that they live and act according to good principles not because they are forced to do so, but because they are inspired by loyalty to the school,

[1] See p. 130, footnote.

by 'team spirit', by a sense of solidarity and common purpose; whereas at other schools these results have to be achieved by fear of punishment and stern measures. But in neither case is it contemplated that a man might, without losing face, or incurring contempt, or a diminution of his human essence, withdraw from public life altogether, and pursue private ends, live in a room of his own, in the company of personal friends, as Epicurus later advocated, and perhaps the Cynic and Cyrenaic disciples of Socrates had preached before him. As for Otanes, he wished neither to rule nor to be ruled—the exact opposite of Aristotle's notion of true civic liberty. Perhaps this attitude did begin to occur in the ideas of unpolitical thinkers in Herodotus' day: of Antiphon the Sophist, for example, and possibly in some moods of Socrates himself. But it remains isolated and, until Epicurus, undeveloped. In other words, it seems to me that the issue of individual freedom, of the frontiers beyond which public authority, whether lay or ecclesiastical, should not normally be allowed to step, had not clearly emerged at this stage; the central value attached to it may, perhaps (as I remarked in the penultimate paragraph of my lecture), be the late product of a capitalist civilization, an element in a network of values that includes such notions as personal rights, civil liberties, the sanctity of the individual personality, the importance of privacy, personal relations, and the like. I do not say that the ancient Greeks did not in fact enjoy a great measure of what we should today call individual liberty.[1] My thesis is only that the notion had not explicitly emerged, and was therefore not central to Greek culture, or, perhaps, any other ancient civilization known to us.

One of the by-products or symptoms of this stage of social development is that, for instance, the issue of free will (as opposed to that of voluntary action) is not felt to be a problem before the Stoics; the corollary of which seems to be that variety for its own sake—and the corresponding abhorrence of uniformity—is not a prominent ideal, or perhaps an explicit ideal at all, before the Renaissance, or even, in its full form, the beginning of the

---

[1] Professor A. W. Gomme and others have provided a good deal of evidence for the hypothesis that they did.

eighteenth century. Issues of this type seem to arise only when forms of life, and the social patterns that are part of them, after long periods in which they have been taken for granted, are upset, and so come to be recognized and become the subject of conscious reflection. There are many values which men have disputed, and for and against which they have fought, that are not mentioned in some earlier phase of history, either because they are assumed without question, or because men are, whatever the cause, in no condition to conceive of them. It may be that the more sophisticated forms of individual liberty did not impinge upon the consciousness of the masses of mankind simply because they lived in squalor and oppression. Men who live in conditions where there is not sufficient food, warmth, shelter, and the minimum degree of security can scarcely be expected to concern themselves with freedom of contract or of the press.

It may make matters clearer if at this point I mention what seems to me yet another misconception—namely the identification of freedom with activity as such. When, for example, Dr. Erich Fromm, in his moving tracts for the times, speaks of true freedom as the spontaneous, rational activity of the total, integrated personality, and is partly followed in this by Professor Bernard Crick, I disagree with them.[1] The freedom of which I speak is opportunity for action, rather than action itself. If, although I enjoy the right to walk through open doors, I prefer not to do so, but to sit still and vegetate, I am not thereby rendered less free. Freedom is the opportunity to act, not action itself; the possibility of action, not necessarily that dynamic realization of it which both Fromm and Crick identify with it. If apathetic neglect of various avenues to a more vigorous and generous life—however much this may be condemned on other grounds—is not considered incompatible with the notion of being free, then I have nothing to quarrel with in the formulations of either of these writers. But I fear that Dr. Fromm would consider such abdication as a symptom of lack of integration, which for him is indispensable to—perhaps identical with—freedom; while Professor Crick would look upon such apathy as too inert and timid

[1] In his inaugural lecture to the University of Sheffield in 1966.

to deserve to be called freedom. I find the ideal advocated by these champions of the full life sympathetic; but to identify it with freedom seems to me conflation of two values. To say that freedom is activity as such is to make the term cover too much; it tends to obscure and dilute the central issue—the right and freedom to act—about which men have argued and fought during almost the whole of recorded history.

To return to concepts of liberty. Much has been made by my opponents of the distinction (regarded by them as specious or exaggerated) that I have tried to draw between two questions: 'By whom am I governed?' and 'How much am I governed?' Yet I confess that I cannot see either that the two questions are identical, or that the difference between them is unimportant. It still seems to me that the distinction between the two kinds of answer, and therefore between the different senses of 'liberty' involved, is neither trivial nor confused. Indeed, I continue to believe that the issue is a central one both historically and conceptually, both in theory and practice. Let me say once again that 'positive' and 'negative' liberty, in the sense in which I use these terms, start at no great logical distance from each other. The questions 'Who is master?' and 'Over what area am I master?' cannot be kept wholly distinct. I wish to determine myself, and not be directed by others, no matter how wise and benevolent; my conduct derives an irreplaceable value from the sole fact that it is my own, and not imposed upon me. But I am not, and cannot expect to be, wholly self-sufficient or socially omnipotent.[1] I cannot remove all the obstacles in my path that stem from the conduct of my fellows. I can try to ignore them, treat them as illusory, or 'intermingle' them and attribute them to my own inner principles, conscience, moral sense; or try to dissolve my sense of personal identity in a common enterprise, as an element in a larger self-directed whole. Nevertheless, despite such heroic efforts to transcend or dissolve the conflicts and resistance of

[1] It has been suggested that liberty is always a triadic relation: one can only seek to be free from X to do or be Y; hence 'all liberty' is at once negative and positive or, better still, neither (see G. C. McCallum, jr., *Philosophical Review*, vol. 76, no. 3, 1967, pp. 312–34). This seems to me an error. A man struggling against his chains or a people against enslavement need not consciously aim at any definite further state. A man need not know how he will use his freedom; he just wants to remove the yoke. So do classes and nations.

others, if I do not wish to be deceived, I shall recognize the fact
that total harmony with others is incompatible with self-identity;
that if I am not to be dependent on others in every respect, I shall
need some area within which I am not, and can count on not
being, freely interfered with by them. The question then arises:
how wide is the area over which I am, or should be, master? My
thesis is that historically the notion of 'positive' liberty—in
answer to the question 'Who is master?'—diverged from that of
'negative' liberty, designed to answer 'Over what area am I
master?'; and that this gulf widened as the notion of the self
suffered a metaphysical fission into, on the one hand, a 'higher',
or a 'real', or an 'ideal' self, set up to rule 'lower', 'empirical',
'psychological' self or nature, on the other; into 'myself at my
best' as master over my inferior day-to-day self; into Coleridge's
great *I AM* over less transcendent incarnations of it in time and
space. A genuine experience of inner tension may lie at the root
of this ancient and pervasive metaphysical image of the two
selves, the influence of which has been vast over language,
thought, and conduct; however this may be, the 'higher' self
duly became identified with institutions, churches, nations, races,
states, classes, cultures, parties, and with vaguer entities, such
as the general will, the common good, the enlightened forces of
society, the vanguard of the most progressive class, Manifest
Destiny. My thesis is that, in the course of this process, what
had begun as a doctrine of freedom turned into a doctrine of
authority and, at times, of oppression, and became the favoured
weapon of despotism, a phenomenon all too familiar in our own
day. I was careful to point out that this could equally have been
the fate of the doctrine of negative liberty. Among the dualists
who distinguished the two selves, some—in particular Jewish
and Christian theologians, but also Idealist metaphysicians in
the nineteenth century—speak of the need to release the 'higher'
or 'ideal' self from obstacles in its path, e.g. interference by,
'slavery to', the 'lower' self; and some saw this base entity
incarnated in institutions serving irrational or wicked passions
and other forces of evil likely to obstruct the proper development
of the 'true' or 'higher' self, or 'myself at my best'. The history
of political doctrines might (like that of some protestant sects)

have taken this 'negative' form. The point, however, is that it did so relatively seldom—as, for example, in early liberal, anarchist, and some types of populist writings. But for the most part, freedom was identified by metaphysically inclined writers, with the realization of the real self not so much in individual men as incarnated in institutions, traditions, forms of life wider than the empirical spatio-temporal existence of the finite individual. Freedom is identified by such thinkers most often, it seems to me, with the 'positive' activity of these institutional ('organic') forms of life, growth, etc., rather than with mere ('negative') removal of obstacles even from the paths of such 'organisms', let alone from those of individuals—such an absence of obstacles being regarded as, at best, means to, or conditions of, freedom; not as freedom itself.

It is doubtless well to remember that belief in negative freedom is compatible with, and (so far as ideas influence conduct) has played its part in, generating great and lasting social evils. My point is that it was much less often defended or disguised by the kind of specious arguments and sleights-of-hand habitually used by the champions of 'positive' freedom in its more sinister forms. Advocacy of non-interference (like 'social Darwinism') was, of course, used to support politically and socially destructive policies which armed the strong, the brutal, and the unscrupulous against the humane and the weak, the able and ruthless against the less gifted and the less fortunate. Freedom for the wolves has often meant death to the sheep. The bloodstained story of economic individualism and unrestrained capitalist competition does not, I should have thought, today need stressing. Nevertheless, in view of the astonishing opinions which some of my critics have imputed to me, I should, perhaps, have been wise to underline certain parts of my argument. I should have made even clearer that the evils of unrestricted *laissez-faire*, and of the social and legal systems that permitted and encouraged it, led to brutal violations of 'negative' liberty—of basic human rights (always a 'negative' notion: a wall against oppressors), including that of free expression or association without which there may exist justice and fraternity and even happiness of a kind, but not democracy. And I should perhaps have stressed (save that I thought this too obvious to need saying) the failure of such systems to provide the minimum conditions in which alone any degree of significant 'negative' liberty can be exercised by individuals or groups, and without which it is of little or no value to those who may theoretically possess it. For what are rights without the power to implement them? I had supposed that enough had been said by almost every serious modern writer concerned with this subject about the fate of personal liberty during the reign of unfettered economic individualism—about the condition of the injured majority, principally in the towns, whose children were destroyed in mines or mills, while their parents lived in poverty, disease, and ignorance, a situation in which the enjoyment by the poor and the weak of legal rights to spend their money as they pleased or to choose the education they wanted (which Cobden and Herbert Spencer and their disciples offered them with every appearance of sincerity) became an odious mockery. All this is notoriously true. Legal liberties are compatible with extremes of exploitation, brutality, and injustice. The case for intervention, by the state or other effective agencies, to secure conditions for both positive, and at least a minimum degree of negative, liberty for individuals, is overwhelmingly strong. Liberals like Tocqueville and J. S. Mill, and even Benjamin Constant (who prized negative liberty beyond any modern writer), were not unaware of this. The case for social legislation or planning, for the welfare state and socialism, can be constructed with as much validity from considerations of the claims of negative liberty as from those of its positive brother; and if, historically, it was not made so frequently, that was because the kind of evil against which the concept of negative liberty was directed as a weapon was not *laissez-faire*, but despotism. The rise and fall of the two concepts can largely be traced to the specific dangers which, at a given moment, threatened a group or society most: on the one hand excessive control and interference, or, on the other, an uncontrolled 'market' economy. Each concept seems liable to perversion into the very vice which it was created to resist. But whereas liberal ultra-individualism could scarcely be said to be a rising force at present, the rhetoric of 'positive' liberty, at least in its distorted form, is in far greater evidence, and continues to play its historic role (in both capitalist and anti-capitalist societies) as a cloak for despotism in the name of a wider freedom.

'Positive' liberty, conceived as the answer to the question, 'By whom am I to be governed?', is a valid universal goal. I do not know why I should have been held to doubt this, or, for that matter, the further proposition, that democratic self-government is a fundamental human need, something valuable in itself, whether or not it clashes with the claims of negative liberty or of any other goal; valuable intrinsically and not only for the reasons advanced in its favour by, for example, Constant—that without it, negative liberty may be too easily crushed; or by Mill, who thinks it an indispensable means—but still only a means—to the attainment of happiness. I can only repeat that the perversion of the notion of positive liberty into its opposite—the apotheosis of authority—did occur, and has for a long while been one of the most familiar and depressing phenomena of our time. For whatever reason or cause, the notion of 'negative' liberty (conceived as the answer to the question 'How much am I to be governed?'), however disastrous the consequences of its unbridled forms, has not historically been twisted by its theorists as often or as effectively into anything so darkly metaphysical or socially sinister or remote from its original meaning as its 'positive' counterpart. The first can be turned into its opposite and still exploit the favourable associations of its innocent origins. The second has, much more frequently, been seen, for better and for worse, for what it was; there has been no lack of emphasis, in the last hundred years, upon its more disastrous implications. Hence, the greater need, it seems to me, to expose the aberrations of positive liberty than those of its negative brother.

Nor do I wish to deny that new ways in which liberty, both in its positive and its negative sense, can be, and has been, curtailed have arisen since the nineteenth century. In an age of expanding economic productivity there exist ways of curtailing both types of liberty—for example, by permitting or promoting a situation in which entire groups and nations are progressively shut off from benefits which have been allowed to accumulate too exclusively in the hands of other groups and nations, the rich and strong—a situation which, in its turn, has produced (and was itself produced by) social arrangements that have caused walls to arise around men, and doors to be shut to the development of individuals and classes. This has been done by social and economic policies that were sometimes openly discriminatory, at other times camouflaged, by the rigging of educational policies and of the means of influencing opinion, by legislation in the sphere of morals, and similar measures, which have blocked and diminished human freedom at times as effectively as the more overt and brutal methods of direct oppression—slavery and imprisonment—against which the original defenders of liberty lifted their voices.[1]

Let me summarize my position thus far. The extent of a man's negative liberty is, as it were, a function of what doors, and how many, are open to him; upon what prospects they open; and how open they are. This formula must not be pressed too far, for not all doors are of equal importance, inasmuch as the paths on which they open vary in the opportunities they offer. Consequently, the problem of how an over-all increase of liberty in particular circumstances is to be secured, and how it is to be distributed (especially in situations, and this is almost invariably the case, in which the opening of one door leads to the lifting of other barriers and the lowering of still others), how, in a word, the maximization of opportunities is in any concrete case to be achieved, can be an agonizing problem, not to be solved by any

[1] Not that such open violence has been lacking in our own country, practised at times under the noble banner of the suppression of arbitrary rule and the enemies of liberty and the emancipation of hitherto enslaved populations and classes. On this I agree with a great deal of what has been said on this subject by Professor A. S. Kaufman ('Professor Berlin on Negative Freedom', *Mind*, April 1962, pp. 241-4). Some of his points may be found in an earlier attack by Professor Marshall Cohen ('Berlin and the Liberal Tradition', *Philosophical Quarterly*, 1957, pp. 216-28). Some of Mr. Kaufman's objections have, I hope, been answered already. There is one point, however, on which I must take further issue with him. He appears to regard constraint or obstruction not brought about by human means as being forms of deprivation of social or political freedom. I do not think that this is compatible with what is normally meant by political freedom— the only sense of it with which I am concerned. Mr. Kaufman speaks (op. cit., p. 241) of 'obstructions to the human will, which have nothing to do with a community's pattern of power relations' as obstacles to (political or social) liberty. Unless, however, such obstructions do, in the end, spring from power relations, they do not seem to be relevant to the existence of social or political liberty. I cannot see how one can speak of 'basic human rights' (to use Mr. Kaufman's phrase) as violated by what he calls 'non-human

hard-and-fast rule.¹ What I am mainly concerned to establish is
that, whatever may be the common ground between them, and
whichever is liable to graver distortion, negative and positive
liberty are not the same thing. Both are ends in themselves.
These ends may clash irreconcilably. When this happens,
questions of choice and preference inevitably arise. Should
democracy in a given situation be promoted at the expense of
individual freedom? or equality at the expense of artistic achieve-
ment; or mercy at the expense of justice; or spontaneity at the

. . . interference'. If I stumble and fall, and so find my freedom of movement frustrated,
I cannot, surely, be said to have suffered any loss of basic human rights. Failure to discriminate between human and non-human obstacles to freedom seems to me to mark the
beginning of the great confusion of types of freedom, and of the no less fatal identification
of conditions of freedom with freedom itself, which is at the root of some of the fallacies
with which I am concerned.

¹ Mr. David Nicholls in an admirable survey, 'Positive Liberty, 1880–1914', *American
Political Science Review*, March 1962, thinks that I contradict myself in quoting with
approval Bentham's 'Every law is an infraction of liberty', since some laws increase the
total amount of liberty in a society. I do not see the force of this objection. Every law
seems to me to curtail *some* liberty, although it may be a means to increasing another.
Whether it increases the total sum of attainable liberty will of course depend on the
particular situation. Even a law which enacts that no one shall coerce anyone in a given
sphere, while it obviously increases the freedom of the majority, is an 'infraction' of the
freedom of potential bullies and policemen. Infraction may, as in this case, be highly
desirable, but it remains 'infraction'. There is no reason for thinking that Bentham, who
favoured laws, meant to say more than this.

In his article Mr. Nicholls quotes T. H. Green's statement (in 'Liberal Legislation
and the Freedom of Contract'): 'The mere removal of compulsion, the mere enabling
a man to do as he likes, is in itself no contribution to true freedom . . . the ideal
of true freedom is the maximum of power for all members of human society alike to
make the best of themselves.' (T. H. Green, *Works*, iii, 371–2.) This is a classical statement of positive liberty, and the crucial terms are, of course, 'true freedom' and 'the
best of themselves'. Perhaps I need not enlarge again upon the fatal ambiguity of
these words. As a plea for justice, and a denunciation of the monstrous assumption that
workmen were (in any sense that mattered to them) free agents in negotiating with
employers in his time, Green's essay can scarcely be improved upon. The workers, in
theory, probably enjoyed wide negative freedom. But since they lacked the means of its
realization, it was a hollow gain. Hence I find nothing to disagree with in Green's
recommendations; only with the metaphysical doctrine of the two selves—the individual
streams versus the social river in which they should be merged, a dualistic fallacy used
too often to support a variety of despotisms. Nor, of course, do I wish to deny that
Green's views were exceptionally enlightened, and this holds of many of the critics of
liberalism in Europe and America in the last hundred years or so. Nevertheless, words
are important, and a writer's opinions and purposes are not sufficient to render the use of
a misleading terminology harmless either in theory or in practice. The record of liberalism
is no better in this respect than that of most other schools of political thought.

expense of efficiency; or happiness, loyalty, innocence at the expense of knowledge and truth? The simple point which I am concerned to make is that where ultimate values are irreconcilable, clear-cut solutions cannot, in principle, be found. To decide rationally in such situations is to decide in the light of general ideals, the over-all pattern of life pursued by a man or a group or a society. If the claims of two (or more than two) types of liberty prove incompatible in a particular case, and if this is an instance of the clash of values at once absolute and incommensurable, it is better to face this intellectually uncomfortable fact than to ignore it, or automatically attribute it to some deficiency on our part which could be eliminated by an increase in skill or knowledge;[1] or, what is worse still, suppress one of the competing values altogether by pretending that it is identical with its rival—and so end by distorting both. Yet, it appears to me, it is exactly this that philosophical monists who demand final solutions—tidiness and harmony at any price—have done and are doing still. I do not, of course, mean this as an argument against the proposition that the application of knowledge and skill can, in particular cases, lead to satisfactory solutions. When such dilemmas arise it is one thing to say that every effort must be made to resolve them, and another that it is certain *a priori* that a correct, conclusive solution must always in principle be discoverable—something that the older rationalist metaphysics appeared to guarantee.

Hence, when Mr. Spitz[2] maintains that the frontier falls not so much between positive and negative liberty, but 'in determination of which complex of particular liberties and concomitant restraints is most likely to promote those values that, in Berlin's theory, are distinctively human', and, in the course of his interesting and suggestive review, declares that the issue depends on one's view of human nature, or of human goals (on which men differ), I do not dissent. But when he goes on to say that, in my attempt to cope with the relativity of values, I fall back on the views of J. S. Mill, he seems to me mistaken on an important issue. Mill does seem to have convinced himself that

[1] As was done by Condorcet and his disciples.
[2] 'The Nature and Limits of Freedom', *Dissent*, vol. viii, Winter 1962, pp. 78-86.

there exists such a thing as attainable, communicable, objective truth in the field of value judgments; but that the conditions for its discovery do not exist save in a society which provides a sufficient degree of individual liberty, particularly of inquiry and discussion. This is simply the old objectivist thesis, in an empirical form, with a special rider about the need for individual liberty as a necessary condition for the attainment of this final goal. My thesis is not this at all; but that, since some values may conflict intrinsically, the very notion that a pattern must in principle be discoverable in which they are all rendered harmonious is founded on a false *a priori* view of what the world is like. If I am right in this, and the human condition is such that men cannot always avoid choices, they cannot avoid them not merely for the obvious reasons which philosophers have seldom ignored, namely that there are many possible courses of action and forms of life worth living, and therefore to choose between them is part of being rational or capable of moral judgment; they cannot avoid choice for one central reason (which is, in the ordinary sense, conceptual, not empirical), namely that ends collide; that one cannot have everything. Whence it follows that the very concept of an ideal life, a life in which nothing of value need ever be lost or sacrificed, in which all rational (or virtuous, or otherwise legitimate) wishes must be capable of being truly satisfied—this classical vision is not merely utopian, but incoherent. The need to choose, to sacrifice some ultimate values to others, turns out to be a permanent characteristic of the human predicament. If this is so, it undermines all theories according to which the value of free choice derives from the fact that without it we cannot attain to the perfect life; with the implication that once such perfection has been reached the need for choice between alternatives withers away. On this view, choice, like the party system, or the right to vote against the nominees of the ruling party, becomes obsolete, in the perfect Platonic or theocratic or Jacobin or communist society, where any sign of the recrudescence of disagreement is a symptom of error and vice. For there is only one possible path for the perfectly rational man, since there are now no beguiling illusions, no conflicts, no incongruities, no surprises, no genuine, unpredictable novelty;

everything is still and perfect in the universe governed by what Kant called the Holy Will. Whether or not this calm and tideless sea is conceivable or not, it does not resemble the real world in terms of which alone we conceive men's nature and their values. Given things as we know them, and have known them during recorded human history, capacity for choosing is intrinsic to rationality, if rationality entails normal ability to apprehend the real world. To move in a frictionless medium, desiring only what one can attain, not tempted by alternatives, never seeking incompatible ends, is to live in a coherent fantasy. To offer it as the ideal is to seek to dehumanize men, to turn them into the brainwashed, contented beings of Aldous Huxley's celebrated totalitarian nightmare. To contract the areas of human choice is to do harm to men in an intrinsic, Kantian, not merely utilitarian, sense. The fact that the maintenance of conditions making possible the widest choice must be adjusted—however imperfectly—to other needs, for social stability, predictability, order, and so on, does not diminish their central importance. There is a minimum level of opportunity for choice—not of rational or virtuous choice alone—below which human activity ceases to be free in any meaningful sense. It is true that the cry for individual liberty has often disguised desire for privilege, or for power to oppress and exploit, or simply fear of social change. Nevertheless the modern horror of uniformity, conformism, and mechanization of life is not groundless.

As for the issue of relativity and the subjective nature of values, I wonder whether this has not, for the sake of argument, been exaggerated by philosophers: whether men and their outlooks have differed, over wide stretches of space and time, as greatly as has at times been represented. But on this point—how unchanging, how 'ultimate', how universal and 'basic' human values are—I feel no certainty. If values had varied very widely between cultures and periods, communication would have been harder to achieve, and our historical knowledge, which depends on some degree of ability to understand the goals and motives and ways of life at work in cultures different from our own, would turn out to be an illusion. So, of course, would the findings of historical sociology from which the very concept of social relativity largely derives. Scepticism, driven to extremes, defeats itself by becoming self-refuting.

As for the question of what in fact are the values which we regard as universal and 'basic'—presupposed (if that is the correct logical relation) by the very notions of morality and humanity as such—this seems to me a question of a quasi-empirical kind. That is to say, it seems to be a question for the answer to which we must go to historians, anthropologists, philosophers of culture, social scientists of various kinds, scholars who study the central notions and central ways of be-haviour of entire societies, revealed in monuments, forms of life, social activity, as well as more overt expressions of belief such as laws, faiths, philosophies, literature. I describe this as *quasi*-empirical, because concepts and categories that dominate life and thought over a very large portion (even if not the whole) of the globe, and for very long stretches (even if not the whole) of recorded history, are difficult, and in practice impossible to think away; and in this way differ from the more flexible and changing constructions and hypotheses of the natural sciences.

There is one further point which may be worth reiterating. It is important to discriminate between liberty and the conditions of its exercise. If a man is too poor or too ignorant or too feeble to make use of his legal rights, the liberty that these rights confer upon him is nothing to him, but it is not thereby annihilated. The obligation to promote education, health, justice, to raise standards of living, to provide opportunity for the growth of the arts and the sciences, to prevent reactionary political or social or legal policies or arbitrary inequalities, is not made less stringent because it is not necessarily directed to the promotion of liberty itself, but to conditions in which alone its possession is of value, or to values which may be independent of it. And still, liberty is one thing, and the conditions for it are another. To take a concrete example: it is, I believe, desirable to introduce a uniform system of general primary and secondary education in every country, if only in order to do away with distinctions of social status that are at present created or promoted by the exis-tence of a social hierarchy of schools in some Western countries, notably my own. If I were asked why I believe this, I should give the kind of reasons mentioned by Mr. Spitz,[1] e.g. the intrinsic claims of social equality; the evils arising from differences of status created by a system of education governed by the financial resources or the social position of parents rather than the ability and the needs of the children; the ideal of social solidarity; the need to provide for the bodies and minds of as many human beings as possible, and not only of members of a privileged class; and, what is more relevant here, the need to provide the maximum number of children with opportunities for free choice, which equality in education is likely to increase. If I were told that this must severely curtail the liberty of parents who claim the right not to be interfered with in this matter—that it was an elementary right to be allowed to choose the type of education to be given to one's child, to determine the intellectual, religious, social, economic conditions in which the child is to be brought up—I should not be ready to dismiss this outright. But I should maintain that when (as in this case) values genuinely clash, choices must be made. In this case the clash arises between the need to preserve the existing liberty of some parents to determine the type of education they seek for their children; the need to promote other social purposes; and, finally, the need to create conditions in which those who lack them will be provided with opportunities to exercise those rights (freedom to choose) which they legally possess, but cannot, without such opportunities, put to use. Useless freedoms should be made usable, but they are not identical with the conditions indispensable for their utility. This is not a merely pedantic distinction, for if it is ignored, the meaning and value of freedom of choice is apt to be downgraded. In their zeal to create social and economic conditions in which alone freedom is of genuine value, men tend to forget freedom itself; and if it is remembered, it is liable to be pushed aside to make room for these other values with which the reformers or revolutionaries have become preoccupied.

Again, it must not be forgotten that even though freedom without sufficient material security, health, knowledge, in a society that lacks equality, justice, mutual confidence, may be

[1] Op. cit.

virtually useless, the reverse can also be disastrous. To provide for material needs, for education, for such equality and security as, say, children have at school or laymen in a theocracy, is not to expand liberty. We live in a world characterized by régimes (both right- and left-wing) which have done, or are seeking to do, precisely this; and when they call it freedom, this can be as great a fraud as the freedom of the pauper who has a legal right to purchase luxuries. Indeed, one of the things that Dostoevsky's celebrated fable of the Grand Inquisitor in *The Brothers Karamazov* is designed to show is precisely that paternalism can provide the conditions of freedom, yet withhold freedom itself.

A general consideration follows. If we wish to live in the light of reason, we must follow rules or principles; for that is what being rational is. When these rules or principles conflict in concrete cases, to be rational is to follow the course of conduct which least obstructs the general pattern of life in which we believe. The right policy cannot be arrived at in a mechanical or deductive fashion: there are no hard-and-fast rules to guide us; conditions are often unclear, and principles incapable of being fully analysed or articulated. We seek to adjust the unadjustable, we do the best we can. Those, no doubt, are in some way fortunate who have brought themselves, or have been brought by others, to obey some ultimate principle before the bar of which all problems can be brought. Single-minded monists, ruthless fanatics, men possessed by an all-embracing coherent vision, do not know the doubts and agonies of those who cannot wholly blind themselves to reality. But even those who are aware of the complex texture of experience, of what is not reducible to generalization or capable of computation, can, in the end, justify their decisions only by their coherence with some over-all pattern of a desirable form of personal or social life, of which they may become fully conscious only, it may be, when faced with the need to resolve conflicts of this kind. If this seems vague, it is so of necessity. The notion that there must exist final objective answers to normative questions, truths that can be demonstrated or directly intuited, that it is in principle possible to discover a harmonious pattern in which all values are reconciled, and that it is towards this unique goal that we must make; that we can uncover some single central principle that shapes this vision, a principle which, once found, will govern our lives—this ancient and almost universal belief, on which so much traditional thought and action and philosophical doctrine rests, seems to me invalid, and at times to have led (and still to lead) to absurdities in theory and barbarous consequences in practice.[1]

The fundamental sense of freedom is freedom from chains, from imprisonment, from enslavement by others. The rest is extension of this sense, or else metaphor. To strive to be free is to seek to remove obstacles; to struggle for personal freedom is to seek to curb interference, exploitation, enslavement by men whose ends are theirs, not one's own. Freedom, at least in its political sense, is co-terminous with the absence of bullying or domination. Nevertheless, freedom is not the only value that can or should determine behaviour. Moreover to speak of freedom as an end is much too general. I should like to say once again to my critics that the issue is not one between negative freedom as an absolute value and other, inferior values. It is more complex and more painful. One freedom may abort another; one freedom may obstruct or fail to create conditions which make other freedoms, or a larger degree of freedom, or freedom for more persons, possible; positive and negative freedom may collide; the freedom of the individual or the group may not be fully compatible with a full degree of participation in a common life, with its demands for co-operation, solidarity, fraternity. But beyond all these there is an acuter issue: the paramount need to satisfy the claims of other, no less ultimate, values: justice, happiness, love, the realization of capacities to create new things and experiences and ideas, the discovery of the truth. Nothing is gained by identifying freedom proper, in either of its senses, with these values, or with the conditions of freedom, or by confounding types of freedom with one another. The fact that given examples of negative freedom (especially where they coincide with powers and rights)—say the freedom of parents or schoolmasters to determine the education of children, of employers to

---

[1] The classical—and still, it seems to me, the best—exposition of this state of mind is to be found in Max Weber's distinction between the ethics of conscience and the ethics of responsibility in 'Politics as a Vocation' (Max Weber, *Essays in Sociology*, ed. H. H. Gerth and C. W. Mills).

exploit or dismiss their workers, of slave-owners to dispose of their slaves, of the torturer to inflict pain on his victims—may, in many cases, be wholly undesirable, and should in any sane or decent society be curtailed or suppressed, does not render them genuine freedoms any the less; nor does that fact justify us in so reformulating the definition of freedom that it is always represented as something good without qualification—always leading to the best possible consequences, always likely to promote my 'highest' self, always in harmony with the true laws of my own 'real' nature or those of my society and so on, as has been done in many a classical exposition of freedom, from Stoicism to the social doctrines of our day, at the cost of obscuring profound differences.

If either clarity of thought or rationality in action is not to be hopelessly compromised, such distinctions are of critical importance. Individual freedom may or may not clash with democratic organization, and the positive liberty of self-realization with the negative liberty of non-interference. Emphasis on negative liberty, as a rule, leaves more paths for individuals or groups to pursue; positive liberty, as a rule, opens fewer paths, but with better reasons or greater resources for moving along them; the two may or may not clash. Some of my critics are made indignant by the thought that a man may, on this view, have more 'negative' liberty under the rule of an easy-going or inefficient despot than in a strenuous, but intolerant, egalitarian democracy. But there is an obvious sense in which Socrates would have had more liberty —at least of speech, and even of action—if, like Aristotle, he had escaped from Athens, instead of accepting the laws, bad as well as good, enacted and applied by his fellow citizens in the democracy of which he possessed, and consciously accepted, full membership. Similarly, a man may leave a vigorous and genuinely 'participatory' democratic state in which the social or political pressures are too suffocating for him, for a climate where there may be less civic participation, but more privacy, a less dynamic and all-embracing communal life, less gregariousness but also less surveillance. This may appear undesirable to those who look on distaste for public life or society as a symptom of *malaise*, of a deep alienation. But temperaments differ, and too much enthusiasm for common norms can lead to intolerance and disregard for the inner life of man. I understand and share the indignation of democrats; not only because any negative liberty that I may enjoy in an easy-going or inefficient despotism is precarious, or confined to a minority, but because despotism is irrational and unjust and degrading as such: because it denies human rights even if its subjects are not discontented; because participation in self-government, is, like justice, a basic human requirement, an end in itself. Jacobin 'repressive tolerance' destroys individual liberty as effectively as a despotism (however tolerant) destroys positive liberty and degrades its subjects. Those who endure the defects of one system tend to forget the shortcomings of the other. In different historical circumstances some régimes grow more oppressive than others, and to revolt against them is braver and wiser than to acquiesce. Nevertheless, in resisting great present evils, it is as well not to be blinded to the possible danger of the total triumph of any one principle. It seems to me that no sober observer of the twentieth century can avoid qualms in this matter.[1]

What is true of the confusion of the two freedoms, or of identifying freedom with its conditions, holds in even greater measure of the stretching of the word freedom to include an amalgam of other desirable things—equality, justice, happiness, knowledge, love, creation, and other ends that men seek for their own sakes. This confusion is not merely a theoretical error. Those who are obsessed by the truth that negative freedom is worth little without sufficient conditions for tis active exercise, or without the satisfaction of other human aspirations, are liable to minimize its importance, to deny it the very title of freedom, to transfer it to something that they regard as more precious,

[1] This, indeed, was the point of the penultimate paragraph of p. 171, which was widely taken as an unqualified defence of 'negative' against 'positive' liberty. This was not my intention. This much criticized passage was meant as a defence, indeed, but of a pluralism, based on the perception of incompatibility between the claims of equally ultimate ends, against any ruthless monism which solves such problems by eliminating all but one of the rival claimants. I have therefore revised the text to make it clear that I am not offering a blank endorsement of the 'negative' concept as opposed to its 'positive' twin brother, since this would itself constitute precisely the kind of intolerant monism against which the entire argument is directed.

and finally to forget that without it human life, both social and individual, withers away. If I have been too vehement in the defence of it—only one, I may be reminded, among other human values—and have not insisted as much as my critics demand that to ignore other values can lead to evils at least as great, my insistence upon it in a world in which conditions for freedom may demand an even higher priority does not seem to me to invalidate my general analysis and argument.

Finally one may ask what value there is in liberty as such. Is it a response to a basic need of men, or only something presupposed by other fundamental demands? And further, is this an empirical question, to which psychological, anthropological, sociological, historical facts are relevant? Or is it a purely philosophical question, the solution of which lies in the correct analysis of our basic concepts, and for the answer to which the production of examples, whether real or imaginary, and not factual evidence demanded by empirical inquiries, is sufficient and appropriate? 'Freedom is the essence of man'; '*Frey seyn ist nichts, frey werden ist der Himmel*' (to be free is nothing, to become free is very heaven); 'Every man has a right to life, liberty, and a pursuit of happiness.' Do these phrases embody propositions resting on some empirical foundation, or have they some other logical status? Are they propositions or disguised commands, emotive expressions, declarations of intent or commitment? What role, if any, does evidence—historical, psychological, sociological— play in establishing truth or validity in these matters? Could it be the case that if the evidence of the facts should go against us, we should have to revise our ideas, or withdraw them altogether, or at best concede that they—these propositions if they are are propositions—hold only for particular societies, or particular times and places, as some relativists claim?[1] Or is their authority

---

[1] Joseph de Maistre once observed that, when Rousseau asked why it was that men who were born free were nevertheless everywhere in chains, this was like asking why it was that sheep, who were born carnivorous, nevertheless everywhere nibbled grass. Similarly the Russian radical Alexander Herzen observed that we classify creatures by zoological types, according to the characteristics and habits that are most frequently found to be conjoined. Thus, one of the defining attributes of fish is their liability to live in water; hence, despite the existence of flying fish, we do not say of fish in general that their nature or essence—the 'true' end for which they were created—is to fly, since most fish fail to achieve this and do not display the slightest tendency in this direction. Yet

shown by philosophical analysis which convinces us that indifference to freedom is not compatible with being human, or,
at least, fully human—whether by human beings we mean the
average members of our own culture, or men in general, everywhere, at all times? To this it is sufficient to say that those who
have ever valued liberty for its own sake believed that to be free
to choose, and not to be chosen for, is an inalienable ingredient
in what makes human beings human; and that this underlies both
the positive demand to have a voice in the laws and practices of
the society in which one lives, and to be accorded an area, artificially carved out, if need be, in which one is one's own master,
a 'negative' area in which a man is not obliged to account for his
activities to any man so far as this is compatible with the existence
of organized society.

I should like to add one final qualification. Nothing that I
assert in the essay on two concepts of liberty about the frontiers
of individual liberty (and this applies to the liberty of groups and
associations too) should be taken to mean that freedom in any of
its meanings is either inviolable, or sufficient, in some absolute
sense. It is not inviolable, because abnormal conditions may
occur, in which even the sacred frontiers of which Constant
speaks, e.g. those violated by retrospective laws, punishment of
the innocent, judicial murder, information laid against parents
by children, the bearing of false witness, may have to be dis-
regarded if some sufficiently terrible alternative is to be averted.
Mr. McFarlane[1] urges this point against me, correctly it seems
to me. Nevertheless, the exception proves the rule: precisely
because we regard such situations as being wholly abnormal, and
such measures as abhorrent, to be condoned only in emergencies

in the case of men, and men alone, we say that the nature of man is to seek freedom,
even though only very few men in the long life of our race have in fact pursued it, while
the vast majority at most times have showed little taste for it, and seem contented to be
ruled by others, seeking to be well governed by those who provide them with sufficient
food, shelter, rules of life, but not to be self-governed. Why should man alone, Herzen
asked, be classified in terms of what at most small minorities here or there have ever
sought for its own sake, still less actively fought for? This sceptical reflection was uttered
by a man whose entire life was dominated by a single-minded passion—the pursuit of
liberty, personal and political, of his own and other nations, to which he sacrificed his
public career and his private happiness.

[1] Op. cit.

so critical that the choice is between great evils, we recognize that under normal conditions, for the great majority of men, at most times, in most places, these frontiers are sacred, that is to say, that to overstep them leads to inhumanity. Conversely, the minimum area that men require if such dehumanization is to be averted, a minimum which other men, or institutions created by them, are liable to invade, is no more than a minimum; its frontiers are not to be extended against sufficiently stringent claims on the part of other values, including those of positive liberty itself. Nevertheless the proper concept of degrees of individual liberty still seems to me to consist in the extent of the area in which choices are open. This minimum area may be incompatible with arrangements required by other social ideals, theocratic or aristocratic or technocratic and the like, but this claim is what the demand for individual liberty entails. Least of all does it call for abdication by individuals or groups from democratic self-government of the society, after their own nicely calculated corner has been made secure and fenced in against others, leaving all the rest to the play of power politics. An indefinite expansion of the area in which men can freely choose between various possible courses of action may plainly not be compatible with the realization of other values. Hence, things being as they are, we are compelled to adjust claims, compromise, establish priorities, engage in all those practical operations that social and even individual life has, in fact, always required.

If it is maintained that the identification of the value of liberty with the value of a field of free choice amounts to a doctrine of self-realization, whether for good or evil ends, and that this is closer to positive than to negative liberty, I shall offer no great objection; only repeat that, as a matter of historical fact, distortions of this meaning of positive liberty (or self-determination) even by so well-meaning a liberal as T. H. Green, so original a thinker as Hegel, or so profound a social analyst as Marx, obscured this thesis and at times transformed it into its opposite. Kant, who stated his moral and social position a good deal less equivocally, denounced paternalism, since self-determination is precisely what it obstructs; even if it is indispensable for curing certain evils, it is, for opponents of tyranny, at best a necessary evil; as are all great accumulations of power as such. Those who maintain[1] that such concentrations are sometimes required to remedy injustices or to increase the insufficient liberties of individuals or groups tend to ignore or play down the reverse of the coin: that much power (and authority) is also, as a rule, a standing threat to fundamental liberties. All those who have protested against tyranny in modern times, from Montesquieu to the present day, have struggled with this problem. The doctrine that accumulations of power can never be too great, provided that they are rationally controlled and used, ignores the central reason for pursuing liberty in the first place—that all paternalist governments, however benevolent, cautious, dis-interested, and rational, have tended, in the end, to treat the majority of men as minors, or as being too often incurably foolish or irresponsible; or else as maturing so slowly as not to justify their liberation at any clearly foreseeable date (which, in practice, means at no definite time at all). This is a policy which degrades men, and seems to me to rest on no rational or scientific founda-tion, but, on the contrary, on a profoundly mistaken view of the deepest human needs.

I have, in the essays that follow, attempted to examine some of the fallacies that rest on misunderstanding of certain central human needs and purposes—central, that is, to our normal notion of what it is to be a human being; a being endowed with a nucleus of needs and goals, a nucleus common to all men, which may have a shifting pattern, but one whose limits are determined by the basic need to communicate with other similar beings. The notion of such a nucleus and such limits enters into our conception of the central attributes and functions in terms of which we think of men and societies.

I am only too fully conscious of some of the difficulties and obscurities which my thesis still contains. But short of writing another book, I could do no more than deal with those criticisms which seemed to me at once the most frequent and the least effective, resting as they do on an over-simple application of particular scientific or philosophical principles to social and

[1] e.g. L. J. McFarlane, op. cit., and the majority of democratic theorists.

political problems. But even here I am well aware of how much more needs to be done, especially on the issue of free will, the solution of which seems to me to require a set of new conceptual tools, a break with traditional terminology, which no one, so far as I know, has yet been able to provide.

POLITICAL IDEAS IN THE TWENTIETH CENTURY[1]

'Anyone desiring a quiet life has done badly to be born in the
twentieth century.'   L. TROTSKY

I

HISTORIANS of ideas, however scrupulous and minute they
may feel it necessary to be, cannot avoid perceiving their material
in terms of some kind of pattern. To say this is not necessarily to
subscribe to any form of Hegelian dogma about the dominant
role of laws and metaphysical principles in history—a view
increasingly influential in our time—according to which there is
some single explanation of the order and attributes of persons,
things, and events. Usually this consists in the advocacy of some
fundamental category or principle which claims to act as an infallible guide both to the past and to the future, a magic lens reveal-
ing 'inner', inexorable, all-pervasive historical laws, invisible to
the naked eye of the mere recorder of events, but capable, when
understood, of giving the historian a unique sense of certainty—
certainty not only of what in fact occurred, but of the reason why
it could not have occurred otherwise, affording a secure knowledge which the mere empirical investigator, with his collections
of data, his insecure structure of painstakingly accumulated
evidence, his tentative approximations and perpetual liability to
error and reassessment, can never hope to attain.[2]

---

[1] This article was written in 1949 at the request of the Editor of the American Journal
Foreign Affairs, for its Mid-century Issue. Its tone was to some extent due to the policies
of the Soviet régime during Stalin's last years. Since then a modification of the worst
excesses of that dictatorship has fortunately taken place; but the general tendency with
which the issue was concerned seems to me, if anything, to have gained, if not in intensity,
then in extent: some of the new national states of Asia and Africa seem to show no
greater concern for civil liberties, even allowing for the exigencies of security and
planning which these states need for their development or survival, than the régimes
they have replaced.

[2] I do not, of course, attribute this view either to Hegel or to Marx, whose doctrines
are both more complex and far more plausible; only to the *terribles simplificateurs* among
their followers.

The notion of 'laws' of this kind is rightly condemned as a species of metaphysical fantasy; but the contrary notion of bare facts—facts which are nothing but facts, hard, inescapable, untainted by interpretation or arrangement in man-made patterns—is equally mythological. To comprehend and contrast and classify and arrange, to see in patterns of lesser or greater complexity, is not a peculiar kind of thinking, it is thinking itself. We accuse historians of exaggeration, distortion, ignorance, bias, or departure from the facts, not because they select, compare, and set forth in a context and order which are in part, at least, of their own choosing, in part conditioned by the circumstances of their material and social environment or their character or purpose—we accuse them only when the result deviates too far, contrasts too harshly with the accepted canons of verification and interpretation which belong to their own time and place and society. These canons and methods and categories are those of the normal rational outlook of a given period and culture, at their best a sharpened, highly trained form of this outlook, which takes cognizance of all the relevant scientific techniques available, but is itself not one of them. All the criticisms directed against this or that writer for an excess of bias or fancy, or too weak a sense of evidence, or too limited a perception of connexions between events, are based not upon some absolute standard of truth, of strict 'factuality', of a rigid adherence to a permanently fixed ideal method of 'scientifically' discovering the past *wie es eigentlich gewesen*, in contrast with mere theories about it, for there is in the last analysis no meaning in the notion of 'objective' criticism in this timeless sense. They rest rather on the most refined concept of accuracy and objectivity and scrupulous 'fidelity to the facts' which obtain in a given society at a given period, within the subject in question.

When the great romantic revolution in the writing of history transferred emphasis from the achievements of individuals to the growth and influence of institutions conceived in much less personal terms, the degree of 'fidelity to the facts' was not thereby automatically altered. The new kind of history, the account of the development, let us say, of public and private law, or government, or literature, or social habits during some given period of time, was not necessarily less or more accurate or 'objective' than earlier accounts of the acts and fate of Alcibiades or Marcus Aurelius or Calvin or Louis XIV. Thucydides or Tacitus or Voltaire were not subjective or vague or fanciful in a sense in which Ranke or Savigny or Michelet were not. The new history was merely written from what is nowadays called a different 'angle'. The kinds of fact the new history was intended to record were different, the emphasis was different, a shift of interest had occurred in the questions asked and consequently in the methods used. The concepts and terminology reflect an altered view of what constitutes evidence and therefore, in the end, of what are the 'facts'. When the 'romances' of chroniclers were criticized by 'scientific' historians, at least part of the implied reproach lay in the alleged discrepancies in the work of the older writers from the findings of the most admired and trusted sciences of a later period; and these were in their turn due to the change in the prevalent conceptions of the patterns of human development—to the change in the models in terms of which the past was perceived, those artistic, theological, mechanical, biological, or psychological models which were reflected in the fields of inquiry, in the new questions asked and the new types of technique used, to answer questions felt to be more interesting or important than those which had become outmoded.

The history of these changes of 'models' is to a large degree the history of human thought. The 'organic' or the Marxist methods of investigating history certainly owed part of their vogue to the prestige of the particular natural sciences, or the particular artistic techniques, upon whose model they were supposedly or genuinely constructed; the increased interest, for example, both in biology and in music, from which many basic metaphors and analogies derived, is relevant to the historical writing of the nineteenth century, as the new interest in physics and mathematics is to the philosophy and history of the eighteenth; and the deflationary methods and ironical temper of the historians who wrote after the war of 1914-18 were conspicuously influenced by—and accepted in terms of—the new psychological and sociological techniques which had gained public confidence during this period. The relative dominance of, say, social, economic, and political concepts and presuppositions in a once admired historical work throws more light upon the general characteristics of its time and for this reason is a more reliable index to the standards adopted, the questions asked, the respective roles of 'facts' and 'interpretation', and, in effect, to the entire social and political outlook of an age, than the putative distance of the work in question from some imaginary, fixed, unaltering ideal of absolute truth, metaphysical or scientific, empirical or *a priori*. It is in terms of such shifts in the methods of treating the past (or the present or the future) and of idioms and catchwords, the doubts and hopes, fears and exhortations which they expressed, that the development of political ideas and the conceptual apparatus of a society and of its most gifted and articulate representatives can best be judged. No doubt the concepts in terms of which people speak and think may be symptoms and effects of other processes social, psychological, physical, the discovery of which is the task of this or that empirical science. But this does not detract from their importance and paramount interest for those who wish to know what constitutes the conscious experience of the most characteristic men of an age or a society, whatever its causes and whatever its fate. And we are, of course, for obvious reasons of perspective, in a better situation to determine this in the case of past societies than for our own. The historical approach is inescapable: the very sense of contrast and dissimilarity with which the past affects us provides the only relevant background against which the features peculiar to our own experience stand out in sufficient relief to be adequately discerned and described.

The student of the political ideas of, for example, the mid-nineteenth century must indeed be blind if he does not, sooner or later, become aware of the profound differences in ideas and terminology, in the general view of things—the ways in which the elements of experience are conceived to be related to one another—which divide that not very distant age from our own. He understands neither that time nor his own if he does not perceive the contrast between what was common to Comte and Mill, Mazzini and Michelet, Herzen and Marx, on the one hand, and to Max Weber and William James, Tawney and Beard,

Lytton Strachey and Namier, on the other; the continuity of the European intellectual tradition without which no historical understanding at all would be possible is, at shorter range, a succession of specific discontinuities and dissimilarities. Consequently, the remarks which follow deliberately ignore the similarities in favour of the specific differences in political outlook which characterize our own time, and to a large degree, solely our own.

II

The two great liberating political movements of the nineteenth century were, as every history book informs us, humanitarian individualism and romantic nationalism. Whatever their differences—and they were notoriously profound enough to lead to a sharp divergence and ultimate collision of these two ideals— they had this in common: they believed that the problems both of individuals and of societies could be solved if only the forces of intelligence and of virtue could be made to prevail over ignorance and wickedness. They believed, as against the pessimists and fatalists, both religious and secular, whose voices, audible indeed a good deal earlier, began to sound loudly only toward the end of the century, that all clearly understood questions could be solved by human beings with the moral and intellectual resources at their disposal. No doubt different schools of thought returned different answers to these varying problems; utilitarians said one thing, and neo-feudal romantics— Tory democrats, Christian Socialists, Pan-Germans, Slavophiles —another. Liberals believed in the unlimited power of education and the power of rational morality to overcome economic misery and inequality. Socialists, on the contrary, believed that without radical alterations in the distribution and control of economic resources no amount of change of heart or mind on the part of individuals could be adequate; or, for that matter, occur at all. Conservatives and Socialists believed in the power and influence of institutions and regarded them as a necessary safeguard against the chaos, injustice, and cruelty caused by uncontrolled individualism; anarchists, radicals, and liberals looked upon institutions as such with suspicion as being obstructive to the realization of that free (and, in the view of most such thinkers, rational) society which the will of man could both conceive and build, if it were not for the unliquidated residue of ancient abuses (or un-reason) upon which the existing rulers of society —whether individuals or administrative machines—leaned so heavily, and of which so many of them indeed were typical expressions.

Arguments about the relative degree of the obligation of the individual to society, and *vice versa*, filled the air. It is scarcely necessary to rehearse these familiar questions, which to this day form the staple of discussion in the more conservative institutions of Western learning, to realize that however wide the disagreements about the proper answers to them, the questions themselves were common to Liberals and Conservatives alike. There were, of course, even at that time isolated irrationalists—Stirner, Kierkegaard, in certain moods Carlyle; but in the main all the parties to the great controversies, even Calvinists and ultramontane Catholics, accepted the notion of man as resembling in varying degrees one or the other of two idealized types. Either he is a creature free and naturally good, but hemmed in and frustrated[1] by obsolete or corrupt or sinister institutions masquerading as saviours, protectors, and repositories of sacred traditions; or he is a being within limits, but never wholly, free, and to some degree, but never entirely, good, and consequently unable to save himself by his own wholly unaided efforts; and therefore rightly seeking salvation within the great frameworks— states, churches, unions. For only these great edifices promote solidarity, security, and sufficient strength to resist the shallow joys and dangerous, ultimately self-destructive, liberties peddled by those conscienceless or self-deceived individualists who, in the name of some bloodless intellectual dogma, or noble enthusiasm for an ideal unrelated to human lives, ignore or destroy the rich texture of social life heavy with treasures from the past— blind leaders of the blind, robbing men of their most precious resources, exposing them again to the perils of a life solitary, brutish, nasty, and short. Yet there was at least one premiss

---

[1] According to some, for historically or metaphysically inevitable reasons or causes which, however, soon or late will lose their potency.

common to all the disputants, namely the belief that the problems were real, that it took men of exceptional training and intelligence to formulate them properly, and men with exceptional grasp of the facts, will-power, and capacity for effective thought to find and apply the correct solutions.

These two great currents finally ended in exaggerated and indeed distorted forms as Communism and Fascism—the first as the treacherous heir of the liberal internationalism of the previous century, the second as the culmination and bankruptcy of the mystical patriotism which animated the national movements of the time. All movements have origins, forerunners, imperceptible beginnings: nor does the twentieth century seem divided from the nineteenth by so universal an explosion as the French Revolution, even in our day the greatest of all historical landmarks. Yet it is a fallacy to regard Fascism and Communism as being in the main only more uncompromising and violent manifestations of an earlier crisis, the culmination of a struggle fully discernible long before. The differences between the political movements of the twentieth century and the nineteenth are very sharp, and they spring from factors whose full force was not properly realized until our century was well under way. For there is a barrier which divides what is unmistakably past and done with from that which most characteristically belongs to our day. The familiarity of this barrier must not blind us to its relative novelty. One of the elements of the new outlook is the notion of unconscious and irrational influences which outweigh the forces of reason; another the notion that answers to problems exist not in rational solutions, but in the removal of the problems themselves by means other than thought and argument. The interplay between the old tradition, which saw history as the battle-ground between the easily identifiable forces of light and darkness, reason and obscurantism, progress and reaction; or alternatively between spiritualism and empiricism, intuition and scientific method, institutionalism and individualism—the conflict between this order and, on the other hand, the new factors violently opposed to the humanist psychology of *bourgeois* civilization is to a large extent the history of political ideas in our time.

III

And yet to a casual observer of the politics and the thought of the twentieth century it might at first seem that every idea and movement typical of our time is best understood as a natural development of tendencies already prominent in the nineteenth century. In the case of the growth of international institutions, for instance, this seems a truism. What are the Hague Court, the old League of Nations and its modern successor, the numerous pre-war and post-war international agencies and conventions for political, economic, social, and humanitarian purposes— what are they, if not the direct descendants of that liberal internationalism—Tennyson's 'Parliament of Man'—which was the staple of all progressive thought and action in the nineteenth century, and indeed of much in the century before it? The language of the great founders of European liberalism—Condorcet, for example, or Helvétius—does not differ greatly in substance, nor indeed in form, from the most characteristic moments in the speeches of Woodrow Wilson or Thomas Masaryk. European liberalism wears the appearance of a single coherent movement, little altered during almost three centuries, founded upon relatively simple intellectual foundations, laid by Locke or Grotius or even Spinoza; stretching back to Erasmus and Montaigne, the Italian Renaissance, Seneca, and the Greeks. In this movement there is in principle a rational answer to every question. Man is, in principle at least, everywhere and in every condition, able, if he wills it, to discover and apply rational solutions to his problems. And these solutions, because they are rational, cannot clash with one another, and will ultimately form a harmonious system in which the truth will prevail, and freedom, happiness, and unlimited opportunity for untrammelled self-development will be open to all.

The consciousness of history which grew in the nineteenth century modified the severe and simple design of the classical theory as it was conceived in the eighteenth century. Human progress was presently seen to be conditioned by factors of greater complexity than had been conceived of in the spring-time of liberal individualism: education, rationalist propaganda, even legislation, were perhaps not always, nor everywhere, quite enough. Such factors as the particular and special influences by which various societies were historically shaped—some due to physical conditions, others to socio-economic forces or to more elusive emotional and what were vaguely classified as 'cultural' factors—were presently allowed to have greater importance than they were accorded in the over-simple schemas of Condorcet or Bentham. Education, and all forms of social action, must, it was now thought, be fitted to take account of historical needs which made men and their institutions somewhat less easy to mould into the required pattern than had been too optimistically assumed in earlier and more naïve times.

Nevertheless, the original programme continued in its various forms to exercise an almost universal spell. This applied to the Right no less than to the Left. Conservative thinkers, unless they were concerned solely with obstructing the liberals and their allies, believed and acted upon the belief that, provided no excessive violence was done to slow but certain processes of 'natural' development, all might yet be well; the faster must be restricted from pushing aside the slower, and in this way all would arrive in the end. This was the doctrine preached by Bonald early in the century, and it expressed the optimism of even the stoutest believers in original sin. Provided that traditional differences of outlook and social structure were protected from what conservatives were fond of describing as the 'unimaginative', 'artificial', 'mechanical' levelling processes favoured by the liberals; provided that the infinity of 'intangible' or 'historic' or 'natural' or 'providential' distinctions (which to them seemed to constitute the essence of fruitful forms of life) were preserved from being transformed into a uniform collection of homogeneous units moving at a pace dictated by some 'irrelevant' or 'extraneous' authority, contemptuous of prescriptive or traditional rights and habits. Provided that adequate safeguards were instituted against too reckless a trampling upon the sacred past —with these guarantees—rational reforms and changes were allowed to be feasible and even desirable. Given these safeguards, conservatives no less than liberals were prepared to look upon the conscious direction of human affairs by qualified experts with a considerable degree of approval; and not merely by experts, but by a growing number of individuals and groups, drawn from, and representing, wider and wider sections of a society which was progressively becoming more and more enlightened.

This is a mood and attitude common to a wider section of opinion in the later nineteenth century in Europe, and not merely in the West but in the East too, than historians, affected by the political struggles of a later or earlier period, have allowed. One of the results of it—in so far as it was a causal factor and not merely a symptom of the process—was the wide development of political representation in the West whereby in the end all classes of the population in the succeeding century began to attain to power, sooner or later, in one country or another. The nineteenth century was full of unrepresented groups engaged in the struggle for life, self-expression, and later for control. Its representatives counted among them heroes and martyrs and men of moral and artistic power whom a genuine struggle of this kind brings forth. The twentieth century, by satisfying much of the social and political hunger of the Victorian period, did indeed witness a striking improvement in the material condition of the majority of the peoples of Western Europe, due in large measure to the energetic social legislation which transformed the social order.

But one of the least predicted results of this trend (although isolated thinkers like Tocqueville, Burckhardt, Herzen, and, of course, Nietzsche had more than an inkling of it) was a decline in the quality of moral passion and force and of romantic, artistic rebelliousness which had marked the early struggles of the dis-satisfied social groups during their heroic period when, deeply divergent though they were, they fought together against tyrants, priests, and militant philistines. Whatever the injustices and miseries of our time—and they are plainly no fewer than those of the immediate past—they are less likely to find expression in monuments of noble eloquence, because that kind of inspiration seems to spring only from the oppression or suppression of entire classes of society.[1] There arrives a brief moment when, as indeed

[1] Hence, perhaps, the very different quality of the tone and substance of social protest, however legitimate, in the West in our time, as compared to that of Asian or African critics who speak for societies where large sections of the population are still crushed or submerged.

Marx with much insight pointed out, the leaders of the most articulate, and socially and economically most developed, of these suppressed groups are lifted by the common mood and for a moment speak not for their own class or milieu alone, but in the name of all the oppressed; for a brief instant their utterance has a universal quality.

But a situation where all or nearly all the great sections of society have been, or are on the point of being, in at any rate the formal possession of power is unfavourable to that truly disinterested eloquence—disinterested partly at least because fulfilment is remote, because principles shine forth most clearly in the darkness and void, because the inner vision is still free from the confusions and obscurities, the compromises and blurred outlines of the external world inevitably forced upon it by the beginnings of practical action. No body of men which has tasted power, or is within a short distance of doing so, can avoid a certain degree of that cynicism which, like a chemical reaction, is generated by the sharp contact between the pure ideal, nurtured in the wilderness, and its realization in some unpredicted form which seldom conforms to the hopes or fears of earlier times. It therefore takes an exceptional effort of the imagination to discard the context of later years, to cast ourselves back into the period when the views and movements which have since triumphed and lost their glamour long ago were still capable of stirring so much vehement idealistic feeling: when, for example, nationalism was not in principle felt to be incompatible with a growing degree of internationalism, or civil liberties with a rational organization of society; when this was believed by some conservatives almost as much as their rivals, and the gap between the moderates of both sides was only that between the plea that reason must not be permitted to increase the pace of progress beyond the limits imposed by 'history' and the counterplea that *la raison a toujours raison*, that memories and shadows were less important than the direct perception of the real world in the clear light of day. This was a time when liberals in their turn themselves began to feel the impact of historicism, and to admit the need for a certain degree of adjustment and even control of social life, perhaps by the hated state itself, if only to mitigate the inhumanity of unbridled private enterprise, to protect the liberties of the weak, to safeguard those basic human rights without which there could be neither happiness nor justice nor freedom to pursue that which made life worth living.

The philosophical foundations of these liberal beliefs in the mid-nineteenth century were somewhat obscure. Rights described as 'natural' or 'inherent', absolute standards of truth and justice, were not compatible with tentative empiricism and utilitarianism; yet liberals believed in both. Nor was faith in full democracy strictly consistent with belief in the inviolable rights of minorities or dissident individuals. But so long as the right-wing opposition set itself against all these principles, the contradictions could, on the whole, be allowed to lie dormant, or to form the subject of peaceful academic disputes, not exacerbated by the urgent need for immediate practical application. Indeed, the very recognition of inconsistencies in doctrine or policy further enhanced the role of rational criticism, by which, in the end, all questions could and would one day be settled. Socialists for their part resembled the conservatives in believing in the existence of inexorable laws of history, and, like them, accused the liberals of legislating 'unhistorically' for timeless abstractions —an activity for which history would not neglect to take due revenge. But they also resembled the liberals in believing in the supreme value of rational analysis, in policies founded on theoretical considerations deduced from 'scientific' premises, and with them accused the conservatives of misinterpreting 'the facts' to justify the miserable *status quo*, of condoning misery and injustice; not indeed like the liberals by ignoring history, but by misreading it in a manner consciously or unconsciously calculated to preserve their own power upon a specious moral basis. But genuinely revolutionary as some among them were, and a thoroughly new phenomenon in the Western world, the majority of them shared with the parties which they attacked the common assumption that men must be spoken and appealed to in terms of the needs and interests and ideals of which they were, or could be made to be, conscious.

Conservatives, liberals, radicals, socialists differed in their interpretation of historical change. They disagreed about what were the deepest needs, interests, ideals of human beings, about who held them, and how deeply or widely or for what length of time, about the method of their discovery, or their validity in this or that situation. They differed about the facts, they differed about ends and means, they seemed to themselves to agree on almost nothing. But what they had in common—too obviously to be fully aware of it themselves—was the belief that their age was ridden with social and political problems which could be solved only by the conscious application of truths upon which all men endowed with adequate mental powers could agree. The Marxists did indeed question this in theory, but not in practice: even they did not seriously attack the thesis that when ends were not yet attained and choice of means was limited, the proper way of setting about adapting the means to the ends was by the use of all the skill and energy and intellectual and moral insight available. And while some regarded these problems as akin to those of the natural sciences, some to those of ethics or religion, while others supposed that they were altogether *sui generis* and called for altogether unique solutions, they were agreed—it seemed too obvious to need stating—that the problems themselves were genuine and urgent and intelligible in more or less similar terms to all clear-headed men, that all answers were entitled to a hearing, and that nothing was gained by ignorance or the supposition that the problems did not exist.

This set of common assumptions—they are part of what the word 'enlightenment' means—were, of course, deeply rationalistic. They were denied implicitly by the whole Romantic movement, and explicitly by isolated thinkers—Carlyle, Dostoevsky, Baudelaire, Schopenhauer, Nietzsche. And there were obscurer prophets—Büchner, Kierkegaard, Leontiev—who protested against the prevailing orthodoxy with a depth and originality which became clear only in our own time. Not that these thinkers represent any one single movement, or even an easily identifiable 'trend'; but in one relevant particular they display an affinity. They denied the importance of political action based on rational considerations, and to this extent they were rightly abhorred by the supporters of respectable conservatism. They said or implied that rationalism in any form was a fallacy derived from a false analysis of the character of human beings, because the springs of human action lay in regions unthought of by the sober thinkers whose views enjoyed prestige among the serious public. But their voices were few and discordant, and their eccentric views were ascribed to psychological aberrations. Liberals, however much they admired their artistic genius, were revolted by what they conceived as a perverted view of mankind, and either ignored it or rejected it violently. Conservatives looked upon them as allies against the exaggerated rationalism and infuriating optimism of both liberals and socialists, but treated them nervously as queer visionaries, a little unhinged, not to be imitated or approached too closely. The socialists looked on them as so many deranged reactionaries, scarcely worth their powder and shot. The main currents both on the Right and on the Left flowed round and over these immovable, isolated rocks with their absurd appearance of seeking to arrest or deflect the central current. What were they, after all, but survivals of a darker age, or interesting misfits, sad and at times fascinating casualties of the advance of history, worthy of sympathetic insight—men of talent or even genius born out of their time, gifted poets, remarkable artists, but surely not thinkers worthy of detailed attention on the part of serious students of social and political life?

There was (it is worth saying again) a somewhat sinister element dimly discernible from its very beginning in Marxism—in the main a highly rationalistic system—which seemed hostile to this entire outlook, denying the primacy of the individual's reason in the choice of ends and in effective government alike. But the worship of the natural sciences as the sole proper model for political theory and action which Marxism shared with its liberal antagonists was unpropitious to a clearer perception of its own full nature; and so this aspect of it lay largely unrecognized until Sorel brought it to life and combined it with the Bergsonian anti-rationalism by which his thought is very strongly coloured; and until Lenin, stemming from a different tradition, with his genius for organization half instinctively recognized its superior insight into the irrational springs of human conduct, and translated it into effective practice. But Lenin did not, and his followers to this day do not, seem fully aware of the degree to which this essentially romantic element in Marxism influenced their actions. Or, if aware, they did not and do not admit it. This was so when the twentieth century opened.

IV

Chronological frontiers are seldom landmarks in the history of ideas, and the current of the old century, to all appearances irresistible, seemed to flow peacefully into the new. Presently the picture began to alter. Humanitarian liberalism encountered more and more obstacles to its reforming zeal from the conscious or unconscious opposition both of governments and other centres of social power, as well as the passive resistance of established institutions and habits. The militants among them found themselves compelled to use increasingly radical means in organizing the classes of the population on whose behalf it fought into something sufficiently powerful to work effectively against the old establishment.

The history of the transformation of gradualist and Fabian tactics into the militant formations of Communism and Syndicalism, as well as the milder formations of Social Democracy and trade unionism, is a history not so much of principles as of their interplay with new material facts. In a sense Communism is doctrinaire humanitarianism driven to an extreme in the pursuit of effective offensive and defensive methods. No movement at first sight seems to differ more sharply from liberal reformism than does Marxism, yet the central doctrines—human perfectibility, the possibility of creating a harmonious society by a natural means, the belief in the compatibility (indeed the inseparability) of liberty and equality—are common to both. The historical transformation may occur continuously, or in sudden revolutionary leaps, but it must proceed in accordance with an intelligible, logically connected pattern, abandonment of which is always foolish, always utopian. No one doubted that Liberalism and Socialism were bitterly opposed both on ends and in methods: yet at their edges they shaded off into one another.[1] Marxism is

---

[1] The history and the logic of the transformation of liberalism in the nineteenth century into socialism in the twentieth is a complex and fascinating subject of cardinal importance; but cannot, for reasons of space and relevance, even be touched upon in this short essay.

a doctrine which, however strongly it may stress the class-conditioned nature of action and thought, nevertheless in theory sets out to appeal to reason, at least among the class destined by history to triumph—the proletariat. In the Communist view the proletariat alone can face the future without flinching, because it need not be driven into falsification of the facts by fear of what the future may bring. And, as a corollary, this applies also to those intellectuals who have liberated themselves from the prejudices and rationalizations—the 'ideological distortions' of their economic class—and have aligned themselves with the winning side in the social struggle. To them, since they are fully rational, the privileges of democracy and of free use of all their intellectual faculties may be accorded. They are to Marxists what the enlightened *philosophes* were to the Encyclopedists: their task is to free men from 'false consciousness' and help to realize the means that will transform all those who are historically capable of it into their own liberated and rational likeness.

But in 1903 there occurred an event which marked the culmination of a process which has altered the history of our world. At the conference of the Russian Social Democratic Party held in that year, which began in Brussels and ended in London, during the discussion of what seemed at first a purely technical question—how far centralization and hierarchical discipline should govern the behaviour of the Party—a delegate named Posadovsky inquired whether the emphasis laid by the 'hard' Socialists—Lenin and his friends—upon the need for the exercise of absolute authority by the revolutionary nucleus of the Party might not prove incompatible with those fundamental liberties to whose realization Socialism, no less than liberalism, was officially dedicated. He asked whether the basic, minimum civil liberties—'the inviolability of the person'—should not be infringed and even violated if the party leaders so decided. He was answered by Plekhanov, one of the founders of Russian Marxism, and its most venerated figure, a cultivated, fastidious, and morally sensitive scholar of wide outlook, who had for twenty years lived in Western Europe and was much respected by the leaders of Western Socialism, the very symbol of civilized 'scientific' thinking among Russian revolutionaries. Plekhanov, speaking solemnly, and with a splendid disregard for grammar, pronounced the words, *Salus revolutiae suprema lex*.[1] Certainly, if the revolution demanded it, everything—democracy, liberty, the rights of the individual—must be sacrificed to it. If the democratic assembly elected by the Russian people after the revolution proved amenable to Marxist tactics, it would be kept in being as a Long Parliament; if not, it would be disbanded as quickly as possible. A Marxist revolution could not be carried through by men obsessed by scrupulous regard for the principles of *bourgeois* liberals. Doubtless whatever was valuable in these principles, like everything else good and desirable, would ultimately be realized by the victorious working class; but during the revolutionary period preoccupation with such ideals was evidence of a lack of seriousness.

Plekhanov, who was brought up in a humane and liberal tradition, did, of course, later retreat from this position himself. The mixture of utopian faith and brutal disregard for civilized morality proved in the end too repulsive to a man who had spent the greater part of his civilized and productive life among Western workers and their leaders. Like the vast majority of Social Democrats, like Marx and Engels themselves, he was too European to try to realize a policy which, in the words of Shigalev in Dostoevsky's *The Possessed*, 'starting from unlimited liberty ends in unlimited depotism'. But Lenin[2] accepted the premisses, and being logically driven to conclusions repulsive to most of his colleagues, accepted them easily and without apparent qualms. His assumptions were, perhaps, in some sense, still those of the optimistic rationalists of the eighteenth and nineteenth centuries: the coercion, violence, executions, the total suppression of individual differences, the rule of a small, virtually self-appointed minority, were necessary only in the interim period, only so long as there was a powerful enemy to be destroyed. It was necessary only in order that the majority of mankind, once it was liberated from the exploitation of fools by knaves and of weak knaves by more powerful ones, could develop—trammelled no longer by ignorance or idleness or vice, free at last to realize to their fullest extent the infinitely rich potentialities of human nature. This dream may indeed have affinities with the dreams of

[1] But see Appendix.   [2] Like Posadovsky himself.

Diderot or St.-Simon or Kropotkin, but what marked it as something relatively novel was the assumption about the means required to translate it into reality. And the assumption, although apparently concerned solely with methods, and derived from Babeuf or Blanqui or Tkachov or the French Communards,[1] was very different from the practical programme set forth by the most 'activist' and least 'evolutionary' Western Socialists towards the end of the nineteenth century. The difference was crucial and marked the birth of the new age.

What Lenin demanded was unlimited power for a small body of professional revolutionaries, trained exclusively for one purpose, and ceaselessly engaged in its pursuit by every means in their power. This was necessary because democratic methods, and the attempts to persuade and preach used by earlier reformers and rebels, were ineffective; and this in its turn was due to the fact that they rested on a false psychology, sociology, and theory of history—namely the assumption that men acted as they did because of conscious beliefs which could be changed by argument. For if Marx had done anything, he had surely shown that such beliefs and ideals were mere 'reflections' of the condition of the socially and economically determined classes of men, to some one of which every individual must belong. A man's beliefs, if Marx and Engels were right, flowed from the situation of his class, and could not alter—so far, at least, as the mass of men was concerned—without a change in that situation. The proper task of a revolutionary therefore was to change the 'objective' situation, i.e. to prepare the class for its historical task in the overthrow of the hitherto dominant classes.

Lenin went further than this. He acted as if he believed not merely that it was useless to talk and reason with persons precluded by class interest from understanding and acting upon the truths of Marxism, but that the mass of the proletarians themselves were too benighted to grasp the role which history had called on them to play. He saw the choice as being one between education, the stimulation among the army of the dispossessed of a 'critical spirit' (which would awaken them intellectually, but might lead to a vast deal of discussion and controversy similar to

[1] Or, as is quite likely, from Marx's own writings in 1847-51.

that which divided and enfeebled the intellectuals), and the turning of them into an obedient force held together by a military discipline and a set of perpetually ingeminated formulae (at least as powerful as the patriotic patter used by the Tsarist régime) to shut out independent thought. If the choice had to be made, then it was mere irresponsibility to stress the former in the name of some abstract principle such as democracy or enlightenment. The important thing was the creation of a state of affairs in which human resources were developed in accordance with a rational pattern. Men were moved more often by irrational than reasonable solutions. The masses were too stupid and too blind to be allowed to proceed in the direction of their own choosing. Tolstoy and the populists were profoundly mistaken: the simple agricultural labourer had no deep truths, no valuable way of life, to impart; he and the city worker and the simple soldier were fellow serfs in a condition of abject poverty and squalor, caught in a system which bred fratricidal strife among themselves; they could be saved only by being ruthlessly ordered by leaders who had acquired a capacity for knowing how to organize the liberated slaves into a rational planned system.

Lenin himself was in certain respects oddly utopian. He started with the egalitarian belief that with education, and a rational economic organization, almost anyone could be brought in the end to perform almost any task efficiently. But his practice was strangely like that of those irrationalist reactionaries who believed that man was everywhere wild, bad, stupid, and unruly, and must be held in check and provided with objects of uncritical worship. This must be done by a clear-sighted band of organizers, whose tactics—if not ideals—rested on the truths perceived by élitists—men like Nietzsche, Pareto, or the French absolutist thinkers from De Maistre to Maurras, and indeed Marx himself—men who had grasped the true nature of social development, and in the light of their discovery saw the liberal theory of human progress as something unreal, thin, pathetic, and absurd. Whatever his crudities and errors, on the central issue Hobbes, not Locke, turned out to be right: men sought neither happiness nor liberty nor justice, but, above and before all, security. Aristotle, too, was right: a great number of men were slaves by nature, and when liberated from their chains did not possess the moral and intellectual resources with which to face the prospect of responsibility, of too wide a choice between alternatives; and therefore, having lost one set of chains, inevitably searched for another or forged new chains themselves. It follows that the wise revolutionary legislator, so far from seeking to emancipate human beings from the framework without which they feel lost and desperate, will seek rather to erect a framework of his own, corresponding to the new needs of the new age brought about by natural or technological change. The value of the framework will depend upon the unquestioning faith with which its main features are accepted; otherwise it no longer possesses sufficient strength to support and contain the wayward, potentially anarchical and self-destructive creatures who seek salvation in it. The framework is that system of political, social, economic, and religious institutions, those 'myths', dogmas, ideals, categories of thought and language, modes of feeling, scales of values, 'socially approved' attitudes and habits (called by Marx 'superstructure') that represent 'rationalizations', 'sublimations', and symbolic representations, which cause men to function in an organized way, prevent chaos, fulfil the function of the Hobbesian state. This view which inspires Jacobin tactics, though not, of course, either Jacobin or Communist doctrines, is not so very remote from De Maistre's central and deliberately unprobed mystery—the supernatural authority whereby and in whose name rulers can rule and inhibit their subjects' unruly tendencies, above all the tendency to ask too many questions, to question too many established rules. Nothing can be permitted which might even a little weaken that sense of reliability and security which it is the business of the framework to provide. Only thus (in this view) can the founder of the new free society control whatever threatens to dissipate human energy or to slow down the relentless treadmill which alone prevents men from stopping to commit acts of suicidal folly, which alone protects them from too much freedom, from too little restraint, from the vacuum which mankind, no less than nature, abhors.

Henri Bergson had (following the German romantics) been speaking of something not too unlike this when he had contrasted the flow of life with the forces of critical reason which cannot create or unite, but only divide, arrest, make dead, disintegrate. Freud, too, contributed to this; not in his work of genius as the greatest healer and psychological theorist of our time, but as the originator, however innocent, of the misapplication of rational psychological and social methods by muddle-headed men of good will and quacks and false prophets of every hue. By giving currency to exaggerated versions of the view that the true reasons for men's beliefs were most often very different from what they themselves thought them to be, being frequently caused by events and processes of which they were neither aware nor in the least anxious to be aware, these eminent thinkers helped, however unwittingly, to discredit the rational foundations from which their own doctrines derived their logical force. For it was but a short step from this to the view that what made men most permanently contented was not—as they themselves supposed— the discovery of solutions to the questions which perplexed them, but rather some process, natural or artificial, whereby the problems were made to vanish altogether. They vanished because their psychological 'sources' had been diverted or dried up, leaving behind only those less exacting questions whose solutions did not demand resources beyond the patient's strength.

That this short way with the troubled and the perplexed which underlay much traditionalist, anti-rationalist, right-wing thought should have influenced the Left was new indeed. It is this change of attitude to the function and value of the intellect that is perhaps the best indication of the great gap which divided the twentieth century from the nineteenth.

V

The central point which I wish to make is this: during all the centuries of recorded history the course of intellectual endeavour, the purpose of education, the substance of controversies about the truth or value of ideas, presupposed the existence of certain crucial questions, the answers to which were of paramount importance. How valid, it was asked, were the various claims to provide the best methods of arriving at knowledge and truth made by such great and famous disciplines as metaphysics, ethics, theology, and the sciences of nature and of man? What was the right life for men to lead, and how was it discovered? Did God exist, and could His purposes be known or even guessed at? Did the universe, and in particular human life, have a purpose? If so, whose purpose did it fulfil? How did one set about answering such questions? Were they, or were they not, analogous to the kind of questions to which the sciences or common sense provided satisfactory, generally accepted, replies? If not, did it make sense to ask them?

And as in metaphysics and ethics, so in politics too. The political problem was concerned, for example, with establishing why any individual or individuals should obey other individuals or associations of individuals. All the classical doctrines which deal with the familiar topics of liberty and authority, sovereignty and natural rights, the ends of the state and the ends of the individual, the General Will and the rights of minorities, secularism and theocracy, functionalism and centralization—all these are various ways of attempting to formulate methods in terms of which this fundamental question can be answered in a manner compatible with the other beliefs and the general outlook of the inquirer and his generation. Great and sometimes mortal conflicts have arisen over the proper techniques for the answering of such questions. Some sought answers in sacred books, others in direct personal revelation, some in metaphysical insight, others in the pronouncements of infallible sages or in speculative systems or in laborious empirical investigations. The questions were of vital importance for the conduct of life. There were, of course, sceptics in every generation who suggested that there were, perhaps, no final answers, that solutions hitherto provided depended on highly variable factors such as the climate in which the theorist's life was lived, or his social or economic or political condition, or that of his fellows, or his or their emotional disposition, or the kinds of intellectual interests which absorbed him or them. But such sceptics were usually treated as either frivolous and therefore unimportant, or else as unduly disturbing and even dangerous; in times of instability they were liable to persecution. But even they—even Sextus Empiricus or Montaigne or Hume—did not actually doubt the importance of the questions themselves. What they doubted was the possibility of obtaining final and absolute solutions.

It was left to the twentieth century to do something more drastic than this. For the first time it was now conceived that the most effective way of dealing with questions, particularly those recurrent issues which had perplexed and often tormented original and honest minds in every generation, was not by employing the tools of reason, still less those of the more mysterious capacities called 'insight' and 'intuition', but by obliterating the questions themselves. And this method consists not in removing them by rational means—by proving, for example, that they are founded on intellectual error or verbal muddles or ignorance of the facts—for to prove this would in its turn presuppose the need for rational methods of philosophical or psychological argument. Rather it consists in so treating the questioner that problems which appeared at once overwhelmingly important and utterly insoluble vanish from the questioner's consciousness like evil dreams and trouble him no more. It consists, not in developing the logical implications and elucidating the meaning, the context, or the relevance and origin of a specific problem—in seeing what it 'amounts to'—but in altering the outlook which gave rise to it in the first place. Questions for whose solution no ready-made technique could easily be produced are all too easily classified as obsessions from which the patient must be cured. Thus if a man is haunted by the suspicion that, for example, full individual liberty is not compatible with coercion by the majority in a democratic state, and yet continues to hanker after both democracy and individual liberty, it may be possible by appropriate treatment to rid him of his *idée fixe*, so that it will disappear, to return no more. The worried questioner of political institutions is thereby relieved of his burden and freed to pursue socially useful tasks, unhampered by disturbing and distracting reflections which have been eliminated by the eradication of their cause.

The method has the bold simplicity of genius: it secures agreement on matters of political principle by removing the psychological possibility of alternatives, which itself depends, or is held to depend, on the older form of social organization, rendered obsolete by the revolution and the new social order. And this is how Communist and Fascist states—and all other quasi- and semi-totalitarian societies and secular and religious creeds—have in fact proceeded in the task of imposing political and ideological conformity.

For this the works of Karl Marx are certainly no more responsible than the other tendencies of our time. Marx was a typical nineteenth-century social theorist, in the same sense as Mill or Comte or Buckle. A policy of deliberate psychological conditioning was as alien to him as to them. He believed that many of the questions of his predecessors were quite genuine, and thought that he had solved them. He supported his solutions with arguments which he certainly supposed to conform to the best scientific and philosophical canons of his time. Whether his outlook was in fact as scientific as he claimed, or his solutions as plausible, is another question. What matters is that he recognized the genuineness of the questions he was attempting to answer and offered a theory with a claim to being scientific in the accepted sense of the term; and thereby poured much light (and some darkness) on many vexed problems, and led to much fruitful (and sterile) revaluation and reinterpretation.

But the practice of Communist states and, more logically, of Fascist states (since they openly deny and denounce the value of the rational question-and-answer method) has not been the training of the critical, or solution-finding, powers of their citizens, nor yet the development in them of any capacity for special insights or intuitions regarded as likely to reveal the truth. It consists in something which any nineteenth-century thinker with respect for the sciences would have regarded with genuine horror—the training of individuals incapable of being troubled by questions which, when raised and discussed, endanger the stability of the system; the building and elaboration of a strong framework of institutions, 'myths', habits of life and thought intended to preserve it from sudden shocks or slow decay. This is the intellectual outlook which attends the rise of totalitarian ideologies—the substance of the hair-raising satires of George

Orwell and Aldous Huxley—the state of mind in which trouble-some questions appear as a form of mental perturbation, noxious to the mental health of individuals and, when too widely dis-cussed, to the health of societies. This is an attitude, far removed from Marx or Freud, which looks on all inner conflict as an evil, or at best as a form of futile self-frustration; which considers the kind of friction, the moral or emotional or intellectual collisions, the particular kind of acute mental discomfort which rises to a condition of agony from which great works of the human intellect and imagination have sprung, as being no better than purely destructive diseases—neuroses, psychoses, mental de-rangements, genuinely requiring psychiatric aid; above all as being dangerous deviations from that line to which individuals and societies must adhere if they are to march towards a state of well-ordered, painless, contented, self-perpetuating equilibrium.

This is a truly far-reaching conception, and something more powerful than the pessimism or cynicism of thinkers like Plato or De Maistre, Swift or Carlyle, who looked on the majority of mankind as unalterably stupid or incurably vicious, and therefore concerned themselves with how the world might be made safe for the exceptional, enlightened, or otherwise superior minority or individual. For their view did at least concede the reality of the painful problems, and merely denied the capacity of the majority to solve them; whereas the more radical attitude looks upon intellectual perplexity as being caused either by a technical problem to be settled in terms of practical policy, or else as a neurosis to be cured, that is, made to disappear; if possible without a trace. This leads to a novel conception of the truth and of disinterested ideals in general, which would hardly have been intelligible to previous centuries. To adopt it is to hold that outside the purely technical sphere (where one asks only what are the most efficient means towards this or that practical end) words like 'true', or 'right', or 'free', and the concepts which they denote, are to be re-defined in terms of the only activity recognized as valuable, namely, the organization of society as a smoothly working machine providing for the needs of such of its members as are permitted to survive. The words and ideas in such a society will reflect the outlook of the citizens, being so adjusted as to involve as little friction as possible between, and within, individuals, leaving them free to make the 'optimum' use of the resources available to them.

This is indeed Dostoevsky's utilitarian nightmare. In the course of their pursuit of social welfare, humanitarian liberals, deeply outraged by cruelty, injustice, and inefficiency, discover that the only sound method of preventing these evils is not by providing the widest opportunities for free intellectual or emotional development—for who can tell where this might not lead?—but by eliminating the motives for the pursuit of these perilous ends, by suppressing any tendencies likely to lead to criticism, dissatisfaction, disorderly forms of life. I shall not attempt here to trace historically how this came to pass. No doubt the story must at some stage include the fact that mere disparity in tempo and extent between technical development and social change, together with the fact that the two could not be guaranteed to harmonize—despite the optimistic hopes of Adam Smith—and indeed clashed more and more often, led to increasingly destructive and apparently unavertable economic crises. These were accompanied by social, political, and moral disasters which the general framework—the patterns of behaviour, habits, outlook, language, that is, the 'ideological superstructure' of the victims—could not sustain. The result was a loss of faith in existing political activities and ideals, and a desperate desire to live in a universe which, however dull and flat, was at any rate secure against the repetition of such catastrophes. An element in this was a growing sense of the greater or lesser meaninglessness of such ancient battle-cries as liberty or equality or civilization or truth, since their application to the surrounding scene was no longer as intelligible as it had been in the nineteenth century.

Together with this development, in the majority of cases, there went a reluctance to face it. But the once hallowed phrases were not abandoned. They were used—robbed of their original value—to cover the different and sometimes diametrically opposed notions of the new morality, which, in terms of the old system of values, seemed both unscrupulous and brutal. The Fascists alone did not take the trouble to pretend to retain the old symbols, and while political diehards and the representatives of the more unbridled forms of modern big business clung half cynically, half hopefully, to such terms as freedom or democracy, the Fascists rejected them outright with theatrical gestures of disdain and loathing, and poured scorn upon them as the outworn husks of ideals which had long ago rotted away. But despite the differences of policy concerning the use of specific symbols there is a substantial similarity between all the variants of the new political attitude.

Observers in the twenty-first century will doubtless see these similarities of pattern more easily than we who are involved can possibly do today. They will distinguish them as naturally and clearly from their immediate past—that *hortus inclusus* of the nineteenth century in which so many writers both of history and of journalism and of political addresses today still seem to be living—as we distinguish the growth of romantic nationalism or of naïve positivism from that of enlightened despotism or of patrician republics. Still, even we who live in them can discern something novel in our own times. Even we perceive the growth of new characteristics common to widely different spheres. On the one hand, we can see the progressive and conscious subordination of political to social and economic interests. The most vivid symptoms of this subordination are the open self-identification and conscious solidarity of men as capitalists or workers; these cut across, though they seldom even weaken, national and religious loyalties. On the other, we meet with the conviction that political liberty is useless without the economic strength to use it, and consequently implied or open denial of the rival proposition that economic opportunity is of use only to politically free men. This in its turn carries with it a tacit acceptance of the proposition that the responsibilities of the state to its citizens must and will grow and not diminish, a theorem which is today taken for granted by masters and men alike, in Europe perhaps more unquestioningly than in the United States, but accepted even there to a degree which seemed utopian only thirty, let alone fifty, years ago. This great transformation, with its genuine material gains, and no less genuine growth in social equality in the least liberal societies, is accompanied by something which forms the obverse side of the medal—the elimination, or, at the very best, strong disapproval of those propensities for free inquiry and creation which cannot, without losing their nature, remain as conformist and law-abiding as the twentieth century demands. A century ago Auguste Comte asked why, if there was rightly no demand for freedom to disagree in mathematics, it should be allowed and even encouraged in ethics or the social sciences. And indeed, if the creation of certain 'optimum' patterns of behaviour (and of thought and feeling) in individuals or entire societies is the main goal of social and individual action, Comte's case is unanswerable. Yet it is the extent of this very right to disregard the forces of order and convention, even the publicly accepted 'optimum' goals of action, that forms the glory of that bourgeois culture which reached its zenith in the nineteenth century and of which we have only now begun to witness the beginning of the end.

VI

The new attitude, resting as it does upon the policy of diminishing strife and misery by the atrophy of the faculties capable of causing them, is naturally hostile to, or at least suspicious of, disinterested curiosity (which might end anywhere), and looks upon the practice of all arts not obviously useful to society as being at best forms of social frivolity. Such occupations, when they are not a positive menace, are, in this view, an irritating and wasteful irrelevance, a trivial fiddling, a dissipation or diversion of energy which is in any case difficult enough to accumulate and should therefore be directed wholeheartedly and unceasingly to the task of building and maintaining the well-adjusted— sometimes called the 'integrated'—social whole. In this state of mind it is only natural that such terms as truth or honour or obligation or beauty become transformed into purely offensive or defensive weapons, used by a state or a party in the struggle to create a community impervious to influences beyond its own direct control. This result can be achieved either by rigid censorship and insulation from the rest of the world—a world which remains free at least in the sense that many of its inhabitants continue to say what they wish, in which words are relatively un-organized, with all the unpredictable and consequently 'danger-ous' consequences that flow from this; or else it can be achieved by extending the area of strict control until it stretches over all possible sources of anarchy, i.e. the whole of mankind. Only by one of these two expedients can a state of affairs be achieved in which human behaviour can be manipulated with relative ease by technically qualified specialists—adjusters of conflicts and promoters of peace both of body and of mind, engineers and other scientific experts in the service of the ruling group, psycho-logists, sociologists, economic and social planners, and so on. Clearly this is not an intellectual climate which favours originality of judgement, moral independence, or uncommon powers of insight. The entire trend of such an order is to reduce all issues to technical problems of lesser or greater complexity, in particular the problem of how to survive, get rid of maladjustments, achieve a condition in which the individual's psychological or economic capacities are harnessed to producing the maximum of unclouded social contentment compatible with opposition to all experiment outside the bounds of the system; and this in its turn depends upon the suppression of whatever in the individual might raise doubt or assert itself against the single all-embracing, all-clarifying, all-satisfying plan.

The tendency, present in all stable societies—perhaps in all societies as such—has, owing to the repression of all rival influences, assumed a particularly acute form in, for example, the Soviet Union. There, subordination to the central plan, and the elimination of disturbing forces, whether by education or repression, has been enacted with that capacity for believing in the literal inspiration of ideologies—in the ability and duty of human beings to translate ideas into practice fully, rigorously, and immediately—to which Russian thinkers of all schools seem singularly addicted. The Soviet pattern is clear, simple, and deduced from 'scientifically demonstrated' premisses. The task of realizing it must be entrusted to technically trained believers who look on the human beings at their disposal as material which is infinitely malleable within the confines revealed by the sciences. Stalin's remark that creative artists are 'engineers of human souls' is a very precise expression of this spirit. The presence of something analogous in various Fascist societies, with intuition or instinct substituted for science, and cynicism for hypocrisy, are equally clear for all to see. In Western Europe this tendency has taken the milder form of a shift of emphasis away from disagreement about political principles (and from party struggles which at least in part sprang from genuine differences of outlook) towards disagreements, ultimately technical, about methods—about the best ways of achieving that degree of minimum economic or social stability without which arguments concerned with fundamental principles and the ends of life are felt to be 'abstract', 'academic', and unrelated to the urgent needs of the hour. It leads to that noticeably growing lack of interest in long-term political issues—as opposed to current day-to-day economic or social problems—on the part of the populations of the Western European continent which is occasionally deplored by shocked American and British observers, who mistakenly ascribe it to the growth of cynicism and disenchantment with ideals.

No doubt all abandonment of old values for new may appear to the surviving adherents of the former as conscienceless disregard for morality as such. If so, it is a great delusion. There is all too little disbelief, whether conscienceless or apathetic, in the new values. On the contrary, they are clung to with unreasoning faith and that blind intolerance towards scepticism which springs, as often as not, from an inner bankruptcy or terror, the hope against hope that here at least is a safe haven, narrow, dark, cut off, but secure. Growing numbers of human beings are prepared to purchase this sense of security even at the cost of allowing vast tracts of life to be controlled by persons who, whether consciously or not, act systematically to narrow the horizon of human activity to manageable proportions, to train human beings into more easily combinable parts—interchangeable, almost prefabricated—of a total pattern. In the face of such a strong desire to stabilize, if need be, at the lowest level—upon the floor from which you cannot fall, which cannot betray you, let you down—all the ancient political principles begin to vanish, feeble symbols of creeds no longer relevant to the new realities.

This process does not move at a uniform pace everywhere.

In the United States perhaps, for obvious economic reasons, the nineteenth century survives more powerfully than anywhere else. The political issues and conflicts, the topics of discussion, and the idealized personalities of democratic leaders are more reminiscent of Victorian Europe than anything to be found on that continent now.

Woodrow Wilson was a nineteenth-century liberal in a very full and unqualified sense. The New Deal and the personality of President Roosevelt excited political passions far more like those of the battles which raged round Gladstone or Lloyd George, or the anti-clerical governments at the turn of the century in France, than anything actually contemporary with it in Europe; and this great liberal enterprise, certainly the most constructive compromise between individual liberty and economic security which our own time has witnessed, corresponds more closely to the political and economic ideals of John Stuart Mill in his last, humanitarian-Socialist phase then to left-wing thought in Europe in the thirties. The controversy about international organization, about the United Nations and its subsidiaries, as well as the other post-war international institutions, like the controversies which in the years after 1918 surrounded the League of Nations, are fully intelligible in terms of nineteenth-century political ideals, and therefore occupied far more attention and meant much more in America than in Europe. The United States may have disavowed President Wilson, but it continued to live in a moral atmosphere not very different from that of Wilson's time—the easily recognizable black-and-white moral world of the Victorian values. The events of 1918 preyed on the American conscience for twenty-five years, whereas in Europe the *exalté* atmosphere of 1918–19 was soon dissipated— a brief moment of illumination which in retrospect seems more American than European, the last manifestation in Europe of a great but dying tradition in a world already living, and fully conscious of living, in a new medium, too well aware of its differences from, and resentful of, its past. The break was not sudden and total, a dramatic *coup de théâtre*. Many of the seeds planted in the eighteenth or nineteenth century have flowered only in the twentieth: the political and ethical climate in which trade unions flourished, for instance, in Germany, or England, or France contained as elements the old, familiar doctrines of human rights and duties which were the common property, avowed or not, of almost all parties and views in the liberal, humanitarian, expansionist hundred years of peace and technological progress.

The main current of the nineteenth century does, of course, survive into the present, and especially in America, Scandinavia, and the British Commonwealth; but it is not what is most characteristic of our time. For in the past there were conflicts of ideas; whereas what characterizes our time is less the struggle of one set of ideas against another than the mounting wave of hostility to all ideas as such. Since ideas are considered the source of too much disquiet, there is a tendency to suppress the conflict between liberal claims to individual political rights and the patent economic injustice which can result from their satisfaction (which forms the substance of socialist criticism) by the submersion of both in an authoritarian régime which removes the free area within which such conflict can occur. What is genuinely typical of our time is a new concept of the society, the values of which are analysable not in terms of the desires or the moral sense which inspire the view of its ultimate ends held by a group or an individual, but from some factual hypothesis or metaphysical dogma about history, or race, or national character in terms of which the answers to the question what is good, right, required, desirable, fitting, can be 'scientifically' deduced, or intuited, or expressed in this or that kind of behaviour. There is one and only one direction in which a given aggregate of individuals is conceived to be travelling, driven thither by quasi-occult impersonal forces, such as their class structure, or their collective unconscious, or their racial origin, or the 'real' social or physical roots of this or that 'popular' or 'group' 'mythology'. The direction is alterable, but only by tampering with the hidden cause of behaviour—those who wish to tamper being, according to this view, free to a limited degree to determine their own direction and that of others not by the increase of rationality and by argument addressed to it, but by having a superior understanding of the machinery of social behaviour and skill in manipulating it.

In this sinister fashion have the words of St.-Simon's prophecy finally come true—words which once seemed so brave and optimistic: 'The government of man will be replaced by the administration of things.' The cosmic forces are conceived as omnipotent and indestructible. Hopes, fears, prayers cannot wish them out of existence; but the *élite* of experts can canalize them and control them to some extent. The task of these experts is to adjust human beings to these forces and to develop in them an unshakeable faith in the new order, and unquestioning loyalty to it, which will anchor it securely and for ever. Consequently the technical disciplines which direct natural forces and adjust men to the new order must take primacy over humane pursuits—philosophical, historical, artistic. Such pursuits, at most, will serve only to prop up and embellish the new establishment. Turgenev's naïve materialist, the hero of his novel *Fathers and Sons*, the 'nihilistic' scientist Bazarov, has finally come into his own, as St.-Simon and his more pedestrian follower Comte always felt sure that he would, but for reasons very different from those which seemed plausible a century ago. Bazarov's faith rested on the claim that the dissection of frogs was more important than poetry because it led to the truth, whereas the poetry of Pushkin did not.

The motive at work today is more devastating: anatomy is superior to art because it generates no independent ends of life, provides no experiences which act as independent criteria of good or evil, truth or falsehood, and are therefore liable to clash with the orthodoxy which we have created as the only bulwark strong enough to preserve us from doubts and despairs and all the horrors of maladjustment. To be borne this way and that emotionally or intellectually is a form of *malaise*. Against it nothing will work but the elimination of alternatives so nearly in equal balance that choice between them is—or at least appears to be—possible.

This is, of course, the position of the Grand Inquisitor in Dostoevsky's *Brothers Karamazov*: he said that what men dreaded most was freedom of choice, to be left alone to grope their way in the dark; and the Church by lifting the responsibility from their shoulders made them willing, grateful, and happy slaves. The Grand Inquisitor stood for the dogmatic organization of the life of the spirit: Bazarov for its theoretical opposite—free scientific inquiry, the facing of the 'hard' facts, the acceptance of the truth however brutal or upsetting. By an irony of history (not unforeseen by Dostoevsky) they have formed a pact, they are allies, and today are often indistinguishable. Buridan's ass, we are told, unable to choose between two equidistant bundles of hay, starved to death. Against this fate the only remedy is blind obedience and faith. Whether the refuge is a dogmatic religious faith or a dogmatic faith in social or natural science matters relatively little: for without such obedience and faith there is no confidence and no hope, no optimistic, 'constructive', 'positive' form of life. That the disciples of those who first exposed the idolatry of ideas frozen into oppressive institutions—Fourier, Feuerbach, and Marx—should be the most ferocious supporters of the new forms of 'reification' and 'dehumanization' is indeed an irony of history.

VII

One of the most fascinating and disquieting symptoms of this trend is to be found in the policy of the great philanthropic foundations of the West. The criticism of these institutions most frequently made by both European and American observers is that their aims are too crudely utilitarian: that instead of seeking to support the pursuit of truth or creative activity as such (basic research, for example, or artistic activity) they are dedicated to the most direct and immediate improvement of human life conceived in crudely material terms—physical well-being, solutions to short-term social and economic problems, the manufacture of prophylactics against politically 'undesirable' views, and so on. But these charges seem to me misconceived. The efforts of the celebrated and munificent bodies engaged in this type of activity rest, I am convinced, on a genuine and disinterested desire to serve the deepest interests of mankind, and not merely its material needs. But these interests are all conceived almost entirely in therapeutic terms: tensions (within or between individuals or groups or nations) that need to be released, wounds, conflicts, fixations, 'phobias' and fears, psychical and psycho-physical abnormalities of all sorts which require the aid of specialized healers—doctors, economists, social workers, teams of diagnosticians or engineers or other masters of the craft of helping the sick and the perplexed—individual and collective sources of practical wisdom of every kind. To the degree to which such suffering exists and can be treated by the applied sciences— genuine physical or mental sickness, poverty, social and economic inequality, squalor, misery, oppression, which men and money, experts and equipment, can cure or alleviate—such policies are, of course, entirely beneficent and their organized support is a great moral asset to an age and a country. But the reverse of this coin is the tendency—difficult to avoid, but disastrous—to assimilate all men's primary needs to those that are capable of being met by these methods: the reduction of all questions and aspirations to dislocations which the expert can set right. Some believe in coercion, others in gentler methods; but the conception of human needs in their entirety as those of the inmates of a prison or a reformatory or a school or a hospital, however sincerely it may be held, is a gloomy, false, and ultimately degraded view, resting on denial of the rational and productive nature of all, or even the majority of, men. The resistance to it, whether in the form of attacks on American 'materialism' (when it springs from a genuine, if naïve, and often crude form of altruistic idealism) or on communist or nationalist fanaticism (when it is, more often than not, a misconceived, over-pragmatic search for human emancipation), derives from an obscure realization that both these tendencies—which spring from a common root—are hostile to the development of men as creative and self-directing beings. If men are indeed such beings, even this tendency, overwhelming as it seems to be at present, will not, in the end, prove fatal to human progress. This circular argument, which is, in essence, that of all critical rationalists—of Marx (at any rate in his youth) and Freud as well as Spinoza and Kant, Mill and Tocqueville—if it is valid, offers some ground for a cautious and highly qualified optimism about the moral and intellectual future of the human race.

VIII

At this point it might be said that the situation I have described is not altogether new. Has not every authoritarian institution, every irrationalist movement, been engaged upon something of this kind—the artificial stilling of doubts, the attempt either to discredit uncomfortable questions or to educate men not to ask them? Was this not the practice of the great organized churches, indeed of every institution from the national state to small sectarian establishments? Was this not the attitude of the enemies of reason from the earliest mystery cults to the romanticism, anarchistic nihilism, surrealism, neo-Oriental cults of the last century and a half? Why should our age be specially accused of addiction to the particular tendency which formed a central theme of social doctrines which go back to Plato, or the sect of the medieval Assassins, or much Eastern thought and mysticism?

But there are two great differences which separate the political characteristics of our age from their origins in the past. In the first place, the reactionaries or romantics of previous periods, however much they might have advocated the superior wisdom of institutional authority or the revealed word over that of individual reason, did not in their moments of wildest unreason minimize the importance of the questions to be answered. On the contrary, they maintained that so crucial was it to obtain the correct answer that only hallowed institutions, or inspired leaders, or mystical revelation, or divine grace could vouchsafe a solution of sufficient depth and universality. No doubt an order of importance of questions underlies any established social system—a hierarchical order the authority of which is itself not open to question. Moreover, the obscurity of some among the answers offered has in every age concealed their lack of truth or their irrelevance to the questions which they purported to solve. And perhaps much hypocrisy has traditionally been necessary to secure their success. But hypocrisy is very different from cynicism or blindness. Even the censors of opinion and the enemies of the truth felt compelled to pay formal homage to the vital importance of obtaining true answers to the great problems by the best available means. If their practice belied this, at least there was something to be belied: traitors and heretics often keep alive the memory—and the authority—of the beliefs which they are intent on betraying.

The second difference consists in the fact that in the past such attempts to obscure the nature of the issues were mostly associated with the avowed enemies of reason and individual freedom. The alignment of forces has been clear at any rate since the Renaissance; progress and reaction, however much these words have been abused, are not empty concepts. On one side stood the supporters of authority, unreasoning faith, suspicious of, or openly opposed to, the uncontrolled pursuit of truth or the free realization of individual ideals. On the other, whatever their differences, were those supporters of free inquiry and self-expression who looked upon Voltaire and Lessing, Mill and Darwin, even Ibsen as their prophets. Their common quality—perhaps their only common quality—was some degree of devotion to the ideals of the Renaissance and a hatred of all that was associated, whether justly or not, with the Middle Ages—darkness, suppression, the stifling of all heterodoxy, the hatred of the flesh and of gaiety, of freedom of thought and expression, and of the love of natural beauty. There were of course many who cannot be classified so simply or so crudely; but until our own day the lines were drawn sharply enough to determine clearly the position of the men who most deeply influenced their age. A combination of devotion to scientific principles with 'obscurantist' social theory seemed altogether unthinkable. Today the tendency to circumscribe and confine and limit, to determine the range of what may be asked and what may not, to what may be believed and what may not, is no longer a distinguishing mark of the old 'reactionaries'. On the contrary, it comes as powerfully from the heirs of the radicals, rationalists, 'progressives' of the nineteenth century as from the descendants of their enemies. There is a persecution not only of science, but by science or at least in its name; and this is a nightmare scarcely foreseen by the most Cassandra-like prophets of either camp.

We are often told that the present is an age of cynicism and despair, of crumbling values and the dissolution of the fixed standards and landmarks of Western civilization. But this is neither true nor even plausible. So far from showing the loose texture of a collapsing order, the world is today stiff with rigid rules and codes and ardent, irrational religions. So far from evincing the toleration which springs from cynical disregard of the ancient sanctions, it treats heterodoxy as the supreme danger.

Whether in the East or West, the danger has not been greater since the ages of faith. Conformities are called for much more eagerly today than yesterday; loyalties are tested far more severely; sceptics, liberals, individuals with a taste for private life and their own inner standards of behaviour, if they do not take care to identify themselves with an organized movement, are objects of fear or derision and targets of persecution for either side, execrated or despised by all the embattled parties in the great ideological wars of our time. And although this is less acute in societies traditionally averse to extremes—Great Britain, say, or Denmark or Switzerland—this makes little difference to the general pattern. In the world today individual stupidity and wickedness are forgiven more easily than failure to be identified with a recognized party or attitude, to achieve an approved political or economic or intellectual status. In earlier periods, when more than one authority ruled human life, a man might escape the pressure of the state by taking refuge in the fortress of the opposition—of an organized church or a dissident feudal establishment. The mere fact of conflict between authorities allowed room for a narrow and shifting, but still never entirely non-existent, no-man's-land, where private lives might still precariously be lived, because neither side dared to go too far for fear of too greatly strengthening the other. Today the very virtues of even the best intentioned paternalistic state, its genuine anxiety to reduce destitution and disease and inequality, to penetrate all the neglected nooks and crannies of life which may stand in need of its justice and its bounty—its very success in those beneficent activities—have narrowed the area within which the individual may commit blunders, and curtailed his liberties in the interest (the very real interest) of his welfare or of his sanity, his health, his security, his freedom from want and fear. His area of choice has grown smaller not in the name of some opposing principle—as in the Dark Ages or during the rise of the nationalities—but in order to create a situation in which the very possibility of opposed principles, with all their unlimited capacity to cause mental stress and danger and destructive collisions, is eliminated in favour of a simpler and better regulated life, a robust faith in an efficiently working order, untroubled by agonizing moral conflict.

Yet this is not a gratuitous development: the social and economic situation in which we are placed, the failure to harmonize the effects of technical progress with the forces of political and economic organization inherited from an earlier phase, do call for a measure of social control to prevent chaos and destitution that can be no less fatal to the development of human faculties than blind conformity. It is neither realistic nor morally conceivable that we should give up our social gains and meditate for an instant the possibility of a return to ancient injustice and inequality and hopeless misery. The progress of technological skill makes it rational and indeed imperative to plan, and anxiety for the success of a particular planned society naturally inclines the planners to seek insulation from dangerous, because incalculable, forces which may jeopardize the plan. And this is a powerful incentive to 'autarky' and 'socialism in one country', whether imposed by conservatives, or New Dealers, or isolationists, or Social Democrats, or, indeed, imperialists. And this in its turn generates artificial barriers and increasingly restricts the planners' own resources. In extreme cases this policy leads to repression of the discontented and a perpetual tightening of discipline, until it absorbs more and more of the time and ingenuity of those who originally conceived it only as a means to a minimum of efficiency. Presently it grows to be a hideous end in itself, since its realization leads to a vicious circle of repression in order to survive and of survival mainly to repress. So the remedy grows to be worse than the disease, and takes the form of those orthodoxies which rest on the simple puritanical faith of individuals who never knew or have forgotten what *douceur de vivre*, free self-expression, the infinite variety of persons and of the relationships between them, and the right of free choice, difficult to endure but more intolerable to surrender, can ever have been like.

The dilemma is logically insoluble: we cannot sacrifice either freedom or the organization needed for its defence, or a minimum standard of welfare. The way out must therefore lie in some logically untidy, flexible, and even ambiguous compromise. Every situation calls for its own specific policy, since out of the crooked timber of humanity, as Kant once remarked, no straight thing was ever made. What the age calls for is not (as we are so often told) more faith, or stronger leadership, or more scientific organization. Rather is it the opposite—less Messianic ardour, more enlightened scepticism, more toleration of idiosyncrasies, more frequent *ad hoc* measures to achieve aims in a foreseeable future, more room for the attainment of their personal ends by individuals and by minorities whose tastes and beliefs find (whether rightly or wrongly must not matter) little response among the majority. What is required is a less mechanical, less fanatical application of general principles, however rational or righteous, a more cautious and less arrogantly self-confident application of accepted, scientifically tested, general solutions to unexamined individual cases. The wicked Talleyrand's '*sur-tout pas trop de zèle*' can be more humane than the demand for uniformity of the virtuous Robespierre, and a salutary brake upon too much control of men's lives in an age of social planning and technology. We must submit to authority not because it is infallible, but only for strictly and openly utilitarian reasons, as a necessary expedient. Since no solution can be guaranteed against error, no disposition is final. And therefore a loose texture and toleration of a minimum of inefficiency, even a degree of indulgence in idle talk, idle curiosity, aimless pursuit of this or that without authorization—'conspicuous waste' itself—may allow more spontaneous, individual variation (for which the individual must in the end assume full responsibility), and will always be worth more than the neatest and most delicately fashioned imposed pattern. Above all, it must be realized that the kinds of problems which this or that method of education or system of scientific or religious or social organization is guaranteed to solve are not *eo facto* the only central questions of human life. Injustice, poverty, slavery, ignorance—these may be cured by reform or revolution. But men do not live only by fighting evils. They live by positive goals, individual and collective, a vast variety of them, seldom predictable, at times incompatible. It is from intense preoccupation with these ends, ultimate, incommensurable, guaranteed neither to change nor to stand still—it is through the absorbed individual or collective pursuit of these, unplanned and at times without wholly adequate technical equipment, more often than not without conscious hope of success, still less of the approbation of the official auditor, that the best moments come in the lives of individuals and peoples.

HISTORICAL INEVITABILITY[1]

> '. . . those vast impersonal forces . . .'
>
> T. S. ELIOT, *Notes towards the Definition of Culture*

I

WRITING some ten years ago in his place of refuge during the German occupation of northern Italy, Mr. Bernard Berenson set down his thoughts on what he called the 'Accidental View of History': 'It led me', he declared, 'far from the doctrine, lapped up in my youth about the inevitability of events and the Moloch still devouring us today, "historical inevitability". I believe less and less in these more than doubtful and certainly dangerous dogmas, which tend to make us accept whatever happens as irresistible and foolhardy to oppose.'[2] The famous critic's words are particularly timely at a moment when there is, at any rate among philosophers of history, if not among historians, a tendency to return to the ancient view that all that is, is ('objectively viewed') best; that to explain is ('in the last resort') to justify; or that to know all is to forgive all; ringing fallacies (charitably described as half-truths) which have led to special pleading and, indeed, obfuscation of the issue on a heroic scale. This is the theme on which I should like to speak; but before doing so, I must express my gratitude to the Director of this great institution and his colleagues for the honour which they have done me by inviting me to deliver this, the first of the Auguste Comte Memorial Lectures. For, indeed, Comte is worthy of commemoration and praise. He was in his own day a very celebrated thinker, and if his works are today seldom mentioned, at any rate in this country, that is partly due to the fact that he has done his work too well. For Comte's views have

---

[1] This Auguste Comte Memorial Trust Lecture was delivered on 12 May 1953 at the London School of Economics and Political Science, and published by the Oxford University Press in the following year.

[2] Bernard Berenson, *Rumor and Reflection*, p. 110 (Simon and Schuster, New York, 1952).

affected the categories of our thought more deeply than is commonly supposed. Our view of the natural sciences, of the material basis of cultural evolution, of all that we call progressive, rational, enlightened, Western; our view of the relationships of institutions and of public symbolism and ceremonial to the emotional life of individuals and societies, and consequently our view of history itself, owes a good deal to his teaching and his influence. His grotesque pedantry, the unreadable dullness of much of his writing, his vanity, his eccentricity, his solemnity, the pathos of his private life, his dogmatism, his authoritarianism, his philosophical fallacies, all that is bizarre and utopian in his character and writings, need not blind us to his merits. The father of sociology is by no means the ludicrous figure he is too often represented as being. He understood the role of natural science and the true reasons for its prestige better than most contemporary thinkers. He saw no depth in mere darkness; he demanded evidence; he exposed shams; he denounced intellectual impressionism; he fought many metaphysical and theological mythologies, some of which, but for the blows he struck, might have been with us still; he provided weapons in the war against the enemies of reason, many of which are far from obsolete today. Above all he grasped the central issue of all philosophy—the distinction between words (or thoughts) that are about words, and words (or thoughts) that are about things, and thereby helped to lay the foundation of what is best and most illuminating in modern empiricism; and, of course, he made a great mark on historical thinking. He believed in the application of scientific, i.e. naturalistic, canons of explanation in all fields: and saw no reason why they should not apply to relations of human beings as well as relations of things.

This doctrine was not original, and by his time growing somewhat out of date; the writings of Vico had been rediscovered; Herder had transformed the concepts of nation, society, and culture; Ranke and Michelet were changing both the art and the science of history. The notion that human history could be turned into a natural science by the extension to human beings of a kind of sociological zoology, analogous to the study of bees and beavers, which Condorcet had so ardently advocated and so confidently prophesied—this simple behaviourism had provoked a reaction against itself. It was seen to be a distortion of the facts, a denial of the evidence of direct experience, a deliberate suppression of much of what we knew about ourselves, our motives, purposes, choices, perpetrated in order to achieve by hook or by crook a single, unitary method in all knowledge. Comte did not commit the enormities of a La Mettrie or a Büchner. He did not say that history was, or was reducible to, a kind of physics; but his conception of sociology pointed in that direction—of one complete and all-embracing pyramid of scientific knowledge; one method; one truth; one scale of rational, 'scientific' values. This naïve craving for unity and symmetry at the expense of experience is with us still.

II

The notion that one can discover large patterns or regularities in the procession of historical events is naturally attractive to those who are impressed by the success of the natural sciences in classifying, correlating, and above all predicting. They consequently seek to extend historical knowledge to fill gaps in the past (and, at times, to build into the limitless gap of the future) by applying 'scientific' method: by setting forth, armed with a metaphysical or empirical system, from such islands of certain, or virtually certain, knowledge of the facts as they claim to possess. And no doubt a great deal has been done, and will be done, in historical as in other fields by arguing from the known to the unknown, or from the little known to the even less known.[1]

[1] I do not wish here to enter into the question of what such procedures are, e.g. of what is meant by speaking of history as a science—whether the methods of historical discovery are inductive, or 'deductive-hypothetical', or analogical, or to what degree they are or should be similar to the methods of the natural sciences, and to which of these methods, and in which of the natural sciences; for there plainly exists a greater variety of methods and procedures than is usually provided for in textbooks on logic or scientific method. It may be that the methods of historical research are, in at least some respects, unique, and some of them are more unlike than like those of the natural sciences; while others resemble given scientific techniques, particularly when they approach such ancillary inquiries as archaeology or palaeography or physical anthropology. Or again they may depend upon the kind of historical research pursued—and may not be the same in demography as in history, in political history as in the history of art, in the history of technology as in the history of religion. The 'logic' of various human studies has been

But whatever value the perception of patterns or uniformities may have in stimulating or verifying specific hypotheses about the past or the future, it has played, and is increasingly playing, another and more dubious role in determining the outlook of our time. It has affected not merely ways of observing and describing the activities and characters of human beings, but moral and political and religious attitudes towards them. For among the questions which are bound to arise in any consideration of how and why human beings act and live as they do, are questions of human motive and responsibility. In describing human behaviour it has always been artificial and over-austere to omit questions of the character, purposes, and motives of individuals. And in considering these one automatically evaluates not merely the degree and kind of influence of this or that motive or character upon what happens, but also its moral or political quality in terms of whatever scale of values one consciously or semi-consciously accepts in one's thought or action. How did this or that situation arise? Who or what was or is (or will be, or could be) responsible for a war, a revolution, an economic collapse, a renaissance of arts and letters, a discovery or an invention or a spiritual transformation altering the lives of men? It is by now a familiar story that there exist personal and impersonal theories of history. On the one hand, theories according to which the lives of entire peoples and societies have been decisively influenced by exceptional individuals[1]—or, alternatively, doctrines according to which what happens occurs as a result not of the wishes and purposes of identifiable individuals, but of those of large numbers of unspecified persons, with the qualification that these collective wishes and goals are not solely or even largely determined by impersonal factors, and are therefore not wholly or even largely deducible from knowledge of natural forces alone,

insufficiently examined, and convincing accounts of its varieties with an adequate range of concrete examples drawn from actual practice are much to be desired.

[1] Indeed, the very notion of great men, however carefully qualified, however sophisticated, embodies this belief; for this concept, even in its most attenuated form, would be empty unless it were thought that some men played a more decisive role in the course of history than others. The notion of greatness, unlike those of goodness or wickedness or talent or beauty, is not a mere characteristic of individuals in a more or less private context, but is, as we ordinarily use it, directly connected with social effectiveness, the capacity of individuals to alter things radically on a large scale.

such as environment, or climate, or physical, physiological, and psychological processes. On either view, it becomes the business of historians to investigate who wanted what, and when, and where, in what way; how many men avoided or pursued this or that goal, and with what intensity; and, further, to ask under what circumstances such wants or fears have proved effective, and to what extent, and with what consequences.

Against this kind of interpretation, in terms of the purposes and characters of individuals, there is a cluster of views (to which the progress of the natural sciences has given a great and growing prestige) according to which all explanations in terms of human intentions rest on a mixture of vanity and stubborn ignorance. These views rest on the assumption that belief in the importance of the motives is delusive; that the behaviour of men is in fact made what it is by causes largely beyond the control of individuals; for instance by the influence of physical factors or of environment or of custom; or by the 'natural' growth of some larger unit—a race, a nation, a class, a biological species; or (according to some writers) by some entity conceived in even less empirical terms—a 'spiritual organism', a religion, a civilization, a Hegelian (or Buddhist) World Spirit; entities whose careers or manifestations on earth are the object either of empirical or of metaphysical inquiries—depending on the cosmological outlook of particular thinkers. Those who incline to this kind of impersonal interpretation of historical change, whether because they believe that it possesses greater scientific value (i.e. enables them to predict the future or 'retrodict' the past more successfully or precisely), or because they believe that it embodies some crucial insight into the nature of the universe, are committed by it to tracing the ultimate responsibility for what happens to the acts or behaviour of impersonal or 'trans-personal' or 'super-personal' entities or 'forces' whose evolution is identified with human history. It is true that the more cautious and clear-headed among such theorists try to meet the objections of empirically minded critics by adding in a footnote, or as an after-thought, that, whatever their terminology, they are on no account to be taken to believe that there literally exist such creatures as civilizations or races or spirits of nations living side by side with the individuals who compose them; and they add that they fully realize that all institutions 'in the last analysis' consist of individual men and women, and are not themselves personalities but only convenient devices—idealized models, or types, or labels, or metaphors—different ways of classifying, grouping, explaining, or predicting the properties or behaviour of individual human beings in terms of their more important (i.e. historically effective) empirical characteristics. Nevertheless these protestations too often turn out to be mere lip-service to principles which those who profess them do not really believe. Such writers seldom write or think as if they took these deflationary caveats over-seriously; and the more candid or naïve among them do not even pretend to subscribe to them. Thus nations or cultures or civilizations for Schelling or Hegel (and Spengler; and one is inclined, though somewhat hesitantly, to add Professor Arnold Toynbee) are certainly not merely convenient collective terms for individuals possessing certain characteristics in common; but seem more 'real' and more 'concrete' than the individuals who compose them. Individuals remain 'abstract' precisely because they are mere 'elements' or 'aspects', 'moments' artificially abstracted for *ad hoc* purposes, and literally without reality (or, at any rate, 'historical' or 'philosophical' or 'real' being) apart from the wholes of which they form a part, much as the colour of a thing, or its shape, or its value are 'elements' or 'attributes' or 'modes' or 'aspects' of concrete objects—isolated for convenience, and thought of as existing independently, on their own, only because of some weakness or confusion in the analysing intellect. Marx and Marxists are more ambiguous. We cannot be quite sure what to make of such a category as a social 'class' whose emergence and struggles, victories and defeats, condition the lives of individuals, sometimes against, and most often independently of, such individuals' conscious or expressed purposes. Classes are never proclaimed to be literally independent entities: they are constituted by individuals in their interaction (mainly economic). Yet to seek to explain, or put a moral or political value on the actions of individuals by examining such individuals one by one, even to the limited extent to which such examination is possible, is considered by Marxists to be not merely impracticable and time-wasting (as indeed it may be), but absurd in a more fundamental sense—because the 'true' (or 'deeper') causes of human behaviour lie not in the specific circumstances of an individual life or in the individual's thoughts or volitions (as a psychologist or biographer or novelist might describe them) but in a pervasive interrelationship between a vast variety of such lives with their natural and man-made environment. Men do as they do, and think as they think, largely as a 'function of' the inevitable evolution of the 'class' as a whole—from which it follows that the history and development of classes can be studied independently of the biographies of their component individuals. It is the 'structure' and the 'evolution' of the class alone that (causally) matters in the end. This is, *mutatis mutandis*, similar to the belief in the primacy of collective patterns taken by those who attribute active properties to race or culture, whether they be benevolent internationalists like Herder who thought that different peoples can and should admire, love, and assist one another as individuals can and do, because peoples are in some sense individuals (or super-individuals); or by the ferocious champions of national or racial self-assertion and war, like Gobineau or Houston Stewart Chamberlain or Hitler. And the same note, sometimes mild and civilized, sometimes harshly aggressive, is heard in the voices of all those upholders of collectivist *mystiques* who appeal from individual to tradition, or to the collective consciousness (or 'Unconscious') of a race or a nation or a culture, or, like Carlyle, feel that abstract nouns deserve capital letters, and tell us that Tradition or History (or 'the past', or the species, or 'the masses') is wiser than we, or that the great society of the quick and the dead, of our ancestors and of generations yet unborn, has larger purposes than any single creature, purposes of which our lives are but a puny fragment, and that we belong to this larger unity with the 'deepest' and perhaps least conscious parts of ourselves.[1]

---

[1] We are further told that we belong to such wholes and are 'organically' one with them, whether we know it or not; and that we have such significance as we do only to the degree to which we are sensitive to, and identify ourselves with, these unanalysable, imponderable, scarcely explicable relationships; for it is only in so far as we belong to an

There are many versions of this belief, with varying proportions of empiricism and mysticism, 'tender'- and 'tough'-mindedness, optimism and pessimism, collectivism and individualism; but what all such views have in common is the fundamental distinction on which they rest between, on the one hand, 'real' and 'objective', and, on the other, 'subjective' or 'arbitrary' judgments, based respectively on acceptance or rejection of this ultimately mystical act of self-identification with a reality which transcends empirical experience.

For Bossuet, for Hegel, for Marx,[1] for Spengler (and for almost all thinkers for whom history is 'more' than past events, namely a theodicy) this reality takes on the form of an objective 'march of history'. The process may be thought of as being in time and space or beyond them; as being cyclical or spiral or rectilinear, or as occurring in the form of a peculiar zigzag movement, sometimes called dialectical; as continuous and uniform, or irregular, broken by sudden leaps to 'new levels'; as due to the changing forms of one single 'force', or of conflicting elements locked (as in some ancient myth) in an eternal Pyrrhic struggle; as the history of one deity or 'force' or 'principle', or of several; as being destined to end well or badly; as holding out to human beings the prospect of eternal beatitude, or eternal damnation, or of both in turn, or of neither. But whatever version of the story is accepted—and it is never a scientific, that is, empirically testable

entity greater than ourselves, and are thereby carriers of 'its' values, instruments of 'its' purposes, living 'its' life, suffering and dying for 'its' richer self-realization, that we are, or are worth, anything at all. This familiar line of thought should be distinguished from the no less familiar but less ethically charged supposition that men's outlooks and behaviour are largely conditioned by the habits of other past and present members of their society; that the hold of prejudice and tradition is very strong; that there may be inherited characteristics both mental and physical; and that any effort to influence human beings and to judge their conduct must take such non-rational factors into account. For whereas the former view is metaphysical and normative (what Karl Popper calls 'essentialist'), the latter is empirical and descriptive; and while the former is largely found as an element in the kind of ethical or political anti-individualism held by romantic nationalists, Hegelians, and other transcendentalists, the latter is a sociological and psychological hypothesis which doubtless carries its own ethical and political implications, but rests its claim on observation of empirical facts, and can be confirmed or refuted or rendered less or more plausible by it. In their extreme forms these views contradict each other; in their softer and less consistent forms they tend to overlap, and even coalesce.

[1] Or, some prefer to say, Engels.

theory, stated in quantitative terms, still less a description of
what our eyes see and our ears hear[1]—the moral of it is always
one and the same: that we must learn to distinguish the 'real'
course of things from the dreams and fancies and 'rationalizations' which we construct unconsciously for our solace or amuse-
ment; for these may comfort us for a while, but will betray us
cruelly in the end. There is, we are told, a nature of things and it
has a pattern in time: 'things are what they are' said a sober English philosopher over two centuries ago 'and their consequences
will be what they will be; why then should we seek to be deceived?'
What, then, must we do to avoid deception? At the very least—
if we cannot swallow the notion of super-personal 'spirits' or
'forces'—we must admit that all events occur in discoverable,
uniform, unaltering patterns; for if some did not, how could we
find the laws of such occurrences? And without universal order—
a system of true laws—how could history be 'intelligible'? how
could it 'make sense', 'have meaning', be more than a picaresque
account of a succession of random episodes, a mere collection (as
Descartes, for this very reason, seems to have thought) of old
wives' tales? Our values—what we think good and bad, important
and trivial, right and wrong, noble and contemptible—all these
are conditioned by the place we occupy in the pattern, on the
moving stair. We praise and blame, worship and condemn whatever fits or does not fit the interests and needs and ideals that we
seek to satisfy—the ends that (being made as we are) we cannot
help pursuing—according to our lights, that is, our own perception of our condition, our place in 'Nature'. Such attitudes are held to be 'rational' and 'objective' to the degree to
which we perceive this condition accurately, that is, understand
where we are in terms of the great world plan, the movement
whose regularities we discern as well as our historical sense and

[1] No one has demonstrated this with more devastating lucidity than Professor Karl
Popper. While he seems to me somewhat to underestimate the differences between the methods of natural science and those of history or common sense (Professor
F. v. Hayek's *The Counter-revolution of Science* seems, despite some exaggerations, to
be more convincing on this topic), he has, in his *The Open Society and its Enemies*
and *The Poverty of Historicism*, exposed some of the fallacies of metaphysical 'historicism' with such force and precision, and made so clear its incompatibility with any
kind of scientific empiricism, that there is no further excuse for confounding
the two.

knowledge permit. To each condition and generation its own perspectives of the past and future, depending upon where it has arrived, what it has left behind, and whither it is moving; its values depend on this same awareness. To condemn the Greeks or the Romans or the Assyrians or the Aztecs for this or that folly or vice may be no more than to say that what they did or wished or thought conflicts with our own view of life, which may be the true or 'objective' view for the stage which we have reached, and which is perceived less or more clearly according to the depth and accuracy of our understanding of what this stage is, and of the manner in which it is developing. If the Romans and the Aztecs judged differently from us, they may have judged no less well and truly and 'objectively' to the degree to which they understood their own condition and their own very different stage of development. For us to condemn their scale of values is valid enough for our condition, which is the sole frame of reference we have. And if they had known us they might have condemned us as harshly and, because their circumstances and values were what they inevitably were, with equal validity. According to this view there is nothing, no point of rest outside the general movement, where we or they can take up a stand, no static absolute standards in terms of which things and persons can be finally evaluated. Hence the only attitudes correctly described, and rightly condemned, as relative, subjective, and irrational are forms of failure to relate our judgment to our own truest interests, that is, to what will fulfil our natures most fully—to all that the next step in our inevitable development necessarily holds in store. Some thinkers of this school view subjective aberrations with compassion and condone them as temporary attitudes from which the enlightenment of the future will henceforward preserve mankind. Others gloat exultantly or ironically over the inevitable doom of those who misinterpret, and therefore fall foul of, the inexorable march of events. But whether the tone is charitable or sardonic, whether one condemns the errors of foolish individuals or the blind mob, or applauds their inevitable annihilation, this attitude rests on the belief that everything is caused to occur as it does by the machinery of history itself— by the impersonal forces of class, race, culture, History, Reason,

The Life-Force, Progress, The Spirit of the Age. Given this organization of our lives, which we did not create, and cannot alter, it, and it alone, is ultimately responsible for everything. To blame or praise individuals or groups of individuals for acting rightly or wrongly, so far as this entails a suggestion that they are in some sense genuinely free to choose between alternatives, and may therefore be justly and reasonably blamed or praised for choosing as they did and do, is a vast blunder, a return to some primitive or naïve conception of human beings as being able somehow to evade total determination of their lives by forces natural or supernatural, a relapse into a childish animism which the study of the relevant scientific or metaphysical system should swiftly dispel. For if such choices were real, the determined world structure which alone, on this view, makes complete explanation, whether scientific or metaphysical, possible, could not exist. And this is ruled out as unthinkable, 'reason rejects it', it is confused, delusive, superficial, a piece of puerile megalomania, pre-scientific, unworthy of civilized men.

The notion that history obeys laws, whether natural or supernatural, that every event of human life is an element in a necessary pattern, has deep metaphysical origins: infatuation with the natural sciences feeds this stream, but is not its sole nor, indeed, its principal source. In the first place, there is the teleological outlook whose roots reach back to the beginnings of human thought. It occurs in many versions, but what is common to them all is the belief that men, and all living creatures and perhaps inanimate things as well, not merely are as they are, but have functions and pursue purposes. These purposes are either imposed upon them by a creator who has made every person and thing to serve each a specific goal; or else these purposes are not, indeed, imposed by a creator but are, as it were, internal to their possessors, so that every entity has a 'nature' and pursues a specific goal which is 'natural' to it, and the measure of its perfection consists in the degree to which it fulfils it. Evil, vice, imperfection, all the various forms of chaos and error, are, on this view, forms of frustration, impeded efforts to reach such goals, failures due either to misfortune which puts obstacles in the path of self-fulfilment, or to mis-directed effort to fulfil some goal not 'natural' to the entity in question.

In this cosmology the world of men (and, in some versions, the entire universe) is a single all-inclusive hierarchy; so that to explain why each ingredient of it is as, and where, and when it is, and does what it does, is *eo ipso* to say what its goal is, how far it successfully fulfils it, and what are the relations of co-ordination and subordination between the goals of the various goal-pursuing entities in the harmonious pyramid which they collectively form. If this is a true picture of reality, then historical explanation, like every other form of explanation, must consist, above all, in the attribution to individuals, groups, nations, species, of their proper place in the universal pattern. To know the 'cosmic' place of a thing or a person is to say what it is and does, and at the same time why it should be and do as it is and does. Hence to be and to have value, to exist and to have a function (and to fulfil it less or more successfully) are one and the same. The pattern, and it alone, brings into being, and causes to pass away, and con-fers purpose, that is to say, value and meaning, on all there is. To understand is to perceive patterns. To offer historical explanations is not merely to describe a succession of events, but to make it intelligible; to make intelligible is to reveal the basic pattern; not one of several possible patterns, but the one unique plan which, by being as it is, fulfils only one particular purpose, and consequently is revealed as fitting in a specifiable fashion within the single 'cosmic' over-all schema which is the goal of the universe, the goal in virtue of which alone it is a uni-verse at all, and not a chaos of unrelated bits and pieces. The more thoroughly the nature of this purpose is understood, and with it the patterns it entails in the various forms of human activity, the more explanatory or illuminating—the 'deeper'—the activity of the historian will be. Unless an event, or the character of an individual, or the activity of this or that institution or group or historical personage, is explained as a necessary consequence of its place in the pattern (and the larger, that is, the more comprehensive the schema, the more likely it is to be the true one), no explanation—and therefore no historical account—is being provided. The more inevitable an event or an action or a character can be exhibited as being, the better it has been understood, the profounder the researcher's insight, the nearer we are to the one embracing, ultimate truth.

This attitude is profoundly anti-empirical. We attribute purposes to all things and persons not because we have evidence for this hypothesis; for if there were a question of evidence for it, there could in principle be evidence against it; and then some things and events might turn out to have no purpose and therefore, in the sense used above, be incapable of being fitted into the pattern, that is, of being explained at all; but this cannot be, and is rejected in advance, *a priori*. We are plainly dealing not with an empirical theory but with a metaphysical attitude which takes for granted that to explain a thing—to describe it as it 'truly' is—even to define it more than verbally, that is, superficially— is to discover its purpose. Everything is in principle explicable, for everything has a purpose, although our minds may be too feeble or too distraught to discover in any given case what this purpose is. On such a view to say of things or persons that they exist is to say that they pursue goals; to say that they exist or are real, yet literally lack a purpose, whether imposed from outside or 'inherent' or 'innate', is to say something not false, but literally self-contradictory and therefore meaningless. Teleology is not a theory, or a hypothesis, but a category or a framework in terms of which everything is, or should be, conceived and described. The influence of this attitude on the writing of history from the epic of Gilgamesh to those enjoyable games of patience which Professor Arnold Toynbee plays with the past and future of mankind—and plays with exhilarating skill and imagination—is too familiar to need emphasis. It enters, however unconsciously, into the thought and language of those who speak of the 'rise' and 'fall' of states or movements or classes or individuals as if they obeyed some irresistible rhythm, a rising or falling wave of some cosmic river, an ebb or tide in human affairs, subject to natural or supernatural laws; as if discoverable regularities had been imposed on individuals or 'super-individuals' by a Manifest Destiny, as if the notion of life as a play were more than a vivid metaphor.[1] To those who use this figure history is a piece—or succession of pieces—comical or tragical, a libretto whose heroes and villains, winners and losers, speak their lines and suffer their fate in accordance with the text conceived in terms of them but not by them; for otherwise nothing could be rightly conceived as tragical or comical; no pattern—no rules—no explanation. Historians, journalists, ordinary men speak in these terms; they have become part and parcel of ordinary speech. Yet to take such metaphors and turns of phrase literally; to believe that such patterns are not invented but intuitively discovered or discerned, that they are not only some among many possible tunes which the same sounds can be made to yield to the musical ear, but are in some sense unique; to think that there exists *the* pattern, *the* basic rhythm of history—something which both creates and justifies all that there is—that is to take the game too seriously, to see in it a key to reality. Certainly it is to commit oneself to the view that the notion of individual responsibility is, 'in the end', an illusion. No effort, however ingenious, to re-interpret that much-tormented expression will, within a teleo-logical system, restore its normal meaning to the notion of free choice. The puppets may be conscious and identify them-selves happily with the inevitable process in which they

---

[1] I do not, of course, wish to imply that metaphors and figures of speech can be dis-pensed with in ordinary utterance, still less in the sciences; only that the danger of illicit 'reification'—the mistaking of words for things, metaphors for realities—is even greater in this sphere than is usually supposed. The most notorious cases are, of course, those of the State or the Nation, the quasi-personification of which has rightly made philosophers and even plain men uneasy or indignant for over a century. But many other words and usages offer similar dangers. Historical movements exist, and we must be allowed to call them so. Collective acts do occur; societies do rise, flourish, decay, die. Patterns, 'atmospheres', complex interrelationships of men or cultures are what they are, and cannot be analysed away into atomic constituents. Nevertheless, to take such expressions so literally that it becomes natural and normal to attribute to them causal properties, active powers, transcendent properties, demands for human sacrifice, is to be fatally deceived by myths. 'Rhythms' in history occur, but it is a sinister symptom of one's condition to speak of them as 'inexorable'. Cultures possess patterns, and ages spirits; but to explain human actions as their 'inevitable' consequences or expressions is to be a victim of misuse of words. There is no formula which guarantees a successful escape from either the Scylla of populating the world with imaginary powers and dominions, or the Charybdis of reducing everything to the verifiable behaviour of identifiable men and women in precisely denotable places and times. One can do no more than point to the existence of these perils; one must navigate between them as best one can.

play their parts; but it remains inevitable, and they remain marionettes.

Teleology is not, of course, the only metaphysics of history; side by side with it there has persisted a distinction of appearance and reality even more celebrated but of a somewhat different kind. For the teleological thinker all apparent disorder, inexplicable disaster, gratuitous suffering, unintelligible concatenations of random events, are due not to the nature of things but to our failure to discover their purpose. Everything that seems useless, discordant, mean, ugly, vicious, distorted, is needed, if we but knew it, for the harmony of the whole which only the Creator of the world, or the world itself (if it could become wholly aware of itself and its goals), can know. Total failure is excluded *a priori*, for at a 'deeper' level all processes will always be seen to culminate in success; and since there must always exist a level 'deeper' than that of any given insight, there is in principle no empirical test of what constitutes 'ultimate' success or failure. Teleology is a form of faith capable of neither confirmation nor refutation by any kind of experience; the notions of evidence, proof, probability, and so on, are wholly inapplicable to it.

But there is a second, no less time-honoured view according to which it is not goals, less or more dimly discerned, which explain and justify whatever happens, but a timeless, permanent, transcendent reality, 'above', or 'outside', or 'beyond'; which is as it is for ever, in perfect, inevitable, self-explaining harmony. Each element of it is necessitated to be what it is by its relations to the other elements and to the whole. If the world does not appear to manifest this, if we do not see actual events and persons as connected with each other by those relations of logical necessity which would make it inconceivable that anything could be other than it is, that is due solely to the failure of our own vision. We are blinded by ignorance, stupidity, passion, and the task of explanation in science or in history is the attempt to show the chaos of appearances as an imperfect reflection of the perfect order of reality, so that once more everything falls into its proper place. Explanation is the discovery of the 'underlying' pattern. The ideal is now not a distant prospect beckoning all things and persons towards self-realization, but a self-consistent, eternal, ultimate 'structure of reality', compresent 'timelessly', as it were, with the confused world of the senses which it casts as a distorted image or a feeble shadow, and of which it is at once the origin, the cause, the explanation, and the justification. The relation of this reality to the world of appearances forms the subject-matter of all the departments of true philosophy—of ethics, aesthetics, logic, of the philosophy of history and of law and of politics, according to the 'aspect' of the basic relation that is selected for attention. But under all its various names—form and matter, the one and the many, ends and means, subject and object, order and chaos, change and rest, the perfect and the imperfect, the natural and the artificial, nature and mind—the central issue, that of Reality and Appearance, remains one and the same. To understand truly is to understand it and it alone. It plays the part which the notion of function and purpose plays in teleology. It alone at once explains and justifies.

Finally there is the influence of the natural sciences. At first this seems a paradox: scientific method is surely the very negation of metaphysical speculation. But historically the one is closely interwoven with the other, and, in the field of which I speak, shows important affinities with it, namely, the notion that all that exists is necessarily an object in material nature, and therefore susceptible to explanation by scientific laws. If Newton was able in principle to explain every movement of every particular constituent of physical nature in terms of a small number of laws of great generality, is it not reasonable to suppose that psychological events, which constitute the conscious and unconscious lives of individuals, as well as social facts—the internal relationships and activities and 'experiences' of societies—could be explained by the use of similar methods? It is true that we seem to know a good deal less about the subject-matter of psychology and sociology than about the facts dealt with by physics or chemistry; but is there any objection in principle to the view that a sufficiently scrupulous and imaginative investigation of human beings might, one day, reveal laws capable of yielding predictions as powerful and as precise as those which are now possible in the natural sciences? If psychology and sociology ever attain to their proper stature—and why should they not?—we shall have laws enabling us, at least in theory (for it might still be difficult in practice), to predict (or reconstruct) every detail in the lives of every single human being in the future, present, and past. If this is (as surely it is) the theoretical ideal of such sciences as psychology, sociology, and anthropology, historical explanations will, if they are successful, simply consist in the application of the laws—the established hypotheses—of these sciences to specific individual situations. There will perhaps be 'pure' psychology, sociology, history, i.e. the principles themselves; and there will be their 'application': there will come into being social mathematics, social physics, social engineering, the 'physiology' of every feeling and attitude and inclination, as precise and powerful and useful as their originals in the natural sciences. And indeed this is the very phraseology and the ideal of eighteenth-century rationalists like d'Holbach and d'Alembert and Condorcet. The metaphysicians are victims of a delusion; nothing in nature is transcendent, nothing purposive; everything is measurable; the day will dawn when, in answer to all the painful problems now besetting us, we shall be able to say with Condorcet, 'Calculemus', and return the answers clearly, exactly, and conclusively.

What all these concepts—metaphysical and scientific alike—have in common (despite their even vaster differences) is the notion that to explain is to subsume under general formulae, to represent as examples of laws which cover an infinite number of instances; so that with knowledge of all the relevant laws, and of a sufficient range of relevant facts, it will be possible to tell not merely what happens, but also why; for, if the laws have been correctly established, to describe something is, in effect, to assert that it cannot happen otherwise. The question 'why?' for teleologists means 'in pursuit of what unalterable goal?'; for the non-teleological metaphysical 'realists' it means 'determined unalterably by what ultimate pattern?'; and for the upholders of the Comtean ideals of social statics and dynamics it means 'resulting from what causes?'—actual causes which are as they are, whether they might have been otherwise or not. The inevitability of historical processes, of trends, of 'rises' and 'falls', is merely *de facto* for those who believe that the universe obeys only 'natural

laws' which make it what it is; it is *de jure* as well—the justification as well as the explanation—for those who see such uniformity as not merely something given, brute fact, something
unchangeable and unquestionable, but as patterns, plans, purposes, ideals, as thoughts in the mind of a rational Deity or
Universal Reason, as goals, as aesthetic, self-fulfilling wholes, as
metaphysical rationales, theological other-worldly justifications,
as theodicies, which satisfy the craving to know not merely why
the world exists, but why it is worthy of existence; and why it is
this particular world that exists, rather than some other, or no
world at all; the solution being provided in terms of values which
are either somehow 'embedded' in the facts themselves or 'determine' them from some 'transcendent' height or depth. All these
theories are, in one sense or another, forms of determinism,
whether they be teleological, metaphysical, mechanistic, religious, aesthetic, or scientific. And one common characteristic of
all such outlooks is the implication that the individual's freedom
of choice (at any rate here, below) is ultimately an illusion, that
the notion that human beings could have chosen otherwise than
they did usually rests upon ignorance of facts; with the consequence that any assertion that they should have acted thus or
thus, might have avoided this or that, and deserve (and not
merely elicit or respond to) praise or blame, approval or condemnation, rests upon the presupposition that some area, at any
rate, of their lives is not totally determined by laws, whether
metaphysical or theological or expressing the generalized probabilities of the sciences. And this assumption, it is then maintained,
is patently false. The advance of knowledge constantly brings
new areas of experience under the sway of laws which make
systematic inference and prediction possible. Hence we can, if we
seek to be rational, praise and condemn, warn and encourage,
advocate justice or self-interest, forgive, condone, make resolu-
tions, issue orders, feel justified remorse, only to the degree to
which we remain ignorant of the true nature of the world. The
more we know, the farther the area of human freedom, and consequently of responsibility, is narrowed. For the omniscient
being, who sees why nothing can be otherwise than as it is,
the notions of responsibility or guilt, of right and wrong, are

necessarily empty; they are a mere measure of ignorance, of adolescent illusion; and the perception of this is the first sign of moral and intellectual maturity.

This doctrine has taken several forms. There are those who believe that moral judgments are groundless because we know too much, and there are those who believe that they are unjustified because we know too little. And again, among the former there are those whose determinism is optimistic and benevolent, and those whose determinism is pessimistic, or else confident of a happy ending yet at the same time indignantly or sardonically malevolent. Some look to history for salvation; others for justice; for vengeance; for annihilation. Among the optimistic are the confident rationalists, in particular the heralds and prophets (from Bacon to modern social theorists) of the natural sciences and of material progress, who maintain that vice and suffering are in the end always the product of ignorance. The foundation of their faith is the conviction that it is possible to find out what all men at all times truly want; and also what they can do and what is for ever beyond their power; and, in the light of this, to invent, discover, and adapt means to realizable ends. Weakness and misery, folly and vice, moral and intellectual defects are due to maladjustment. To understand the nature of things is (at the very least) to know what you (and others who, if they are human, will be like you) truly want, and how to get it. All that is bad is due to ignorance of ends or of means; to attain to knowledge of both is the purpose and function of the sciences. The sciences will advance; true ends as well as efficient means will be discovered; knowledge will increase, men will know more, and therefore be wiser and better and happier. Condorcet, whose *Esquisse* is the simplest and most moving statement of this belief, has no doubt that happiness, scientific knowledge, virtue, and liberty are bound as 'by an indissoluble chain', while stupidity, vice, injustice, and unhappiness are forms of a disease which the advance of science will eliminate for ever; for we are made what we are by natural causes; and when we understand them, this alone will suffice to bring us into harmony with 'Nature'. Praise and blame are functions of ignorance; we are what we are, like stones and trees, like bees and beavers, and if it is irrational to blame or demand justice from things or animals, climates or soils or wild beasts when they cause us pain, it is no less irrational to blame the no less determined characters or acts of men. We can regret— and deplore and expose—the depth of human cruelty, injustice, and stupidity, and comfort ourselves with the certainty that with the rapid progress of our new empirical knowledge this will soon pass away like an evil dream; for progress and education, if not inevitable, are at any rate highly probable. The belief in the possibility (or probability) of happiness as the product of rational organization unites all the benevolent sages of modern times, from the metaphysicians of the Italian Renaissance to the evolutionary thinkers of the German *Aufklärung*, from the radicals and utilitarians of pre-revolutionary France to the science-worshipping visionaries of the nineteenth and twentieth centuries. It is the heart of all the utopias from Bacon and Campanella, to Lessing and Condorcet, Saint-Simon and Cabet, Fourier and Owen, culminating in the bureaucratic fantasies of Auguste Comte, with his fanatically tidy world of human beings joyfully engaged in fulfilling their functions, each within his own rigorously defined province, in the rationally ordered, totally unalterable hierarchy of the perfect society. These are the benevolent humanitarian prophets—our own age has known not a few of them, from Jules Verne and H. G. Wells and Anatole France and Bernard Shaw to their unnumbered American disciples—generously disposed towards all mankind, genuinely seeking to rescue every living being from its burden of ignorance, sorrow, poverty, and humiliating dependence on others.

The other variant of this attitude is a good deal less amiable in tone and in feeling. When Hegel, and after him Marx, describe historical processes, they too assume that human beings and their societies are part and parcel of a wider nature, which Hegel regards as spiritual, and Marx as material, in character. Great social forces are at work of which only the acutest and most gifted individuals are ever aware; the ordinary run of men are blind in varying degrees to that which truly shapes their lives, worship fetishes and invent childish mythologies, which they dignify with the title of views or theories in order to explain the world in which they live. From time to time the real forces—impersonal and irresistible—which truly govern the world develop to a point where a new historical advance is 'due'. Then (as both Hegel and Marx notoriously believed) the crucial moments of advance are reached; these take the form of violent, cataclysmic leaps, destructive revolutions which, often with fire and sword, establish a new order upon the ruins of the old. Inevitably, the foolish, obsolete, purblind, home-made philosophies of the denizens of the old establishment are knocked over and swept away together with their possessors. For Hegel, and for a good many others, though by no means all, among the philosophers and poets of the Romantic movement, history is a perpetual struggle of vast spiritual forces embodied now in institutions—churches, races, civilizations, empires, national states—now in individuals of more than human stature—'world-historical figures'—of bold and ruthless genius, towering over, and contemptuous of, their puny contemporaries. For Marx, the struggle is a fight between socially conditioned, organized groups—classes shaped by the struggle for subsistence and survival and consequently for the control of power. There is a sardonic note (inaudible only to their most benevolent and single-hearted followers) in the words of both these thinkers as they contemplate the discomfiture and destruction of the philistines, the ordinary men and women caught in one of the decisive moments of history. Both Hegel and Marx conjure up an image of peaceful and foolish human beings, largely unaware of the part they play in history, building their homes, with touching hope and simplicity, upon the green slopes of what seems to them a peaceful mountain side, trusting in the permanence of their particular way of life, their own economic, social, and political order, treating their own values as if they were eternal standards, living, working, fighting without any awareness of the cosmic processes of which their lives are but a passing stage. But the mountain is no ordinary mountain; it is a volcano; and when (as the philosopher always knew that it would) the inevitable eruption comes, their homes and their elaborately tended institutions and their ideals and their ways of life and values will be blown out of existence in the cataclysm which marks the leap from the 'lower' to a 'higher' stage. When this point is reached, the two great prophets of destruction are in their

element; they enter into their inheritance; they survey the con-
flagration with a defiant, almost Byronic, irony and disdain. To
be wise is to understand the direction in which the world is inexorably moving, to identify oneself with the rising power which
ushers in the new world. Marx—and it is part of his attraction to
those of a similar emotional cast—identifies himself exultantly,
in his way no less passionately than Nietzsche or Bakunin, with
the great force which in its very destructiveness is creative, and
is greeted with bewilderment and horror only by those whose
values are hopelessly subjective, who listen to their consciences,
their feelings, or to what their nurses or teachers tell them, without realizing the glories of life in a world which moves from
explosion to explosion to fulfil the great cosmic design. When
history takes her revenge—and every *enragé* prophet in the nineteenth century looks to her to avenge him against those he hates
most—the mean, pathetic, ludicrous, stifling human anthills will
be justly pulverized; justly, because what is just and unjust, good
and bad, is determined by the goal towards which all creation is
tending. Whatever is on the side of victorious reason is just and
wise; whatever is on the other side, on the side of the world
that is doomed to destruction by the working of the forces of
reason, is rightly called foolish, ignorant, subjective, arbitrary,
blind; and, if it goes so far as to try to resist the forces that are
destined to supplant it, then it—that is to say, the fools and
knaves and mediocrities who constitute it—is rightly called retro-
grade, wicked, obscurantist, perversely hostile to the deepest
interests of mankind.

Different though the tone of these forms of determinism
may be—whether scientific, humanitarian, and optimistic, or
furious, apocalyptic, and exultant—they agree in this: that the
world has a direction and is governed by laws, and that the
direction and the laws can in some degree be discovered by
employing the proper techniques of investigation: and moreover
that the working of these laws can only be grasped by those who
realize that the lives, characters, and acts of individuals, both
mental and physical, are governed by the larger 'wholes' to which
they belong, and that it is the independent evolution of these
'wholes' that constitutes the so-called 'forces' in terms of whose

direction truly 'scientific' (or 'philosophic') history must be formulated. To find the explanation of why given individuals, or groups of them, act or think or feel in one way rather than another, one must first seek to understand the structure, the state of development and the direction of such 'wholes', as for example, the social, economic, political, religious institutions to which such individuals belong; once that is known, the behaviour of the individuals (or the most characteristic among them) should become almost logically deducible, and does not constitute a separate problem. Ideas about the identity of these large entities or forces, and their functions, differ from theorist to theorist. Race, colour, church, nation, class; climate, irrigation, technology, geo-political situation; civilization, social structure, the Human Spirit, the Collective Unconscious, to take some of these concepts at random, have all played their parts in theologico-historical systems as the protagonists upon the stage of history. They are represented as the real forces of which individuals are ingredients, at once constitutive, and the most articulate expressions, of this or that phase of them. Those who are more clearly and deeply aware than others of the part which they play, whether willingly or not, to that degree play it more boldly and effectively; these are the natural leaders. Others, led by their own petty personal concerns into ignoring or forgetting that they are parts of a continuous or convulsive pattern of change, are deluded into assuming that (or, at any rate, into acting as if) they and their fellows are stabilized at some fixed level for ever.

What the variants of either of these attitudes entail, like all forms of genuine determinism, is the elimination of the notion of individual responsibility. It is, after all, natural enough for men, whether for practical reasons or because they are given to reflection, to ask who or what is responsible for this or that state of affairs which they view with satisfaction or anxiety, enthusiasm or horror. If the history of the world is due to the operation of identifiable forces other than, and little affected by, free human wills and free choices (whether these occur or not), then the proper explanation of what happens must be given in terms of the evolution of such forces. And there is then a tendency to say that not individuals, but these larger entities, are ultimately 'responsible'. I live at a particular moment of time in the spiritual and social and economic circumstances into which I have been cast: how then can I help choosing and acting as I do? The values in terms of which I conduct my life are the values of my class, or race, or church, or civilization, or are part and parcel of my 'station'—my position in the 'social structure'. Nobody denies that it would be stupid as well as cruel to blame me for not being taller than I am, or to regard the colour of my hair or the qualities of my intellect or heart as being due principally to my own free choice; these attributes are as they are through no decision of mine. If I extend this category without limit, then whatever is, is necessary and inevitable. This unlimited extension of necessity, on any of the views described above, becomes intrinsic to the explanation of everything. To blame and praise, consider possible alternative courses of action, accuse or defend historical figures for acting as they do or did, becomes an absurd activity. Admiration and contempt for this or that individual may indeed continue, but it becomes akin to aesthetic judgment. We can eulogize or denounce, feel love or hatred, satisfaction and shame, but we can neither blame nor justify. Alexander, Caesar, Attila, Mohammed, Cromwell, Hitler are like floods and earthquakes, sunsets, oceans, mountains; we may admire or fear them, welcome or curse them, but to denounce or extol their acts is (ultimately) as sensible as addressing sermons to a tree (as Frederick the Great pointed out with his customary pungency in the course of his attack on d'Holbach's *System of Nature*).[1]

[1] Determinism is, of course, not identical with fatalism, which is only one, and not the most plausible, species of the vast determinist genus. The majority of determinists seem to maintain that such distinctions as those between voluntary and involuntary behaviour, or between acts and mechanical movements or states, or what a man is and what he is not accountable for, and therefore the very notion of a moral agent, depend on what is or could be affected by individual choice, effort, or decision. They hold that I normally praise or blame a man only if, and because, I think that, what occurred was (or might at any rate in part be) caused by his choice or the absence of it; and should not praise or blame him if his choices, efforts, etc., were conspicuously unable to affect the result that I applaud or deplore; and that this is compatible with the most rigorous determinism, since choice, effort, etc., are themselves causally inevitable consequences of identifiable spatio-temporal antecedents. This (in substance the classical 'dissolution' of the problem of free will by the British empiricists—Hobbes, Locke, Hume, and their modern followers Russell, Schlick, Ayer, Nowell-Smith, Hampshire, etc.) does not seem to me to solve the problem, but merely to push it a step further back. It may be that for legal or other purposes I may define responsibility, moral accountability, etc., on some such lines

To assess degrees of their responsibility, to attribute this or that consequence to their free decision, to set them up as examples or deterrents, to seek to derive lessons from their lives, becomes senseless. We can feel ashamed of our acts or of our states of mind, or of theirs, as a hunchback may be ashamed of his hump; but we cannot feel remorse: for that entails the belief that we not only could have acted otherwise, but also could have freely chosen to do so. These men were what they were; and so are we. They acted as they acted; and so do we. Their behaviour can be explained in terms of whatever fundamental category is to be

as these. But if I were convinced that although acts of choice, dispositional characteristics, etc., did affect what occurred, yet were themselves wholly determined by factors not within the individual's control (including his own motives and springs of action), I should certainly not regard him as morally praiseworthy or blameworthy. In such circumstances the concept of worth and desert, as these terms are now used, would become empty for me.

The same kind of objection seems to me to apply to the connected doctrine that free will is tantamount to capacity for being (causally) affected by praise, blame, persuasion, education, etc. Whether the causes that are held completely to determine human action are physical or psychical or of some other kind, and in whatever pattern or proportion they are deemed to occur, if they are truly causes—if their outcomes are thought to be as unalterable as, say, the effects of physical or physiological causes—this of itself seems to me to make the notion of a free choice between alternatives inapplicable. On this view 'I could have acted otherwise' is made to mean 'I could have acted otherwise if I had chosen', i.e. if there were no insuperable obstacle to hinder me (with the rider that my choice may well be affected by praise, social disapproval, etc.; but if my choice is itself the result of antecedent causes, I am, in the relevant sense, not free. Freedom to act depends not on absence of only this or that set of fatal obstacles to action—physical or biological, let us say—while other obstacles, e.g. psychological ones—character, habits, 'compulsive' motives, etc.—are present; it requires a situation in which no sum total of such causal factors wholly determines the result—in which there remains some area, however narrow, within which choice is not completely determined. This is the minimal sense of 'can' in this context. Kant's argument that where there is no freedom there is no obligation, where there is no independence of causes there is no responsibility and therefore no desert, and consequently no occasion for praise or reproach, carries conviction. If I can correctly say 'I cannot help choosing thus or thus', I am not free. To say that among the factors which determine the situation are my own character, habits, decisions, choices, etc.—which is, of course, conspicuously true—does not alter the case, or render me, in the only relevant sense, free. The feeling of those who have recognized free will as a genuine issue, and were not deceived by the latest efforts to interpret it away, turns out, as so often in the case of major problems which have plagued thoughtful men in every generation, to be sound as against philosophers armed with some all-conquering simple method of sweeping troublesome questions out of sight. Dr. Johnson, as in other matters affecting common-sense notions, here, too, seems to have been guided by a sound linguistic sense. It does not, of course, follow that any of the analyses so far provided of the relevant senses of 'can', 'freedom', 'uncaused', etc. is satisfactory. To cut the knot, as Dr. Johnson did, is not to untie it.

used, whereby history is reducible to a natural science or a metaphysical or theological schema. So much we can do for them, and, to a more limited degree, for ourselves and our contemporaries. This is all that can be done.

Yet we are adjured, oddly enough, by tough-minded determinists in the very name of the scientific status of the subject, to avoid bias; regular appeals are made to historians to refrain from sitting in judgment, to remain objective, not to read the values of the present into the past, or of the West into the East; not to admire or condemn ancient Romans for being like or unlike modern Americans; not to denounce the Middle Ages because they failed to practise toleration as it was conceived by Voltaire, nor applaud the Gracchi because we are shocked by the social injustices of our time, or criticize Cicero because of our own experience of lawyers in politics. What are we to make of such exhortations, or of the perpetual pleas to use our imagination or our powers of sympathy or of understanding in order to avoid the injustice that springs from an insufficient grasp of the aims and codes and customs of cultures distant from us in time or space? What meaning has this, save on the assumption that to give moral praise and blame, to seek to be just, is not totally irrational, that human beings deserve justice as stocks or stones do not, and that therefore we must seek to be fair, and not praise and blame arbitrarily, or mistakenly, through ignorance, or prejudice, or lack of imagination? Yet once we transfer responsibility for what happens from the backs of individuals to the causal or teleological operation of institutions or cultures or psychical or physical factors, what can be meant by calling upon our sympathy or sense of history, or sighing after the ideal of total impartiality, which may not indeed be fully attainable, but to which some come nearer than others? Few are accused of biased accounts of geological changes or lack of intuitive sympathy in describing the effect of the Italian climate upon the agriculture of ancient Rome. To this it may be answered that even if history, like natural science, is satisfaction of curiosity about unalterable processes—merely disfigured by the intrusion of moral judgments—we shall attain a less adequate grasp of even the bare facts unless we have some degree of imaginative insight into ways of life alien, or little known, to us. This is doubtless true; but it does not penetrate to the heart of the objection brought against historians who are accused of prejudice or of colouring their accounts too strongly. It may be (and has doubtless often been said) that Gibbon or Macaulay or Treitschke or the late Mr. Belloc fail to reproduce the facts as we suspect them to have been. To say this is, of course, to accuse the writers of serious inadequacy as historians; but that is not the main gravamen of the charge. It is rather that they are in some sense not merely inaccurate or superficial or incomplete, but that they are unjust; that they are seeking to secure our approval for one side, and, in order to achieve this, unfairly denigrate the other; that in dealing with one side they cite evidence and use methods of inference or presentation which, for no good reason, they deny to the other; and that their motive for doing this derives from their conviction of how men should be, and what they should do; and sometimes also that these convictions spring from views which (judged in terms of the ordinary standards and scales of value which prevail in the societies to which they and we belong) are too narrow; or irrational or inapplicable to the historical period in question; and that because of this they have suppressed or distorted the true facts, as true facts are conceived by the educated society of their, or our, time. We complain, that is to say, not merely of suppression or distortion, but of propagandist aims to which we think this may be due; and to speak of propaganda at all, let alone assume that it can be dangerously effective, is to imply that the notion of injustice is not inoperative, that marks for conduct are, and can properly be, awarded; it is in effect to say that I must either seek not to praise or blame at all, or, if I cannot avoid doing so because I am a human being and my views are inevitably shot through with moral assessments, I should seek to do so justly, with detachment, on the evidence, not blaming men for failing to do the impossible, and not praising them for it either. And this, in its turn, entails belief in individual responsibility—at any rate some degree of it. How great a degree—how wide the realm of possibility—of alternatives freely choosable—will depend on one's reading of nature and history; but it will never be nothing at all. And yet it is this, it seems to me, that is virtually denied by those historians and sociologists, steeped in metaphysical or scientific determinism, who think it right to say that in (what they are fond of calling) 'the last analysis', everything—or so much of it as makes no difference—boils down to the effects of class, or race, or civilization, or social structure. Such thinkers seem to me committed to the belief that although we may not be able to plot the exact curve of each individual life with the data at our disposal and the laws we claim to have discovered, yet, in principle, if we were omniscient, we could do so; and that consequently even that minimum residue of value judgment which no amount of conscious self-discipline and self-effacement can wholly eliminate, which colours and is a part of our very choice of historical material, of our emphasis, however tentative, upon some events and persons as being more important or interesting or unusual than others, must be either the result of our own 'ineluctable' conditioning, or else the fruit of our own incurable vanity and ignorance; and in either case remains in practice unavoidable—the price of our human status, part of the imperfection of man; and must be accepted only because it literally cannot be rejected, because men and their outlooks are what they are, and men judge as they do; because they are finite, and forget, or cannot face, the fact that they are so. This stern conclusion is not, of course, actually accepted by any working historian, or any human being in his non-theoretical moments; even though, paradoxically enough, the arguments by which we are led to such untenable conclusions, by stressing how much narrower is the area of human freedom, and therefore of responsibility, than it was believed to be during the ages of scientific ignorance, have taught many admirable lessons in restraint and humility. But to maintain that, since men are 'determined', history, by which I mean the activity of historians, cannot, strictly speaking, ever be just or unjust but only true or false, wise or stupid, is to expound a noble fallacy, and one that can seldom, if ever, have been acted upon. For its theoretical acceptance, however half-hearted, has led to the drawing of exceedingly civilized consequences, and checked much traditional cruelty and injustice.

III

The proposition that everything that we do and suffer is part of a fixed pattern; that Laplace's observer (supplied with adequate knowledge of facts and laws) could at any moment of historical time describe correctly every past and future event including those of the 'inner' life, that is, human thoughts, feelings, acts, &c.— has often been entertained, and very different implications have been drawn from it; belief in its truth has dismayed some and inspired others. But whether or not determinism is true or even coherent, it seems clear that acceptance of it does not in fact colour the ordinary thoughts of the majority of human beings, including historians, nor even those of natural scientists outside the laboratory. For if it did, the language of the believers would reflect this fact, and be different from that of the rest of us. There is a class of expressions which we constantly use (and can scarcely do without) like 'you should not (or need not) have done this'; 'need you have made this terrible mistake?'; 'I could do it, but I would rather not'; 'why did the King of Ruritania abdicate? Because, unlike the King of Abyssinia, he lacked the strength of will to resist'; '*must* the Commander-in-Chief be quite so stupid?' Expressions of this type plainly involve the notion of more than the merely logical possibility of the realization of alternatives other than those which were in fact realized, namely of differences between situations in which individuals can be reasonably regarded as being responsible for their acts, and those in which they can not. For no one will wish to deny that we do often argue about the best among the possible courses of action open to human beings in the present and past and future, in fiction and in dreams; that historians (and detectives and judges and juries) do attempt to establish, as well as they are able, what these possibilities are; that the ways in which these lines are drawn mark the frontiers between reliable and unreliable history; that what is called realism (as opposed to fancy or ignorance of life or utopian dreams) consists precisely in the placing of what occurred (or might occur) in the context of what could have happened (or could happen) and in the demarcation of this from what could not; that this is what (as I think Sir Lewis Namier once suggested) the sense of history, in the end, comes to; that upon this capacity historical (as well as legal) justice depends; that it alone makes it possible to speak of criticism, or praise and blame, as just or deserved or absurd or unfair; and that this is the sole and obvious reason why accidents, *force majeure*—being unavoidable —are necessarily outside the category of responsibility and consequently beyond the bounds of criticism, of the attribution of praise and blame. The difference between the expected and the exceptional, the difficult and the easy, the normal and the perverse, rests upon the drawing of these same lines. All this seems too self-evident to argue. It seems superfluous to add that all the discussions of historians about whether a given policy could or could not have been prevented, and what view should therefore be taken of the acts and characters of the actors, are intelligible only on the assumption of the reality of human choices. If determinism were a valid theory of human behaviour, these distinctions would be as inappropriate as the attribution of moral responsibility to the planetary system or the tissues of a living cell. These categories permeate all that we think and feel so pervasively and universally that to think them away, and conceive what and how we should be thinking, feeling, and talking without them, or in the framework of their opposites, psychologically greatly strains our capacity—is nearly, if not quite, as impracticable as, let us say, to pretend that we live in a world in which space, time, or number in the normal sense no longer exist. We may indeed always argue about specific situations, about whether a given occurrence is best explained as the inevitable effect of antecedent events beyond human control, or on the contrary as due to free human choice; free not merely in the sense that the case would have been altered if we had chosen—tried to act— differently; but that nothing prevented us from so choosing. It may well be that the growth of science and historical knowledge does in fact tend to show—make probable—that much of what was hitherto attributed to the acts of the unfettered wills of individuals can be satisfactorily explained only by the working of other, 'natural', impersonal factors; that we have, in our ignorance or vanity, extended the realm of human freedom much too far. Yet, the very meaning of such terms as 'cause' and 'inevitable' depends on the possibility of contrasting them with at least their imaginary opposites. These alternatives may be improbable; but they must at least be conceivable, if only for the purpose of contrasting them with causal necessities and law-observing uniformities; unless we attach some meaning to the notion of free acts, i.e. acts not wholly determined by antecedent events or by the nature and 'dispositional characteristics' of either persons or things, it is difficult to see why we come to distinguish acts to which responsibility is attached from mere segments in a physical, or psychical, or psycho-physical causal chain of events —a distinction signified (even if all particular applications of it are mistaken) by the cluster of expressions which deal with open alternatives and free choices. Yet it is this distinction that under-lies our normal attribution of values, in particular the notion that praise and blame can ever be justly (not merely usefully or effectively) given. If the determinist hypothesis were true, and adequately accounted for the actual world, there is a clear sense in which, despite all the extraordinary casuistry which has been brought to avoid this conclusion, the notion of human responsi-bility, as ordinarily understood, would no longer apply to any actual, but only to imaginary or conceivable, states of affairs. I do not here wish to say that determinism is necessarily false, only that we neither speak nor think as if it could be true, and that it is difficult, and perhaps beyond our normal powers, to conceive what our picture of the world would be if we seriously believed it; so that to speak, as some theorists of history (and scientists with a philosophical bent) tend to do, as if one might (in life and not only in the study) accept the determinist hypothesis, and yet to continue to think and speak much as we do at present, is to breed intellectual confusion. If the belief in freedom—which rests on the assumption that human beings do occasionally choose, and that their choices are not wholly accounted for by the kind of causal explanations which are accepted in, say, physics or biology—if this is a necessary illusion, it is so deep and so pervasive that it is not felt as such.[1] No doubt we can try

[1] What can and what cannot be done by particular agents in specific circumstances is an empirical question, properly settled, like all such questions, by an appeal to experience. If all acts were causally determined by antecedent conditions which were themselves

to convince ourselves that we are systematically deluded;[1] but unless we attempt to think out the implications of this possibility, and alter our modes of thoughts and speech to allow for it accordingly, this hypothesis remains hollow; that is, we find it impracticable even to entertain it seriously, if our behaviour is to be taken as evidence of what we can and what we cannot bring ourselves to believe or suppose not merely in theory, but in practice. My submission is that to make a serious attempt to adapt our thoughts and words to the hypothesis of determinism is a fearful task, as things are now, and have been within recorded history. The changes involved are very radical; our moral and psychological categories are, in the end, more flexible than our physical ones, but not much more so; it is not much easier to begin to think out in real terms, to which behaviour and speech would correspond, what the universe of the genuine determinist would be like, than to think out, with the minimum of indispensable concrete detail (i.e. begin to imagine) what it would be like to be in a timeless world, or one with a seventeen-dimensional space. Let those who doubt this try for themselves; the symbols with which we think will hardly lend themselves to the experiment; they, in their turn, are too deeply involved in our normal view of the world, allowing for every difference of period and clime and culture, to be capable of so violent a break. We can, of course, work out the logical implications of any set of internally consistent premisses—logic and mathematics will do any work that is required of them—but this is a very different thing from knowing how the result would look 'in practice', what the concrete innovations are; and, since history is not a deductive science (and even sociology becomes progressively less intelligible as it loses touch with its empirical foundations), such hypotheses, being abstract

similarly determined, and so on *ad infinitum*, such investigations would rest on an illusion. As rational beings we should, in that case, make an effort to disillusion ourselves—to cast off the spell of appearances; but we should surely fail. The delusion, if it is one, belongs to the order of what Kant called 'empirically real' and 'transcendentally ideal'. To try to place ourselves outside the categories which govern our empirical ('real') experience is what he regarded as an unintelligible plan of action. This thesis is surely valid, and can be stated without the paraphernalia of the Kantian system.

[1] This desperate effort to remain at once within and without the engulfing dream, to say the unsayable, is irresistible to German metaphysicians of a certain type: e.g. Schopenhauer and Vaihinger.

models, pure and unapplied, will be of little use to students of human life. Hence the ancient controversy between free will and determinism, while it remains a genuine problem for theologians and philosophers, need not trouble the thoughts of those whose concern is with empirical matters—the actual lives of human beings in the space and time of normal experience. For practising historians determinism is not, and need not be, a serious issue.

Yet, inapplicable as it may be as a theory of human action, specific forms of the deterministic hypothesis have played an arresting, if limited, role in altering our views of human responsibility. The irrelevance of the general hypothesis to historical studies must not blind us to its importance as a specific corrective to ignorance, prejudice, dogmatism, and fantasy on the part of those who judge the behaviour of others.[1] For it is plainly a good thing that we should be reminded by social scientists that the scope of human choice is a good deal more limited than we used to suppose; that the evidence at our disposal shows that many of the acts too often assumed to be within the individual's control are not so—that man is an object in (scientifically predictable) nature to a larger degree than has at times been supposed, that human beings more often than not act as they do because of characteristics due to heredity or physical or social environment or education, or biological or physical characteristics or the interplay of these factors with each other and with the obscurer factors loosely called psychical characteristics; and that the resultant habits of thought, feeling, and expression are[2] as capable of being classified and made subject to hypotheses and systematic laws as the behaviour of material objects. And this certainly alters our ideas about the limits of freedom and responsibility. If we are told that a given case of stealing is due to kleptomania, we protest that the appropriate treatment is not punishment but a remedy for a disease; and similarly, if a destructive act or a vicious character is ascribed to a specific psychological or social cause, we decide, if we are convinced that the explanation is valid, that the agent is not responsible for his acts and consequently deserves therapeutic rather than penal treatment. It is salutary

---

[1] See pp. 68 and 70–71.
[2] At least in principle.

to be reminded of the narrowness of the field within which we can begin to claim to be free; and some would claim that such knowledge is still increasing, and the field still contracting. Where the frontier between freedom and causal laws is to be determined is a crucial practical issue; knowledge of it is a powerful and indispensable antidote to ignorance and irrationality, and offers us new types of explanation—historical, psychological, sociological, biological—which previous generations have lacked. What we cannot alter, or cannot alter as much as we had supposed, cannot be used as evidence for or against us as free moral agents; it can cause us to feel pride, shame, regret, interest, but not remorse; it can be admired, envied, deplored, enjoyed, feared, wondered at, but not (save in some quasi-aesthetic sense) praised or condemned; our tendency to indignation is curbed, we desist from passing judgment. '*Je ne propose rien, je ne suppose rien, je n'impose rien . . . j'expose*,' said a French writer proudly, and such *exposition* meant for him the treatment of all events as causal or statistical phenomena, as scientific material to the exclusion of moral judgment. Historians of this persuasion, anxious to avoid all personal, above all, all moral, judgments, tend to emphasize the immense predominance of impersonal factors in history, of the physical media in which life is lived, the power of geographical, psychological, social factors which are not, at any rate consciously, man-made, and often beyond human control. This does tend to check our arrogance, to induce humility by forcing us to admit that our own outlook and scales of value are neither permanent nor universally accepted, that the over-confident, too complacent, moral classifications of past historians and of their societies sprang all too obviously from specific historical conditions, specific forms of ignorance or vainglory, or from particular temperamental traits in the historian (or moralist), or from other causes and circumstances which, from our vantage point, we perceive to belong to their own place and time, and to have given rise to interpretations which later seem idiosyncratic, smug, shallow, unjust, and often grotesque in the light of our own standards of accuracy or objectivity. And, what is even more important, such a line of approach throws doubt upon all attempts to establish a definitive line between the individual's free choice and his natural or social necessitation, and does this by bringing to light the egregious blunders of some of those who tried to solve this or that problem in the past, and made mistakes of fact which now, all too plainly, seem due to their (unalterable) *milieu*, or character, or interests. And this tends to make us ask whether the same might not be equally true of us and our own historical judgments; and so, by suggesting that every generation is 'subjectively' conditioned by its own and psychological peculiarities, leads us to wonder whether it might not be best to avoid all moral judgment, all ascription of responsibility, might not be safest to confine ourselves to impersonal terms, and leave whatever cannot be said in such terms altogether unsaid. Have we learned nothing from the intolerable moral dogmatism and the mechanical classifications of those historians and moralists and politicians whose views are now so dated, so obsolete, and so justly discredited? And, indeed, who are we to make such a parade of our personal opinions, to give such importance to what are no more than symptoms of our own ephemeral outlook? And what right, in any case, have we to sit in judgment on our fellows whose moral codes are the products of their specific historical environments, as our own are of ours? Is it not better to analyse, to describe, to present the events, and then withdraw and let them 'speak for themselves', refraining from the intolerable presumption of awarding marks, meting out justice, dividing the sheep from the goats according to our own personal criteria, as if these were eternal and not, as in fact they are, neither more nor less valid than those of others with other interests, in other conditions?

Such advice to us (in itself salutary enough) to retain a certain scepticism about our own powers of judgment, especially to beware of ascribing too much authority to our own moral views, comes to us, as you may recollect, from at least two quarters; from those who think that we know too much, and from those who think that we know too little. We know now, say the former, that we are as we are, and our moral and intellectual criteria are what they are, in virtue of the evolving historical situation. Let me once more remind you of their varieties. Some among them, who feel sure that the natural sciences will in the end account for everything, explain our behaviour in terms of natural causes. Others, who accept a more metaphysical interpretation of the world, explain it by speaking of invisible powers and dominions, nations, races, cultures; the spirit of the age, the 'workings', overt and occult, of 'the Classical Spirit', 'the Renaissance', 'the Medieval Mind', 'the French Revolution', 'the Twentieth Century', conceived as impersonal entities, at once patterns and realities, in terms of whose 'structure' or 'purpose' their elements and expressions—men and institutions—must behave as they do. Yet still others speak in terms of some teleological procession, or hierarchy, whereby each man, country, institution, culture, age, fulfil their part in some cosmic drama, and are what they are in virtue of the part cast for them, but not by them, by the divine Dramatist Himself. From this it is not far to the views of those who say that History is wiser than we, that its purposes are unfathomable to us, that we, or some amongst us, are but the means, the instruments, the manifestations, worthy or unworthy, of some vast all-embracing schema of eternal human progress, or of the German Spirit, or of the Proletariat, or of post-Christian civilization, or of Faustian man, or of Manifest Destiny, or of the American Century, or of some other myth or mystery or abstraction. To know all is to understand all; it is to know why things are and must be as they are; therefore the more we know the more absurd we must think those who suppose that things could have been otherwise, and so fall into the irrational temptation to praise or blame. *Tout comprendre, c'est tout pardonner* is transformed into a mere truism. Any form of moral censure—the accusing finger of historians or publicists or politicians, and indeed the agonies of the private conscience, too—tends, so far as possible, to be explained away as one or other sophisticated version of primitive taboos or psychical tensions or conflicts, now appearing as moral consciousness, now as some other sanction, growing out of, and battening upon, that ignorance which alone generates fallacious beliefs in free will and uncaused choice, doomed to disappear in the growing light of scientific or metaphysical truth. Or, again, we find that the adherents of a sociological or historical or anthropological metaphysics tend to interpret the sense of mission and dedication, the voice of duty, all forms of inner compulsion of this type, as being an expression within each individual's conscious life of the 'vast impersonal forces' which control it, and which speak 'in us', 'through us', 'to us', for their own inscrutable purposes. To hear is then literally to obey—to be drawn towards the true goal of our 'real' self, or its 'natural' or 'rational' development—that to which we are called in virtue of belonging to this or that class, or nation, or race, or church, or station in society, or tradition, or age, or character. The explanation, and in some sense the weight of responsibility, for all human action is (at times with ill-concealed relief) transferred to the broad backs of these vast impersonal forces—institutions or historic trends—better made to bear such burdens than a feeble thinking reed like man—a creature that, with a megalomania scarcely appropriate to his physical and moral frailty, claims, as he too often does, to be responsible for the workings of Nature or of the Spirit; and flown with his importance, praises and blames, worships and tortures, murders and immortalizes other creatures like himself for conceiving, willing, or executing policies for which neither he nor they can be remotely responsible; as if flies were to sit in solemn judgment upon each other for causing the revolutions of the sun or the changes of the seasons which affect their lives. But no sooner do we acquire adequate insight into the 'inexorable' and 'inevitable' parts played by all things animate and inanimate in the cosmic process, than we are freed from the sense of personal endeavour. Our sense of guilt and of sin, our pangs of remorse and self-condemnation, are automatically dissolved; the tension, the fear of failure and frustration, disappear as we become aware of the elements of a larger 'organic whole' of which we are variously described as limbs or members, or reflections, or emanations, or finite expressions; our sense of freedom and independence, our belief in an area, however circumscribed, in which we can choose to act as we please, falls from us; in its place we are provided with a sense of a membership in an ordered system, each with a unique position sacred to oneself alone. We are soldiers in an army, and no longer suffer the pains and penalties of solitude; the army is on the march, our goals are set for us, not chosen by us; doubts are stilled by authority. The growth of knowledge brings with it relief from moral burdens, for if powers beyond and above us are at work, it is wild presumption to claim responsibility for their activity or blame ourselves for failing in it. Original sin is thus transferred to an impersonal plane, and acts hitherto regarded as wicked or unjustifiable are seen in a more 'objective' fashion— in a larger context—as part of the process of history which, being responsible for providing us with our scale of values, must not therefore itself be judged in terms of it; and viewed in this new light they turn out no longer wicked but right and good because necessitated by the whole. This is a doctrine which lies at the heart equally of scientific attempts to explain moral sentiments as psychological or sociological 'residues' or the like, and of the metaphysical vision for which whatever is—'truly' is—is good. To understand all is to see that nothing could be otherwise than as it is; that all blame, indignation, protest is mere complaint about what seems discordant, about elements which do not seem to fit, about the absence of an intellectually or spiritually satisfy- ing pattern. But this is always only evidence of failure on the part of the observer, of his blindness and ignorance; it can never be an objective assessment of reality, for in reality everything neces- sarily fits, nothing is superfluous, nothing amiss, every ingredient is 'justified' in being where it is by the demands of the tran- scendent whole; and all sense of guilt, injustice, ugliness, all resistance or condemnation, is mere proof of (at times unavoid- able) lack of vision, misunderstanding, subjective aberration. Vice, pain, folly, maladjustment, all come from failure to under- stand, from failure, in Mr. E. M. Forster's celebrated phrase, 'to connect'. This is the sermon preached to us by great and noble thinkers of very different outlooks, by Spinoza and Godwin, by Tolstoy and Comte, by mystics and rationalists, theologians and scientific materialists, metaphysicians and dogmatic empiricists, American sociologists, Russian Marxists, and German historicists alike. Thus Godwin (and he speaks for many humane and civilized persons) tells us that to understand a human act we must always avoid applying general principles but examine each case in its full individual detail. When we scrupulously examine the texture and pattern of this or that life, we shall not, in our haste and blindness seek to condemn or to punish; for we shall see why this or that man was caused to act in this or that manner by ignorance or poverty or some other moral or intellectual or physical defect, as (Godwin optimistically supposes) we can always see, if we arm ourselves with sufficient patience, knowledge, and sympathy, and we shall then blame him no more than we should an object in nature; and since it is axiomatic that we cannot both act upon our knowledge, and yet regret the result, we can and shall in the end succeed in making men good, just, happy, and wise. So, too, Condorcet and Henri de Saint-Simon, and their disciple, Auguste Comte, starting from the opposite conviction, namely that men are not unique and in need, each one of them, of individual treatment, but, no less than inhabitants of the animal, vegetable, and mineral kingdom, belong to types and obey general laws, maintain no less stoutly that once these laws have been discovered (and therefore applied) this will by itself lead to universal felicity. And this conviction has since been echoed by many idealistic liberals and rationalists, technocrats, positivists, and believers in the scientific organization of society; and in very different keys by theocrats, neo-medieval romantics, authoritarians, and political mystics of various kinds. This, too, is in substance the morality preached if not by Marx, then by most of the disciples of Engels and Plekhanov, by Prussian nationalist historians, by Spengler, and by many another thinker who believes that there is a pattern which he has seen but others have not seen, or at least not so clearly seen, and that by this vision men may be saved. Know and you will not be lost. What it is that we must know differs from thinker to thinker, differs as views of the nature of the world differ. Know the laws of the universe, animate and inanimate, or the principles of growth, or of evolution, or of the rise and fall of civilizations, or the goals towards which all creation tends, or the stages of the Idea, or something less tangible still. Know, in the sense of identifying yourself with it, realizing your oneness with it, for, do what you may, you cannot escape from the laws to which you are subject, of whatever kind they may be, 'mechanistic', 'vitalistic', causal, purposive, imposed, transcendent, immanent, or the 'myriad' impalpable strands which bind you to the past—to your land and to the dead, as Barrès declared; to the *milieu*, the race, and the moment, as Taine asserted; to Burke's great society of the dead and living, who have made you what you are; so that the truth in which you believe, the values in terms of which you judge, from the profoundest principles to the most trivial whims, are part and parcel of the historical continuum to which you belong. Tradition or blood or class or human nature or progress or humanity; the *Zeitgeist* or the social structure or the laws of history, or the true ends of life; know these—be true to them—and you will be free. From Zeno to Spinoza, from the Gnostics to Leibniz, from Thomas Hobbes to Lenin and Freud, the battle-cry has been essentially the same; the object of knowledge and the methods of discovery have often been violently opposed, but that reality is knowable, and that knowledge and only knowledge liberates, and absolute knowledge liberates absolutely—that is common to many doctrines which are so large and valuable a part of Western civilization. To understand is to explain and to explain is to justify. The notion of individual freedom is a delusion. The further we are from omniscience, the wider our notion of our freedom and responsibility and guilt, products of ignorance and fear which populate the unknown with terrifying fictions. Personal freedom is a noble delusion and has had its social value; society might have crumbled without it; it is a necessary instrument—one of the greatest devices of 'the cunning' of Reason or of History, or of whatever other cosmic force we may be invited to worship. But a delusion however noble, useful, metaphysically justified, historically indispensable, is still a delusion. And so individual responsibility and the perception of the difference between right and wrong choices, between avoidable evil and misfortune, are mere symptoms, evidences of vanity, of our imperfect adjustment, of human inability to face the truth. The more we know, the greater the relief from the burden of choice; we forgive others for what they cannot avoid being, and by the same token we forgive ourselves. In ages in which the choices seem peculiarly agonizing, when strongly held ideals cannot be reconciled and collisions cannot be averted, such doctrines seem peculiarly comforting. We escape moral dilemmas by denying their reality; and, by directing our gaze towards the greater wholes, we make them responsible in our place. All we lose is an illusion, and with it the painful and superfluous emotions of guilt and remorse. Freedom notoriously involves responsibility, and it is for many spirits a source of welcome relief to lost the burden of both, not by some ignoble act of surrender, but by daring to contemplate in a calm spirit things as they must be; for this is to be truly philosophical. Thereby we reduce history to a kind of physics; as well blame the galaxy or gamma-rays as Genghis Khan or Hitler. 'To know all is to forgive all' turns out to be, in Professor Ayer's striking phrase (used in another context) nothing but a dramatized tautology.

IV

We have spoken thus far of the view that we cannot praise or blame because we know—or may one day know—or at any rate could know, too much for that. By a queer paradox the same position is reached by some of those who hold what seems at first the diametrical opposite of this position, that we cannot praise or blame not because we know too much, but because we know too little. Historians imbued with a sense of humility before the scope and difficulties of their task, viewing the magnitude of human claims and the smallness of human knowledge and judgment, warn us sternly against setting up our parochial values as universally valid and applying what may, at most, hold for a small portion of humanity for a brief span in some insignificant corner of the universe to all beings in all places and at all times. Tough-minded realists influenced by Marxism and Christian apologists differ profoundly in outlook, in method, in conclusions, but they are at one in this. The former[1] tell us that the social or economic principles, which, for example, Victorian Englishmen accepted as basic and eternal, were but the interests of one particular island community at one particular moment of its social and commercial development, and the truths which they so dogmatically bound upon themselves and upon others, and in the name of which they felt justified in acting as they did, were but their own passing economic or political needs and

---

[1] See, for example, the impressive and influential writings of Professor E. H. Carr on the history of our time.

claims masquerading as universal truths, and rang progressively more hollow in the ears of other nations with increasingly opposed interests, as they found themselves frequently the losers in a game where the rules had been invented by the stronger side. Then the day began to dawn when they in their turn acquired sufficient power, and turned the tables, and transformed international morality, albeit unconsciously, to suit themselves. Nothing is absolute, moral rules vary directly as the distribution of power: the prevalent morality is always that of the victors; we cannot pretend to hold the scales of justice even between them and their victims, for we ourselves belong to one side or the other; *ex hypothesi* we cannot see the world from more than one vantage point at a time. If we insist on judging others in terms of our transient standards we must not protest too much if they, in their turn, judge us in terms of theirs, which sanctimonious persons among us are too swift to denounce for no better reason than that they are not ours. And some among their Christian opponents, starting from very different assumptions, see men as feeble creatures groping in darkness, knowing but little of how things come about, or what in history inexorably causes what, and how things might have turned out but for this or that scarcely perceptible, all but untraceable, fact or situation. Men, they argue, often seek to do what is right according to their lights, but these lights are dim, and such faint illumination as they give reveals very different aspects of life to different observers. Thus, the English follow their own traditions; the Germans fight for the development of theirs; the Russians to break with their own and those of other nations; and the result is often bloodshed, widespread suffering, the destruction of what is most highly valued in the various cultures which come into violent conflict. Man proposes, but it is cruel and absurd to lay upon him—a fragile creature, born to sorrows—responsibility for many of the disasters that occur. For these are entailed by what, to take a Christian historian of distinction, Professor Herbert Butterfield calls the 'human predicament' itself—wherein we often seem to ourselves virtuous enough, but being imperfect, and doomed to stay so by Man's original sin, being ignorant, hasty, vainglorious, self-centred, lose our way, do unwitting harm, destroy what we seek to save and strengthen what we seek to destroy. If we understood more, perhaps we could do better, but our intellect is limited. For Professor Butterfield, if I understand him correctly, the 'human predicament' is a product of the complex interaction of innumerable factors, few among them known, fewer still controllable, the greater number scarcely recognized at all. The least that we can do, therefore, is to acknowledge our condition with due humility, and since we are involved in a common darkness, and few of us stumble in it to much greater purpose than others (at least in the perspective of the whole of human history), we should practise understanding and charity. The least we can do as historians, scrupulous to say no more than we are entitled to say, is to suspend judgment; neither praise nor condemn; for the evidence is always insufficient, and the alleged culprits are like swimmers for ever caught in cross-currents and whirlpools beyond their control.

A not dissimilar philosophy is, it seems to me, to be found in the writings of Tolstoy and other pessimists and quietists, both religious and irreligious. For these, particularly the most conservative among them, life is a stream moving in a given direction, or perhaps a tideless ocean stirred by occasional breezes. The number of factors which cause it to be as it is, is very great, but we know only very few of them. To seek to alter things radically in terms of our knowledge is therefore unrealistic, often to the point of absurdity. We cannot resist the central currents, for they are much stronger than we, we can only tack, only trim to the winds and avoid collisions with the great fixed institutions of our world, its physical and biological laws, and the great human establishments with their roots deep in the past—the empires, the churches, the settled beliefs and habits of mankind. For if we resist these, our small craft will be sunk, and we shall lose our lives to no purpose. Wisdom lies in avoiding situations where we may capsize, in using the winds that blow as skilfully as we can, so that we may last at any rate our own time, preserve the heritage of the past, and not hurry towards a future which will come soon enough, and may be darker even than the gloomy present. On this view it is the human predicament—the disproportion between our vast designs and our feeble means—that is responsible for much of the suffering and injustice of the world. Without help, without divine grace, or one or other form of divine intervention, we shall not, in any case, succeed. Let us then be tolerant and charitable and understanding, and avoid the folly of accusation and counter-accusation which will expose us to the laughter or pity of later generations. Let us seek to discern what we can—some dim outline of a pattern—in the shadows of the past, for even so much is surely difficult enough.

In one important sense, of course, the hard-boiled realists and the Christian pessimists are right. Censoriousness, recrimination, moral or emotional blindness to the ways of life and outlooks and complex predicaments of others, intellectual or ethical fanaticism, are vices in the writing of history as in life. No doubt Gibbon and Michelet, Macaulay and Carlyle, Taine and Trotsky (to mention only the eminent dead) do try the patience of those who do not accept their opinions. Nevertheless this corrective to dogmatic partiality, like its opposite, the doctrine of inevitable bias, by shifting responsibility on to human weakness and ignorance, and identifying the human predicament itself as the ultimate central factor in human history, in the end leads us by a different road to the very same position as the doctrine that to know all is to forgive all; only for the latter it substitutes the formula that the less we know, the fewer reasons we can have for just condemnation; for knowledge can only lead to a clearer realization of how small a part men's wishes or even their unconscious desires play in the life of the universe, and thereby reveals the absurdity of placing any serious responsibility upon the shoulders of individuals, or, for that matter, of classes, or states, or nations.[1]

Two separate strands of thought are involved in the modern plea for a greater effort at understanding, and the fashionable warnings against censoriousness, moralizing, and partisan history. There is, in the first place, the view that individuals and groups always, or at any rate more often than not, aim at what seems to them desirable; but owing to ignorance, or weakness,

[1] I do not, of course, mean to imply, that the great Western moralists, e.g. the philosophers of the medieval Church (and in particular Thomas Aquinas) or those of the Enlightenment, denied moral responsibility; nor that Tolstoy was not agonized by problems raised by it. My thesis is that their determinism committed these thinkers to a dilemma which some among them did not face, and none escaped.

or the complexities of the world which mere human insight and skill cannot adequately understand or control, they feel and act in such a manner that the result is too often disastrous both for themselves and for others, caught in the common human predicament. Yet it is not men's purposes—only the human predicament itself—man's imperfection—that is largely to blame for this. There is, in the second place, the further thesis that in attempting to explain historical situations and to analyse them, to unwind their origins and trace their consequences, and, in the course of this, to fix the responsibility for this or that element in the situation, the historian, however detached, clear-headed, scrupulous, dispassionate he may be, however skilled at imagining himself in other men's shoes, is nevertheless faced with a network of facts so minute, connected by links so many and complex, that his ignorance must always far outweigh his knowledge; consequently his judgment, particularly his evaluative judgment, must always be founded on insufficient data; and if he succeeds in casting even a little light upon some small corner of the vast and intricate pattern of the past, he has done as well as any human being can ever hope to do. The difficulties of disentangling even a minute portion of the truth are so great, that he must, if he is an honest and serious practitioner, soon realize how far he is from being in a position to moralize; consequently to praise and blame, as historians and publicists do so easily and glibly, is presumptuous, foolish, irresponsible, unjust. This prima facie very humane and convincing thesis[1] is, however, not one but two: It is one thing to say that man proposes, but the consequences are too often beyond his control or powers of prediction or prevention; that since human motives have so seldom had any decisive influence on the actual course of events, they should not play any great part in the accounts of the historian; and that since the historian's business is to discover and describe what occurred, and how and why, if he allows his moral opinions of men's characters and motives—those least effective of all historical factors—to colour his interpretations, he thereby exaggerates their importance for purely subjective or psychological reasons.

---

[1] Held, unless I have gravely misunderstood his writings, by Professor Herbert Butterfield.

For to treat what may be morally significant as *eo ipso* historically influential is to distort the facts. That is one perfectly clear position. Quite distinct from it is the other thesis, namely, that our knowledge is never sufficient to justify us in fixing responsibility, if there is any, where it truly belongs. An omniscient being (if that is a tenable notion) could do so, but we are not omniscient, and our attributions are therefore absurdly presumptuous; to realize this and feel an appropriate degree of humility is the beginning of historical wisdom. It may well be that both these theses are true. And it may further be that they both spring from the same kind of pessimistic conviction of human weakness, blindness, and ineffectiveness both in thought and in action. Nevertheless, these melancholy views are two, not one: the first is an argument from ineffectiveness, the second from ignorance: and either might be true and the other false. Moreover, neither seems to accord with common belief, nor with the common practice of either ordinary men or of ordinary historians; each seems plausible and unplausible in its own way, and each deserves its own defence or refutation. There is, however, at least one implication common to them: in both these doctrines individual responsibility is made to melt away. We may neither applaud nor condemn individuals or groups either because they cannot help themselves (and all knowledge is a growing understanding of precisely this), or conversely because we know too little to know either this or its opposite. But then—this surely follows—neither may we bring charges of moralism or bias against those historians who are prone to praise and blame, for we are all in the same boat together, and no one standard can be called objectively superior to any other. For what, on this view, could 'objective' mean? What standard can we use to measure its degrees? It is plain that there can exist no 'super-standard' for the comparison of entire scales of value, which itself derives from no specific set of beliefs, no one specific culture. All such tests must be internal, like the laws of a state that apply only to its own citizens. The case against the notion of historical objectivity is like the case against international law or international morality: that it does not exist. More than this: that the very notion has no meaning, because ultimate standards are what we measure things by, and cannot by definition themselves be measured in terms of anything else.

This is indeed to be hoist by one's own petard. Because all standards are pronounced relative, to condemn bias or moralism in history or to defend them, turn out themselves to express attitudes which, in the absence of a super-standard, cannot be rationally defended or condemned. All attitudes turn out to be morally neutral; but even this cannot be said, for the contradictory of this proposition cannot be refuted. Hence nothing on this topic can be said at all. This is surely a *reductio ad absurdum* of the entire position. A fatal fallacy must be lurking somewhere in the argument of the anti-moralistic school.[1]

Let us consider the normal thoughts of ordinary men on this topic. In ordinary circumstances we do not feel that we are saying something peculiarly hazardous or questionable if we attempt to assess the value of Cromwell's statesmanship, or if we describe

---

[1] The paradox arising out of general scepticism about historical objectivity may perhaps be put in another fashion. One of the principal reasons for complaining about the moralistic attitude of this or that historian is that his scale of values is thought to distort his judgments, to cause him to pervert the truth. But if we start from the assumption that historians, like other human beings, are wholly conditioned to think as they do by specific material (or immaterial) factors, however incalculable or impalpable, then their so-called bias is, like everything else about their thought, the inevitable consequence of their 'predicament', and so equally are our objections to it—our own ideals of impartiality, our own standards of objective truth in terms of which we condemn, say, nationalistic or woodenly Marxist historians, or other forms of animus or *parti pris*. For what is sauce for the subjective goose must be sauce for the objective gander; if we look at the matter from the vantage point of a communist or a chauvinist, our 'objective' attitude is an equal offence against their standards, which is in their own eyes no less self-evident, absolute, valid, &c. In this relativistic view the very notion of an absolute standard, presupposing as it does the rejection of all specific vantage points as such, must, of course, be an absurdity. All complaints about partiality and bias, about moral (or political) propaganda, seem, on this view, beside the point. Whatever does not agree with our views we call misleading, but if this fault is to be called subjectivism, so must the condemnation of it; it ought to follow that no point of view is superior to any other, save in so far as it proceeds from wider knowledge (given that there is a commonly agreed standard for measuring such width). We are what we are, and when and where we are; and when we are historians, we select and emphasize, interpret and evaluate, reconstruct and present facts, as we do, each in his own way. Each nation and culture and class does this in its own way—and on this view all that we are doing when we reject this or that historian as a conscious or unconscious propagandist is solely to indicate our own moral or intellectual or historical distance from him; nothing more: we are merely underlining our personal position. And this seems to be a fatal internal contradiction in the views of those who believe in the historical conditioning of historians and yet protest against moralizing by them, whether they do so contemptuously like Mr. Carr, or sorrowfully like Professor Butterfield.

Pasteur as a benefactor of mankind or condemn Hitler's actions. Nor do we feel that we are saying something strange if we maintain that, let us say, the late Mr. Belloc or Lord Macaulay do not seem to apply the same standards of objective truth, or apply them as impartially, as did, let us say, Ranke, or Bishop Creighton, or M. Elie Halévy. In saying this, what are we doing? Are we merely expressing our private approval or disapproval of Cromwell's or Pasteur's or Hitler's character or activities? Are we merely saying that we agree with Ranke's conclusions or M. Halévy's general tone, that they are more to our taste, please us better (because of our own outlook and temperament) than the tone and conclusions of Macaulay or Mr. Belloc? Yet if there is an unmistakable tinge of reproach in our assessment of, say, Cromwell's policies or of Mr. Belloc's account of those policies, is that no more than an indication that we are not favourably disposed towards one or other of them, that our moral or intellectual ideals differ from what we take to be theirs, with no indication that we think that they could, and moreover should, have acted differently? And if we do imply that their behaviour might, or should, have been different, is that merely a symptom of our psychological inability to realize that they could not (for no one can) have acted differently, or of an ignorance too deep to entitle us to tell how they could, let alone should, have acted? With the further implication that it would be more civilized not to say such things, but to remember that we may all be equally, or almost equally, deluded, and remember, too, that moral responsibility is a pre-scientific fiction, that with the increase of knowledge and a more scrupulous and appropriate use of language such 'value-charged' expressions, and the false notions of human freedom on which they rest, will, it is to be hoped, finally disappear from the vocabulary of enlightened men, at least in their public utterances? For this seems to me to follow directly from the doctrines outlined above. Determinism, whether benevolent or malevolent, no less than the view that our moral judgments are rendered absurd either because we know too much or because we know too little, seems to point to this. It is a view that in its various forms has been held by many civilized and sensitive thinkers, particularly in the present day. Nevertheless it rests on beliefs about the world and about human beings which are too difficult to accept; which are unplausible because they render illegitimate certain basic distinctions which we all draw—distinctions which are inevitably reflected in our everyday use of words. If such beliefs were true, too much that we accept without question would turn out to be sensationally false. Yet these paradoxes are urged upon us, although there is no strong factual evidence or logical argument to force us to embrace them.

It is part of the same tendency to maintain that, even if total freedom from moralizing is not to be looked for in this world (for all human beings inevitably live and think by their own varying moral or aesthetic or religious standards), yet in the writing of history an effort must be made to repress such tendencies. As historians it is our duty only to describe and explain, not to pronounce verdicts. The historian is, we are told, not a judge but a detective; he provides the evidence, and the reader, who has none of the professional responsibilities of the expert, can form what moral conclusions he likes. As a general warning against moralizing history this is, particularly in times of acute partisan emotion, timely enough. But it must not be interpreted literally. For it depends upon a false analogy with some among the more exact of the natural sciences. In these last, objectivity has a specific meaning. It means that methods and criteria of a less or more precisely defined kind are being used with scrupulous care; and that evidence, arguments, conclusions are formulated in the special terminology invented or employed for the specific purpose of each science, and that there is no intrusion (or almost none) of irrelevant considerations or concepts or categories, i.e. those specifically excluded by the canons of the science in question. I am not sure whether history can usefully be called a science at all, but certainly it is not a science in this sense. For it employs few, if any, concepts or categories peculiar to itself. Attempts to construct special sets of concepts and special techniques for history[1] have proved sterile, for they either misdescribed—overschematized—our experience, or they were felt not to provide answers to our questions. We can accuse historians of bias, or

[1] As opposed to making profitable use of other disciplines, e.g. sociology or economics or psychology.

inaccuracy, or stupidity, or dishonesty, as we can accuse one another of these vices in our ordinary daily intercourse; and we can praise them for the corresponding virtues; and usually with the same degree of justice and reason. But just as our ordinary speech would become fantastically distorted by a conscious effort to eliminate from it some basic ingredient—say, everything remotely liable to convey value judgments, our normal, scarcely noticed, moral or psychological attitudes—and just as this is not regarded as indispensable for the preservation of what we should look upon as a normal modicum of objectivity, impartiality, and accuracy, so, for the same reason, no such radical remedy is needed for the preservation of a reasonable modicum of these qualities in the writing of history. There is a sense in which a physicist can, to a large degree, speak with different voices as a physicist and as a human being; although even there the line between the two vocabularies is anything but clear or absolute. It is possible that this may in some measure be true of economists or psychologists; it grows progressively less true as we leave mathematical methods behind us, for example, in palaeography, or the history of science or that of the woollen trade; and it comes perilously near an absurdity when demanded of social or political historians, however skilled in the appropriate techniques, however professional, however rigorous. History is not identical with imaginative literature, but it is certainly not free from what, in a natural science, would be rightly condemned as unwarrantably subjective and even, in an empirical sense of the term, intuitive. Except on the assumption that history must deal with human beings purely as material objects in space—must, in short, be behaviourist—its method can scarcely be assimilated to the standards of an exact natural science.[1] The invocation to his-

[1] That history is in this sense different from physical description is a truth discovered long ago by Vico, and most imaginatively and vividly presented by Herder and his followers, and, despite the exaggerations and extravagances to which it led some nineteenth-century philosophers of history, still remains the greatest contribution of the Romantic movement to our knowledge. What was then shown, albeit often in a very misleading and confused fashion, was that to reduce history to a natural science was deliberately to leave out of account what we know to be true, to suppress great portions of our most familiar introspective knowledge on the altar of a false analogy with the sciences and their mathematical and scientific disciplines. This exhortation to the students of humanity to practise austerities, and commit deliberate acts of self-laceration,

torians to suppress even that minimal degree of moral or psychological insight and evaluation which is necessarily involved in viewing human beings as creatures with purposes and motives (and not merely as causal factors in the procession of events) seems to me to spring from a confusion of the aims and methods of the humane studies with those of natural science. Purely descriptive, wholly depersonalized, history remains, what it has always been, a figment of abstract theory, a violently exaggerated reaction to the cant and vanity of earlier generations.

V

All judgments, certainly all judgments dealing with facts, rest on—embody—generalizations, whether of fact or value or of both, and would make no sense save in terms of such generalizations. This truism, while it does not seem startling in itself, can nevertheless lead to formidable fallacies. Thus some of the heirs of Descartes who assume that whatever is true must be capable of being (at any rate in principle) stated in the form of scientific (i.e. at least quasi-mathematical or mathematically clear) generalizations conclude, as Comte and his disciples did, that the generalizations unavoidable in historical judgments must, to be worth anything, be capable of being so formulated, i.e. as demonstrable sociological laws; while valuations, if they cannot be stated in such terms, must be relegated to some 'subjective' lumber room, as 'psychological' odds and ends, expressions of purely personal attitudes, unscientific superfluities, in principle capable of being eliminated altogether, and must certainly be kept out so far as possible from the objective realm in which they have no place. Every science (we are invited to believe) must sooner or later shake itself free of what are at best irrelevances, at worst serious impediments, to clear vision. This view springs from a very understandable fascination with the morally 'neutral' attitude of natural scientists, and a desire to emulate them in other fields. But it rests on a false analogy. For the generalizations of the

that, like Origen, they might escape all temptation to sin (involved in any lapse from 'neutral' protocols of the data of observation), is to render the writing of history (and, it may be added, of sociology) gratuitously sterile.

historians differ from those of the scientists in that the valuations which they embody, whether moral, political, aesthetic, or (as they often suppose) purely historical, are intrinsic, and not, as in the sciences, external, to the subject-matter. If I am an historian and wish to explain the causes of the great French Revolution, I naturally assume or take for granted certain general propositions. Thus I assume that all the ordinarily accepted physical laws of the external world apply. I also assume that all or most men need and consciously seek food, clothing, shelter, some degree of protection for their persons, and facilities for getting their grievances listened to or redressed. Perhaps I assume something more specific, namely, that persons who have acquired a certain degree of wealth or economic power will not be indefinitely content to lack political rights or social status; or that human beings are prey to various passions—greed, envy, lust for power; or that some men are more ambitious, ruthless, cunning, or fanatical than others; and so forth. These are the assumptions of common experience; some of them are probably false; some are exaggerated, some confused, or inapplicable to given situations. Few among them are capable of being formulated in the form of hypotheses of natural science; still fewer are testable by crucial experiment, because they are not often sufficiently clear and sharp and precisely defined to be capable of being organized in a formal structure which allows of systematic mutual entailments or exclusions, and consequently of strictly logical or mathematical treatment. More than this: if they do prove capable of such formulation they will lose some of their usefulness; the idealized models of economics (not to speak of those of physics or physiology) will be of limited use in historical research or description. These inexact disciplines depend on a certain measure of concreteness, vagueness, ambiguity, suggestiveness, vividness, and so on, embodied in the properties of the language of common sense and of literature and the humanities. Degrees and kinds of precision doubtless depend on the context, the field, the subject-matter; and the rules and methods of algebra lead to absurdities if applied to the art of, say, the novel, which has its own appallingly exacting standards. The precise disciplines of Racine or Proust require a degree of genius, and are as creditable to the intellect (as well as to the imagination) of the human race as those of Newton or Darwin or Hilbert, but these kinds of method (and there is no theoretical limit to their number) are not interchangeable. They may have much or little to learn from each other; Stendhal may have learnt something from the Sensationalists of the eighteenth century, or the *Idéologues* of his own time, or from the *Code Napoléon*. But when Zola seriously contemplated the possibility of a literally 'experimental novel', founded directly on, and controlled by, the results of scientific methods and conclusions, the idea remained largely still-born, as, for similar reasons, the collective novel of the early Russian communist theorists still remains; and that not because we do not (as yet) know a sufficient number of facts (or laws), but because the concepts involved in the worlds described by novelists (or historians) are not the artificially refined concepts of scientific models—the idealized entities in terms of which natural laws are formulated—but a great deal richer in content and less logically simple or streamlined in structure. Some interplay there is, of course, between a given scientific 'world-picture' and views of life in the normal meaning of this word; the former can give very sharp impulsions to the latter. Writers like H. G. Wells or Aldous Huxley would not have described (or so egregiously misunderstood) both social and individual life as at times they did, had they not been influenced by the natural sciences of their day to an excessive degree. But even such writers as these do not actually deduce anything from scientific generalizations; do not in their writings use any semblance of truly scientific methods; for this cannot be done outside its proper field without total absurdity. The relation of the sciences to historical writing is complex and close: but it is certainly not one of identity or even similarity. Scientific method is indispensable in, say, such disciplines as palaeography, or epigraphy, or archaeology, or economics, or in other activities which are propaedeutic to history, and supply it with evidence, and help to solve specific problems. But what they establish can never suffice to constitute an historical narrative. We select certain events or persons because we believe them to have had a special degree of 'influence' or 'power' or 'importance'. These attributes are not, as a rule, quantitatively measurable, or capable of being symbolized in the terminology of an exact, or even semi-exact, science. Yet they can no more be subtracted or abstracted from the facts—from events or persons—than physical or chronological characteristics; they enter even the driest, barest chronicles of events—it is a truism to say this. And is it so very clear that the most obviously moral categories, the notions of good and bad, right and wrong, so far as they enter into our assessments of societies, individuals, characters, political action, states of mind, are in principle utterly different from such indispensable 'non-moral' categories of value as 'important', 'trivial', 'significant', &c.? It might perhaps be maintained that views of what is generally regarded as 'important'—the conquests of Alexander or Genghis Khan, or the fall of the Roman Empire, or the French Revolution, or the rise and fall of Hitler—embody relatively more stable assessments than more obviously 'ethical' valuations, or that there would be more general agreement about the fact that the French or Russian Revolutions are 'major' events (in the sense in which the tune which I hummed yesterday afternoon is not) than about whether Robespierre was a good man or a bad one, or whether it was right or wrong to execute the leaders of the National Socialist régime in Germany. And no doubt some concepts and categories are in this sense more universal or more 'stable' than others.[1] But they are not therefore 'objective' in some absolutely clear sense in which ethical notions are not. For

[1] Such 'stability' is a matter of degree. All our categories are, in theory, subject to change. The physical categories—e.g. the three dimensions and infinite extent of ordinary perceptual space, the irreversibility of temporal processes, the multiplicity and countability of material objects—are perhaps the most fixed. Yet even a shift in these most general characteristics is in principle conceivable. After these come orders and relations of sensible qualities—colours, shapes, tastes, etc.; then the uniformities on which the sciences are based—these can be quite easily thought away in fairy tales or scientific romances. The categories of value are more fluid than these; and within them tastes fluctuate more than rules of etiquette, and these more than moral standards. Within each category some concepts seem more liable to change than others. When such differences of degree become so marked as to constitute what are called differences of kind, we tend to speak of the wider and more stable distinctions as 'objective', of the narrower and less stable as the opposite. Nevertheless there is no sharp break, no frontier. The concepts form a continuous series from the 'permanent' standards to fleeting momentary reactions, from 'objective' truths and rules to 'subjective' attitudes, and they criss-cross each other in many dimensions, sometimes at unexpected angles, to perceive, discriminate, and describe which can be a mark of genius.

our historical language, the words and thoughts with which we attempt to reflect about or describe past events and persons, embody moral concepts and categories—standards both permanent and transient—just as deeply as other notions of value. Our notions of Napoleon or Robespierre as historically important, as worthy of our attention in the sense in which their minor followers are not (as well as the very meaning of terms like 'major' and 'minor'), derive from the fact that the part of the former in forwarding or retarding the interests or the ideals of a great many of their contemporaries (with which our own are bound up) was very considerable; but then so do our 'moral' judgments about them. Where to draw the line—where to exclude judgments as being too subjective to be admitted into an account which we desire to make as 'objective' as possible, that is, as well supported by publicly discoverable, inspectable, comparable facts as we can make it—that is a question for ordinary judgment, that is to say for what passes as such in our society, in our own time and place, among the people to whom we are addressing ourselves, with all the assumptions which are taken for granted, more or less, in normal communication. Because there is no hard and fast line between 'subjective' and 'objective', it does not follow that there is no line at all; and because judgments of 'importance', normally held to be 'objective', differ in some respects from moral judgments which are so often suspected of being merely 'subjective', it does not follow that 'moral' is tantamount to 'subjective': that there is some mysterious property in virtue of which those quasi-aesthetic or political judgments which distinguish essential from inessential, or crucial from trivial, are somehow intrinsic to our historical thinking and description. It does not follow that whereas the ethical implications, concerned with responsibility and moral worth, can somehow be sloughed off as if they constituted an external adjunct, a set of subjective emotional attitudes towards a body of commonly accepted, 'hard', publicly inspectable facts; as if these 'facts' were not themselves shot through with such valuations, as if a hard and fast distinction could be made, by historians or anyone else, between what is truly factual and what is a valuation of the facts, in the sense in which such a valuation truly would be an irrelevant and avoidable intrusion in, say, such fields as physics or chemistry (and doubtfully so in economics or sociology), where 'facts' can and should, according to the rules of these sciences, be described, as far as possible, with no moral overtones.

VI

When everything has been said in favour of attributing responsibility for character and action to natural and institutional causes; when everything possible has been done to correct blind or over-simple interpretations of conduct which fix too much responsibility on individuals and their free acts; when in fact there is strong evidence to show that it was difficult or impossible for men to do otherwise than they did, given their material environment or education or the influence upon them of various 'social pressures'; when every relevant psychological and sociological consideration has been taken into account, every impersonal factor given due weight; after 'hegemonist', nationalist, and other historical heresies have been exposed and refuted; after every effort has been made to induce history to aspire, so far as it can without open absurdity, after the pure, *wertfrei* condition of a science; after all these severities, we continue to praise and to blame. We blame others as we blame ourselves; and the more we know, the more, it may be, are we disposed to blame. Certainly it will surprise us to be told that the better we understand our own actions—our own motives and the circumstances surrounding them—the freer from self-blame we shall inevitably feel. The contrary is surely often true. The more deeply we investigate the course of our own conduct, the more blameworthy our behaviour may seem to us to be, the more remorse we may be disposed to feel; and if this holds for ourselves, it is not reasonable to expect us necessarily, and in all cases, to withhold it from others. Our situations may differ from theirs, but not always so widely as to make all comparisons unfair. We ourselves may be accused unjustly, and so become acutely sensitive to the dangers of unjustly blaming others. But because blame can be unjust and the temptation to utter it too strong, it does not follow that it is never just; and because judgments can be based on ignorance, can spring from violent, or perverse, or silly, or shallow, or unfair notions, it does not follow that the opposites of these qualities do not exist at all; that we are mysteriously doomed to a degree of relativism and subjectivism in history, from which we are no less mysteriously free, or at any rate more free, in our normal daily thought and transactions with one another. Indeed, the major fallacy of this position must by now be too obvious to need pointing out. We are told that we are creatures of nature or environment, or of history, and that this colours our temperament, our judgments, our principles. Every judgment is relative, every evaluation subjective, made what and as it is by the interplay of the factors of its own time and place, individual or collective. But relative to what? Subjective in contrast with what? Made to conform as it does to some ephemeral pattern as opposed to what conceivable timeless independence of such distorting factors? Relative terms (especially pejoratives) need correlatives, or else they turn out to be without meaning themselves, mere gibes, propagandist phrases designed to throw discredit, and not to describe or analyse. We know what we mean by disparaging a judgment or a method as subjective or biased—we mean that proper methods of weighing evidence have been too far ignored; or that what are normally called facts have been overlooked or suppressed or perverted; or that evidence normally accepted as sufficient to account for the acts of one individual or society is, for no good reason, ignored in some other case similar in all relevant respects; or that canons of interpretation are arbitrarily altered from case to case, that is, without consistency or principle; or that we have reasons for thinking that the historian in question wished to establish certain conclusions for reasons other than those constituted by the evidence according to canons of valid inference accepted as normal in his day or in ours, and that this has blinded him to the criteria and methods normal in his field for verifying facts and proving conclusions; or all, or any, of these together; or other considerations like them. These are the kinds of ways in which superficiality is, in practice, distinguished from depth, bias from objectivity, perversion of facts from honesty, stupidity from perspicacity, passion and confusion from detachment and lucidity. And if we grasp these rules correctly, we are fully justified in denouncing breaches of them on the part of anyone; why should we not? But, it may be objected, what of the words such as those we have used so liberally above—'valid', 'normal', 'proper', 'relevant', 'perverted', 'suppression of facts', 'interpretation'—what do they signify? Is the meaning and use of these crucial terms so very fixed and unambiguous? May not that which is thought relevant or convincing in one generation be regarded as irrelevant in the next? What are unquestioned facts to one historian may, often enough, seem merely a suspicious piece of theorizing to another. This is indeed so. Rules for the weighing of evidence do change. The accepted data of one age seem to its remote successors shot through with metaphysical presuppositions so queer as to be scarcely intelligible. All objectivity, we shall again be told, is subjective, is what it is relatively to its own time and place; all veracity, reliability, all the insights and gifts of an intellectually fertile period are such only relatively to their own 'climate of opinion'; nothing is eternal, everything flows. Yet frequently as this kind of thing has been said, and plausible as it may seem, it remains in this context mere rhetoric. We do distinguish facts, not indeed sharply from the valuations which enter into their very texture, but from interpretations of them; the borderline may not be distinct, but if I say that Stalin is dead and General Franco still alive, my statement may be accurate or mistaken, but nobody in his senses could, as words are used, take me to be advancing a theory or an interpretation. But if I say that Stalin exterminated a great many peasant proprietors because in his infancy he had been swaddled by his nurse, and that this made him aggressive, while General Franco has not done so because he did not go through this kind of experience, no one but a very naïve student of the social sciences would take me to be claiming to assert a fact, and that, no matter how many times I begin my sentences with the words 'It is a fact that'. And I shall not readily believe you if you tell me that for Thucydides (or even for some Sumerian scribe) no fundamental distinction existed between relatively 'hard' facts and relatively 'disputable' interpretations. The borderline has, no doubt, always been wide and vague; it may be a shifting frontier; it is affected by the level of generality of the propositions involved; but unless we know where, within certain limits, it lies, we fail to understand descriptive language altogether. The modes of thought of cultures remote from our own are comprehensible to us only to the degree to which we share some, at any rate, of their basic categories; and the distinction between fact and theory is among these. I may dispute whether a given historian is profound or shallow, objective and impartial in his judgments, or borne on the wings of some obsessive hypothesis or overpowering emotion: but what I mean by these contrasted terms will not be utterly different for those who disagree with me, else there would be no argument; and will not, if I can claim to decipher texts at all correctly, be so widely different in different cultures and times and places as to make all communication systematically misleading and delusive. 'Objective', 'true', 'fair', are words of large content, their uses are many, their edges often blurred. Ambiguities and confusions are always possible and often dangerous. Nevertheless such terms do possess meanings, which may, indeed, be fluid, but stay within limits recognized by normal usage, and refer to standards commonly accepted by those who work in relevant fields; and that not merely within one generation or society, but across large stretches of time and space. The mere claim that these crucial terms, these concepts or categories or standards, change in meaning or application, is to assume that such changes can to some degree be traced by methods which themselves are, *pro tanto*, not held liable to such traceable change; for if these change in their turn, then, *ex hypothesi*, they do so in a way scarcely discoverable by us.[1] And if not discoverable, then not discountable, and therefore of no use as a stick with which to beat us for our alleged subjectiveness or relativity, our delusions of grandeur and permanence, of the absoluteness of our standards in a world of ceaseless change. Such charges resemble suggestions sometimes casually advanced, that life is a dream. We protest that 'everything' cannot be a dream, for then,

---

[1] Unless indeed we embark on the extravagant path of formulating and testing the reliability of such methods by methods of methods (at times called the study of methodology), and these by methods of methods of methods; but we shall have to stop somewhere before we lose count of what we are doing: and accept that stage, willy-nilly, as absolute, the home of 'permanent standards'.

with nothing to contrast with dreams, the notion of a 'dream' loses all specific reference. We may be told that we shall have an awakening: that is, have an experience in relation to which the recollection of our present lives will be somewhat as remembered dreams now are, when compared to our normal waking experience at present. That may be true; but as things are, we can have little or no empirical experience for or against this hypothesis. We are offered an analogy one term of which is hidden from our view; and if we are invited, on the strength of it, to discount the reality of our normal waking life, in terms of another form of experience which is literally not describable and not utterable in terms of our daily experience and normal language—an experience of whose criteria for discriminating between realities and dreams we cannot in principle have any inkling—we may reasonably reply that we do not understand what we are asked to do; that the proposal is quite literally meaningless. Indeed, we may advance the old, but nevertheless sound, platitude that one cannot cast doubt on everything at once, for then nothing is more dubious than anything else, and there are no standards of comparison and nothing is altered. So too, and for the same reason, we may reject as empty those general warnings which beg us to remember that all norms and criteria, factual, logical, ethical, political, aesthetic, are hopelessly infected by historical or social or some other kind of conditioning; that all are but temporary makeshifts, none are stable or reliable; for time and chance will bear them all away. But if all judgments are thus infected, there is nothing whereby we can discriminate between various degrees of infection, and if everything is relative, subjective, accidental, biased, nothing can be judged to be more so than anything else. If words like 'subjective' and 'relative', 'prejudiced' and 'biased', are terms not of comparison and contrast—do not imply the possibility of their own opposites, of 'objective' (or at least 'less subjective') of 'unbiased' (or at least 'less biased'), what meaning have they for us? To use them in order to refer to everything whatever, to use them as absolute terms, and not as correlatives, is a rhetorical perversion of their normal sense, a kind of general *memento mori*, an invocation to all of us to remember how weak and ignorant and trivial we are, a stern and virtuous maxim, and merited perhaps, but not a serious doctrine concerned with the question of the attribution of responsibility in history, relevant to any particular group of moralists or statesmen or human beings.

It may, at this stage, be salutary to be reminded once again of the occasions which stimulated respected thinkers to such views. If, moved to indignation by the crudity and lack of scruple of those 'ideological' schools of history which, ignoring all that we know about human beings, paint individuals or classes or societies as heroes and villains, wholly white or unimaginably black, other, more sensitive and honest historians or philosophers of history protest against this, and warn us about the dangers of moralizing, of applying dogmatic standards, we applaud, we subscribe to the protest, yet we must be on our guard lest we protest too much, and, on the plea of curbing excesses, use means which promote some of the diseases of which they purport to be the cure. To blame is always to fail in understanding, say the advocates of toleration; to speak of human responsibility, guilt, crime, wickedness, if only a way of saving oneself the effort, the long, patient, subtle, or tedious labour of unravelling the tangled skein of human affairs. It is always open to us, we shall be told, by a feat of imaginative sympathy to place ourselves in the circumstances of an individual or society; if only we take the trouble to 'reconstruct' the conditions, the intellectual and social and religious 'climate' of another time or place, we shall thereby obtain insight into, or at least a glimpse of, motives and attitudes in terms of which the act we are judging may seem no longer either gratuitous, stupid, wicked, nor, above all, unintelligible. These are proper sentiments. It follows that we must, if we are to judge fairly, have adequate evidence before us; possess sufficient imagination, sufficient sense of how institutions develop, how human beings act and think, to enable us to achieve understanding of times and places and characters and predicaments very unlike our own; not to let ourselves be blinded by prejudice and passion; make every effort to construct cases for those whom we condemn—better cases, as Acton said, than they made or could have made for themselves; not look at the past solely through the eyes of the victors; nor lean over too far towards the vanquished, as if truth and justice were the monopoly of the martyrs and the minorities; and strive to remain fair even to the big battalions. All this cannot be gainsaid: it is true, just, relevant, but perhaps hardly startling. And we can add as a corollary: other times, other standards; nothing is absolute or unchanging; time and chance alter all things; and that too would be a set of truisms. Surely it is not necessary to dramatize these simple truths, which are by now, if anything, too familiar, in order to remember that the purposes, the ultimate ends of life pursued by men, are many, even within one culture and generation; that some of these come into conflict, and lead to clashes between societies, parties, individuals, and not least within individuals themselves; and furthermore that the ends of one age and country differ widely from those of other times and other outlooks. And if we understand how conflicts between ends equally ultimate and sacred, but irreconcilable within the breast of even a single human being, or between different men or groups, can lead to tragic and unavoidable collisions, we shall not distort the moral facts by artificially ordering them in terms of some one absolute criterion; recognizing that (*pace* the moralists of the eighteenth century) not all good things are necessarily compatible with one another; and shall seek to comprehend the changing ideas of cultures, peoples, classes, and individual human beings, without asking which are right, which wrong, at any rate not in terms of some simple home-made dogma. We shall not condemn the Middle Ages simply because they fell short of the moral or intellectual standard of the *révolté* intelligentsia of Paris in the eighteenth century, or denounce these latter because in their turn they earned the disapprobation of moral bigots in England in the nineteenth or in America in the twentieth century. Or, if we do condemn societies or individuals, do so only after taking into account the social and material conditions, the aspirations, codes of value, degree of progress and reaction, measured in terms of their own situation and outlook; and judge them, when we do (and why in the world should we not?), as we judge anyone or anything else: in terms partly of what we like, approve, believe in, and think right ourselves, partly of the views of the societies and individuals in question, and of what we think about such views, and of how far we, being what we are, think it natural or desirable to have a wide variety of views; and of what we think of the importance of motives as against those of consequences, or of the value of consequences as against the quality of motives, and so on. We judge as we judge, we take the risks which this entails, we accept correction wherever this seems valid, we go too far, and under pressure we retract. We make hasty generalizations, we prove mistaken, and if we are honest, we withdraw. We seek to be understanding and just, or we seek to derive practical lessons, or to be amused, and we expose ourselves to praise and blame and criticism and correction and misunderstanding. But in so far as we claim to understand the standards of others, whether members of our own societies or those of distant countries and ages, to grasp what we are told by spokesmen of many different traditions and attitudes, to understand why they think as they think and say what they say, then, so long as these claims are not absurdly false, the 'relativism' and 'subjectivism' of other civilizations do not preclude us from sharing common assumptions, sufficient for some communication with them, for some degree of understanding and being understood. This common ground is what is correctly called objective—that which enables us to identify other men and other civilizations as human and civilized at all. When this breaks down we do cease to understand, and, *ex hypothesi*, we misjudge; but since by the same hypothesis we cannot be sure how far communication has broken down, how far we are being deluded by historical mirages, we cannot always take steps to avert this or discount its consequences. We seek to understand by putting together as much as we can out of the fragments of the past, make out the best, most plausible cases for persons and ages remote or unsympathetic to us or for some reason inaccessible to us; we do our utmost to extend the frontiers of knowledge and imagination; as to what happens beyond all possible frontiers, we cannot tell and consequently cannot care; for it is nothing to us. What we can discern we seek to describe as accurately and fully as possible; as for the darkness which surrounds the field of our vision, it is opaque to us, concerning it our judgments are neither subjective nor objective; what is beyond the horizon of vision cannot disturb us in what we are able to see or seek to know; what we can never know cannot make us doubt or reject that which we do. Some of our judgments are, no doubt, relative and subjective, but others are not; for if none were so, if objectivity were in principle inconceivable, the terms subjective and objective, no longer contrasted, would mean nothing; for all correlatives stand and fall together. So much for the secular argument that we must not judge, lest—all standards being relative—we be judged, with the equally fallacious corollary that no individual in history can rightly be pronounced innocent or guilty, for the values in terms of which he is so described are subjective, spring from self-interest or class interest or a passing phase of a culture or from some other such cause; and the verdict has therefore no 'objective' status and no real authority.

And what of the other argument—the *tout comprendre* maxim? It appeals to the world order. If the world follows a fixed design and every element in it is determined by every other, then to understand a fact, a person, a civilization, is to grasp its relationship to the cosmic design, in which it plays a unique part; and to grasp its meaning is to grasp, as we have shown before, its value, its justification, too. To understand the cosmic symphony wholly is to understand the necessity for every note of it; to protest, condemn, complain is merely to show that one has not understood. In its metaphysical form this theory claims to perceive the 'real' design, so that the outer disorder is but a distorted reflection of the universal order—at once the ground and the purpose of all there is—'within' or 'beyond' or 'beneath'. This is the *philosophia perennis* of Platonists and Aristotelians, Scholastics and Hegelians, Eastern philosophers and contemporary metaphysicians, who distinguish between the harmonious reality which is invisible and the visible chaos of appearances. To understand, to justify, to explain, are identical processes. The empirical versions of this view take the form of belief in some kind of universal sociological causation. Some are optimistic like the theories of Turgot and Comte, emergent evolutionists, scientific utopians, and other convinced believers in the inevitable increase in the quality and variety of human happiness. Alternatively, as in Schopenhauer's version, they may be pessimistic, and hold out the prospect of perpetual suffering which all human efforts to prevent it will only serve to increase. Or they may take a neutral attitude and seek only to establish that there exists an inexorable sequence of cause and effect; that everything, both mental and physical, is subject to discoverable laws; that to understand them is not necessarily to approve, but at least makes it pointless to blame men for not having done better; for there was no other alternative which such men could—causally could—have chosen; so that their historical alibi is unbreakable. We can still, of course, complain in a purely aesthetic fashion. We can complain of ugliness, although we know we cannot alter it; and in the same way we can complain of stupidity, cruelty, cowardice, injustice, and feel anger or shame or despair, while remembering that we cannot put an end to their objects; and in the process of convincing ourselves that we cannot change behaviour, we shall duly cease to speak of cruelty or injustice, but merely of painful or annoying events; and to escape from them we should re-educate ourselves (and assuming, inconsistently enough, like many a Greek sage and eighteenth-century radical, that we are free in matters of education, although rigidly conditioned in almost every other respect) to adjust ourselves into conformity with the universe; and distinguishing what is relatively permanent from what is transient, seek so to form our tastes and views and activities as to fit in with the pattern of things. For if we are unhappy because we cannot have something we want, we must seek happiness by teaching ourselves to want only what we cannot anyhow avoid. That is the lesson of the Stoics, as it is, less obviously, that of some modern sociologists. Determinism is held to be 'demonstrated' by scientific observation; responsibility is a delusion; praise and blame are subjective attitudes put to flight by the advance of knowledge. To explain is to justify; one cannot complain of what cannot be otherwise; and natural morality—the life of reason— is the morality and the life whose values are identified with the actual march of events, whether it be metaphysically deduced from some intuitive insight into the nature of reality and its ultimate purpose, or established by scientific methods. But does any ordinary human being, does any practising historian, begin to believe one word of this strange tale?

VII

Two powerful doctrines are at large in contemporary thought, relativism and determinism. The first of these, for all that it is represented as being an antidote to overweening self-confidence, or arrogant dogmatism, or moral self-satisfaction, is nevertheless founded on a fallacious interpretation of experience; the second, for all that its chains are decked with flowers, and despite its parade of noble stoicism and the splendour and vastness of its cosmic design, nevertheless represents the universe as a prison. Relativism opposes to individual protest and belief in moral principles the resignation or the irony of those who have seen many worlds crumble, many ideals turned tawdry or ridiculous by time. Determinism claims to bring us to our senses by showing where the true, the impersonal and unalterable machinery of life and thought is to be found. The first, when it ceases to be a maxim, or merely a salutary reminder to us of our limitations or of the complexity of the issue, and claims our attention as a serious *Weltanschauung*, rests on the misuse of words, a confusion of ideas, and reliance upon a logical fallacy. The second, when it goes beyond indicating specific obstacles to free choice where examinable evidence for this can be adduced, turns out to rest either on a mythology or a metaphysical dogma. Both have, at times, succeeded in reasoning or frightening men out of their most human moral or political convictions in the name of a deeper and more devastating insight into the nature of things. Yet, perhaps, this is no more than a sign of neurosis and confusion: for neither view seems to be supported by human experience. Why then should either doctrine (but especially determinism) have bound its spell so powerfully on so many otherwise clear and honest minds?

VIII

One of the deepest of human desires is to find a unitary pattern in which the whole of experience, past, present, and future, actual, possible, and unfulfilled, is symmetrically ordered. It is often expressed by saying that once upon a time there was a harmonious unity—'the unmediated whole of feeling and thought', 'the unity of the knower and the known', of 'the outer and the inner', of subject and object, form and matter, self and not-self; that this was somehow broken; and that the whole of human experience has consisted in an endless effort to reassemble the fragments, to restore the unity, and so to escape or 'transcend' categories—ways of thinking—which split and isolate and 'kill' the living reality, and 'dirempt' us from it. We are told of an endless quest to find an answer to the puzzle, return to the seamless whole, to the paradise whence we were expelled, or to inherit one which we have still not done enough to earn. This central conception, whatever its origin or value, is surely at the heart of much metaphysical speculation, of much striving for the unification of the sciences, and of a large proportion of aesthetic and logical, social, and historical thought. But whether or not the discovery of a single pattern of experience offers that satisfaction of our reason to which many metaphysicians aspire, and in the name of which they reject empirical science as a mere *de facto* collocation of 'brute' facts—descriptions of events or persons or things not connected by those 'rational' links which alone reason is held to be able to accept; whether or not this lies at the back of so much metaphysics and religion, it does not alter the order of the actual appearances—the empirical scene—with which alone history can properly claim to deal. From the days of Bossuet to those of Hegel and increasingly thereafter, claims have been made, widely varying in degree of generality and confidence, to be able to trace a structure of history (usually *a priori*, for all protests to the contrary), to discover the one and only true pattern into which alone all facts will be found to fit. But this is not, and can never be, accepted by any serious historian who wishes to establish the truth as it is understood by the best critics of his time, working by standards accepted as realistic by his most scrupulous and enlightened fellow workers. For he does not perceive one unique schema as the truth—the only real framework in which alone the facts truly lie; he does not distinguish the one real, cosmic pattern from false ones, as he certainly seeks to distinguish real facts from fiction. The same facts can be arranged in more than one single pattern, seen from several perspectives, displayed in many lights, all of them valid, although some will be more suggestive or fertile in one field than in another, or unify many fields in some illuminating fashion, or, alternatively, bring out disparities and open chasms. Some of these patterns will lie closer than others to the metaphysical or religious outlook of this or that historian or historical thinker. Yet through it all the facts themselves will remain relatively 'hard'. Relatively, but, of course, not absolutely; and, whenever obsession by a given pattern causes a given writer to interpret the facts too artificially, to fill the gaps in his knowledge too smoothly, without sufficient regard to the empirical evidence, other historians will instinctively perceive that some kind of violence is being done to the facts, that the relation between evidence and interpretation is in some way abnormal; and that this is so not because there is doubt about the facts, but because there is an obsessive pattern at work.[1] Freedom from such *idées fixes*—the degree of such freedom—distinguishes true history from the mythology of a given period; for there is no historical thought, properly speaking, save where facts can be distinguished not merely from fiction, but from theory and interpretation, not, it may be, absolutely, but to a lesser or greater degree. We shall be reminded that there is no sharp break between history and mythology; or history and metaphysics; and that in the same sense there is no sharp line between 'facts' and theories: that no absolute touchstone can in principle be produced; and this is true enough, but from it nothing startling follows. That such differences exist only metaphysicians have disputed; yet history as an independent discipline did, nevertheless, emerge; and that is tantamount to saying that the frontier between facts and cosmic patterns, empirical or metaphysical or theological, indistinct and shifting as it may be, is a genuine concept for all those who take the problems of history seriously. So long as we remain historians the two levels must be kept distinct. The attempt, therefore, to shuffle off responsibility, which, at an empirical level, seems to rest upon this or that historical individual or society or set of opinions held or propagated by them, on to some metaphysical machinery which, because it is impersonal, excludes the very idea of moral responsibility, must always be

---

[1] Criteria of what is a fact or what constitutes empirical evidence are seldom in grave dispute within a given culture or profession.

invalid; and the desire to do so may, as often as not, be written down to the wish to escape from an untidy, cruel, and above all seemingly purposeless world, into a realm where all is harmonious, clear, intelligible, mounting towards some perfect culmination which satisfies the demands of 'reason', or an aesthetic feeling, or a metaphysical impulse or religious craving; above all, where nothing can be the object of criticism or complaint or condemnation or despair.

The matter is more serious when empirical arguments are advanced for an historical determinism which excludes the notion of personal responsibility. We are here no longer dealing with the metaphysics of history—the theodicies, say, of Schelling or Toynbee—as obvious substitutes for theology. We have before us the great sociological theories of history—the materialistic or scientific interpretations which began with Montesquieu and the *philosophes*, and led to the great schools of the nineteenth century, from the Saint-Simonians and Hegelians to the followers of Comte, Marx, Darwin, and the liberal economists; from Freud, Pareto, Sorel to the ideologists of Fascism. Of these Marxism is much the boldest and the most intelligent, but its practitioners, much as they have added to our understanding, have not succeeded in their gallant and powerful attempt to turn history into a science. Arising out of this great movement we have the vast proliferation of anthropological and sociological studies of civilized societies, with their tendency to trace all character and behaviour to the same kind of relatively irrational and unconscious causes as those which are held to have so successfully explained the behaviour of primitive societies; we have witnessed the rebirth of the notion of the 'sociology of knowledge', which suggests that not only our methods but our conclusions and our reasons for believing them, in the entire realm of knowledge, can be shown to be wholly or largely determined by the stage reached in the development of our class or group, or nation or culture, or whatever other unit may be chosen; followed, in due course, by the fusion of these at times unconvincing, but, usually, at least quasi-scientific, doctrines with such non-empirical figments—at times all but personified powers both good and bad—as the 'collectivist spirit', or 'The Myth of the Twentieth Century', or 'The contemporary collapse of values' (sometimes called 'The crisis of faith'), or 'Modern man', or 'The last stage of Capitalism'. All these modes of speech have peopled the air with super-natural entities of great power, Neo-Platonic and Gnostic spirits, angels and demons who play with us as they will, or, at any rate, make demands on us which, we are told, we ignore at our peril. There has grown up in our modern time a pseudo-sociological mythology which, in the guise of scientific concepts, has developed into a new animism—certainly a more primitive and naïve reli-gion than the traditional European faiths which it seeks to replace.[1] This new cult leads troubled persons to ask such questions as 'Is war inevitable?', or 'must collectivism triumph?', or 'is civilization doomed?' These questions, and the tone in which they are posed, and the way in which they are discussed, imply a belief in the occult presence of vast impersonal entities —wars, collectivism, doom—agencies and forces at large in the world, which we have but little power to control or deflect. Sometimes these are said to 'embody themselves' in great men, titanic figures, who, because they are at one with their age, achieve superhuman results—Napoleon, Bismarck, Lenin; sometimes in the actions of classes—the great capitalist combines, which work for ends that their members scarcely understand themselves, ends towards which their economic and social position 'inevitably' drive them; sometimes of huge inchoate entities called 'The masses', which do the work of history, little knowing of what mighty forces they are the 'creative vehicles'. Wars, revolutions, dictatorships, military and economic transformations are apt to be conceived like the genii of some oriental demonology, djinns which, once set free from the jars in which they have been con-fined for centuries, become uncontrollable, and capriciously play with the lives of men and nations. It is perhaps not to be wondered at that, with so luxurious a growth of similes and metaphors, many innocent persons nowadays tend to believe that their lives are dominated not merely by relatively stable, easily identifiable,

---

[1] I need hardly add that responsibility (if I may still venture to use this term) for this cannot be placed at the door of the great thinkers who founded modern sociology—Marx, Durkheim, Weber, nor of the rational and scrupulous followers and critics whose work they have inspired.

material factors—physical nature and the laws dealt with by the natural sciences; but by even more powerful and sinister, and far less intelligible, factors—the impersonal struggles of classes which members of these classes may not intend—the collision of social forces, the incidences of slumps and booms which, like tides and harvests, can scarcely be controlled by those whose lives depend upon them—above all, by inexorable 'societal' and 'behavioural' patterns, to quote but a few sacred words from the barbarous vocabulary of the new mythologies. Cowed and humbled by the panoply of the new divinities, men are eager, and seek anxiously, for knowledge and comfort in the sacred books and in the new orders of priesthood which affect to tell them about the attributes and habits of their new masters. And the books and their expositors do speak words of comfort: demand creates supply. Their message is simple and very ancient. In a world where such monsters clash, individual human beings can have but little responsibility for what they do; the discovery of the new, terrifying, impersonal forces may render life infinitely more dangerous, yet if they serve no other purpose, they do, at any rate, divest their victims of all responsibility—from all those moral burdens which men in less enlightened days used to carry with such labour and anguish. So that what we have lost on the swings we make up on the roundabouts: if we lose freedom of choice, at any rate we can no longer blame or be blamed for a world largely out of our control. The terminology of praise and condemnation turns out to be *eo ipso* uncivilized and obscurantist. To record what occurs and why, in impersonal chronicles, as was done by detached and studious monks in other times of violence and strife, is represented as more honourable and more dignified, and more in keeping with the noble humility and integrity of a scholar who in a time of doubt and crisis will at least preserve his soul if he abstains from the easy path of self-indulgence in moral sentiments. Agonizing doubts about the conduct of individuals caught in historical crises and the feeling of hope and despair, guilt, pride, and remorse which accompanies such reflections are taken from us; like soldiers in an army driven by forces too great to resist, we lose those neuroses which spring from the fear of having to choose among alternatives. Where there is no choice there is no anxiety; and a happy release from responsibility. Some human beings have always preferred the peace of imprisonment, a contented security, a sense of having at last found one's proper place in the cosmos, to the painful conflicts and perplexities of the disordered freedom of the world beyond the walls.

Yet this is odd. For the assumptions upon which this kind of determinism has been erected are, when examined, exceedingly unplausible. What are these forces and these inexorable historical laws? What historiographer, what sociologist, can claim as yet to have produced empirical generalizations comparable to the great uniformities of the natural sciences? It is a commonplace to say that sociology still awaits its Newton, but even this seems much too audacious a claim; it has yet to find its Euclid and its Archimedes, before it can begin to dream of a Copernicus. On one side a patient and useful accumulation of facts and analyses, taxonomy, useful comparative studies, cautious and limited hypotheses, still hamstrung by too many exceptions to have any appreciable predictive power;[1] on the other, imposing, sometimes ingenious, theoretical constructions, obscured by picturesque metaphors and a bold mythology, often stimulating to workers in other fields; and between these, a vast gap, such as has not existed in historical times between the theories and the factual evidence of the natural sciences. It is idle for sociology to plead that she is still young and has a glorious future. The eponymous hero to honour whose memory these words are being uttered, Auguste Comte, founded it a full hundred years ago, and its great nomothetic conquests are still to come.[2] It has affected other disciplines most fruitfully, notably history, to which it has added a dimension;[3] but it has as yet succeeded in discovering so few laws, or wide generalizations supported by adequate evidence, that its plea to be treated as a natural science can scarcely be entertained, nor are these few poor laws sufficiently revolutionary to make it seem an urgent matter to test their truth. In the great and fertile field of sociology (unlike her more speculative but far more

[1] And a collection of isolated insights and *aperçus*, like the dubious 'all power either corrupts or intoxicates', or 'man is a political animal', or 'Der Mensch ist was er ißt'.

[2] I do not mean to imply that other 'sciences'—e.g. 'political science' or social anthropology—have fared much better in establishing laws; but their claims are more modest.

[3] As well as new methods for testing the validity of old conclusions.

effective younger sister, psychology) the loose generalizations of historically trained minds, still, at times, seem more fruitful than their 'scientific' equivalents.

Social determinism is, at least historically, closely bound up with the 'nomothetic' ideals of sociology. And it may, indeed, be a true doctrine. But if it is true, and if we begin to take it seriously, then, indeed, the changes in the whole of our language, our moral terminology, our attitudes toward one another, our views of history, of society, and of everything else will be too profound to be even adumbrated. The concepts of praise and blame, innocence and guilt and individual responsibility from which we started are but a small element in the structure, which would collapse or disappear. If social and psychological determinism were established as an accepted truth, our world would be transformed more radically than was the teleological world of the classical and middle ages by the triumphs of mechanistic principles or those of natural selection. Our words—our modes of speech and thought—would be transformed in literally unimaginable ways; the notions of choice, of responsibility, of freedom, are so deeply embedded in our outlook that our new life, as creatures in a world genuinely lacking in these concepts, can, I should maintain, be conceived by us only with the greatest difficulty.[1] But there is, as yet, no need to alarm ourselves unduly. We are speaking only of pseudo-scientific ideals; the reality is not in sight. The evidence for a thoroughgoing determinism is not to hand; and if there is a persistent tendency to believe in it in some theoretical fashion, that is surely due far more to the lure of a 'scientistic' or metaphysical ideal or to a tendency on the part of those who desire to change society to believe that the stars in their courses are fighting for them. Or it may be due to a longing to lay down moral burdens, or minimize individual responsibility and transfer it to impersonal forces which can be accused of causing all our discontents, rather than to any increase in our powers of critical reflection or improvement in our scientific techniques. Belief in historical determinism of this type is, of course, very widespread, particularly in what I should like to call its 'historiosophical' form, by which I mean

[1] See Introduction, p. x.

metaphysico-theological theories of history, which attract many who have lost their faith in older religious orthodoxies. Yet perhaps this attitude, so prevalent recently, is ebbing; and a contrary trend is discernible today. Our best historians use empirical tests in sifting facts, make microscopic examinations of the evidence, deduce no patterns, and show no false fear in attributing responsibility to individuals. Their specific attributions and analyses may be mistaken, but both they and their readers would rightly reject the notion that their very activity had been superseded and stultified by the advances of sociology, or by some deeper metaphysical insight, like that of oriental stargazers by the discoveries of the disciples of Kepler. In their own queer way, some modern existentialists, too, proclaim the crucial importance of individual acts of choice. The condemnation by some among them of all philosophical systems as equally hollow, and of all moral, as of other doctrines, as equally hollow simply because they are systems and doctrines, may be invalid; but the more serious of them are no less insistent than Kant upon the reality of human autonomy, that is, upon the reality of free self-commitment to an act or a form of life for what it is in itself. Whether recognition of freedom in this last sense does or does not entitle one logically to preach to others, or judge the past, is another matter; at any rate, it shows a commendable strength of intellect to have seen through the pretensions of those all-explanatory, all-justifying theodicies, which promised to assimilate the human sciences to the natural in the quest for a unified schema of all there is. It needs more than infatuation with a programme to overthrow some of the most deeply rooted moral and intellectual habits of human beings, whether they be plumbers or historians. We are told that it is foolish to judge Charlemagne or Napoleon or Genghis Khan or Hitler or Stalin for their massacres, that it is at most a comment upon ourselves and not upon 'the facts'. Likewise we are told that we should not so describe those benefactors of humanity whom the followers of Comte so faithfully celebrated; or at least that to do so is not our business as historians: because as historians our categories are 'neutral' and differ from our categories as ordinary human beings as those of chemists undeniably do. We are also told that as historians it is our task to describe, let us say, the great revolutions of our own time without so much as hinting that certain individuals involved in them not merely caused, but were responsible for, great misery and destruction—using such words according to the standards not merely of the twentieth century which is soon over, or of our declining capitalist society, but of the human race at all the times and in all the places in which we have known it; and told that we should practise such austerities out of respect for some imaginary scientific canon which distinguishes between facts and values very sharply, so sharply that it enables us to regard the former as being objective, 'inexorable' and therefore self-justifying, and the latter merely as a subjective gloss upon events—due to the moment, the *milieu*, the individual temperament—and consequently unworthy of serious scholarship. To this we can only answer that to accept this doctrine is to do violence to the basic notions of our morality, to misrepresent our sense of our past, and to ignore some among the most general concepts and categories of normal thought. Those who are concerned with human affairs are committed to the use of moral categories and concepts which normal language incorporates and expresses. Chemists, philologists, logicians, even sociologists with a strong quantitative bias, by using morally neutral technical terms, can avoid doing so. But historians can scarcely do this. They need not—they are certainly not obliged to—moralize: but neither can they avoid the use of normal language with all its associations and 'built in' moral categories. To seek to avoid this is to adopt another moral outlook, not none at all. The time will come when men will wonder how this strange view, which combines a misunderstanding of relation of value to fact with cynicism disguised as stern impartiality, can ever have achieved such remarkable fame and influence and respectability. For it is not scientific; nor can its reputation be due entirely to a commendable fear of undue arrogance or philistinism or of too bland and uncritical an imposition of our own dogmas and standards upon others. In part it is due to a genuine misunderstanding of the pnilosophical implications of the natural sciences, the great prestige of which has been misappropriated by many a fool and impostor since their earliest triumphs. But principally it seems to me to spring from a desire to resign our responsibility, to cease from judging provided we be not judged ourselves and, above all, are not compelled to judge ourselves—from a desire to flee for refuge to some vast amoral, impersonal, monolithic whole, nature, or history,[1] or class, or race, or the 'harsh realities of our time', or the irresistible evolution of the social structure,[2] that will absorb and integrate us into its limitless, indifferent, neutral texture, which it is senseless to evaluate or criticize, and against which we fight to our certain doom. This is an image which has often appeared in the history of mankind, always at moments of confusion and inner weakness. It is one of the great alibis, pleaded by those who cannot or do not wish to face the fact of human responsibility, the existence of a limited but nevertheless real area of human freedom, either because they have been too deeply wounded or frightened to wish to return to the traffic of normal life, or because they are filled with moral indignation against the false values and the, to them, repellent moral codes of their own society, or class, or profession, and take up arms against all ethical codes as such, as a dignified means of casting off a morality which is to them, perhaps justifiably, repulsive. Nevertheless, such views, although they may spring from a natural reaction against too much moral rhetoric, are a desperate remedy; those who hold them use history as a method of escape from a world which has, for some reason, grown odious to them, into a fantasy where impersonal entities avenge their grievances and set everything right, to the greater or lesser discomfiture of their persecutors, real and imaginary. And in the course of this they describe the normal lives lived by men in terms which fail to mark the most important psychological and moral distinctions known to us. This they do in the service of an imaginary science; and, like the astrologers and soothsayers whom they have succeeded, cast up their eyes to the clouds, and speak in immense, unsubstantiated images and similes, in deeply misleading metaphors and allegories, and make use of hypnotic formulae with

---

[1] 'History has seized us by the throat', Mussolini is reported to have cried on learning of the Allied landing in Sicily. Men could be fought; but once 'History' herself took up arms against one, resistance was vain.

[2] 'The irresistible', Mr. Justice Brandeis is said to have remarked, 'is often only that which is not resisted.'

little regard for experience, or rational argument, or tests of proven reliability. Thereby they throw dust in their own eyes as well as in ours, obstruct our vision of the real world, and further confuse an already sufficiently bewildered public about the relations of morality to politics, and about the nature and methods of the natural sciences and historical studies alike.

TWO CONCEPTS OF LIBERTY[1]

IF men never disagreed about the ends of life, if our ancestors had remained undisturbed in the Garden of Eden, the studies to which the Chichele Chair of Social and Political Theory is dedicated could scarcely have been conceived. For these studies spring from, and thrive on, discord. Someone may question this on the ground that even in a society of saintly anarchists, where no conflicts about ultimate purpose can take place, political problems, for example constitutional or legislative issues, might still arise. But this objection rests on a mistake. Where ends are agreed, the only questions left are those of means, and these are not political but technical, that is to say, capable of being settled by experts or machines like arguments between engineers or doctors. That is why those who put their faith in some immense, world-transforming phenomenon, like the final triumph of reason or the proletarian revolution, must believe that all political and moral problems can thereby be turned into technological ones. That is the meaning of Saint-Simon's famous phrase about 'replacing the government of persons by the administration of things', and the Marxist prophecies about the withering away of the state and the beginning of the true history of humanity. This outlook is called utopian by those for whom speculation about this condition of perfect social harmony is the play of idle fancy. Nevertheless, a visitor from Mars to any British—or American—university today might perhaps be forgiven if he sustained the impression that its members lived in something very like this innocent and idyllic state, for all the serious attention that is paid to fundamental problems of politics by professional philosophers.

Yet this is both surprising and dangerous. Surprising because there has, perhaps, been no time in modern history when so large a number of human beings, both in the East and West, have had their notions, and indeed their lives, so deeply altered, and in

[1] This Inaugural Lecture was delivered before the University of Oxford on 31 October 1958, and published by the Clarendon Press in the same year.

some cases violently upset, by fanatically held social and political doctrines. Dangerous, because when ideas are neglected by those who ought to attend to them—that is to say, those who have been trained to think critically about ideas—they sometimes acquire an unchecked momentum and an irresistible power over multitudes of men that may grow too violent to be affected by rational criticism. Over a hundred years ago, the German poet Heine warned the French not to underestimate the power of ideas: philosophical concepts nurtured in the stillness of a professor's study could destroy a civilization. He spoke of Kant's *Critique of Pure Reason* as the sword with which European deism had been decapitated, and described the works of Rousseau as the blood-stained weapon which, in the hands of Robespierre, had destroyed the old régime; and prophesied that the romantic faith of Fichte and Schelling would one day be turned, with terrible effect, by their fanatical German followers, against the liberal culture of the West. The facts have not wholly belied this prediction; but if professors can truly wield this fatal power, may it not be that only other professors, or, at least, other thinkers (and not governments or Congressional committees), can alone disarm them?

Our philosophers seem oddly unaware of these devastating effects of their activities. It may be that, intoxicated by their magnificent achievements in more abstract realms, the best among them look with disdain upon a field in which radical discoveries are less likely to be made, and talent for minute analysis is less likely to be rewarded. Yet, despite every effort to separate them, conducted by a blind scholastic pedantry, politics has remained indissolubly intertwined with every other form of philosophical inquiry. To neglect the field of political thought, because its unstable subject-matter, with its blurred edges, is not to be caught by the fixed concepts, abstract models, and fine instruments suitable to logic or to linguistic analysis—to demand a unity of method in philosophy, and reject whatever the method cannot successfully manage—is merely to allow oneself to remain at the mercy of primitive and uncriticized political beliefs. It is only a very vulgar historical materialism that denies the power of ideas, and says that ideals are mere material interests in disguise.

It may be that, without the pressure of social forces, political ideas are stillborn: what is certain is that these forces, unless they clothe themselves in ideas, remain blind and undirected.

This truth has not escaped every Oxford teacher, even in our own day. It is because he has grasped the importance of political ideas in theory and practice, and has dedicated his life to their analysis and propagation, that the first holder of this Chair has made so great an impact upon the world in which he has lived. The name of Douglas Cole is known wherever men have political or social issues at heart. His fame extends far beyond the confines of this university and country. A political thinker of complete independence, honesty, and courage, a writer and speaker of extraordinary lucidity and eloquence, a poet and a novelist, a uniquely gifted teacher and *animateur des idées*, he is, in the first place, a man who has given his life to the fearless support of principles not always popular, and to the unswerving and passionate defence of justice and truth, often in circumstances of great difficulty and discouragement. These are the qualities for which this most generous and imaginative English socialist is today chiefly known to the world. Not the least remarkable, and perhaps the most characteristic, fact about him is that he has achieved this public position without sacrificing his natural humanity, his spontaneity of feeling, his inexhaustible personal goodness, and above all his deep and scrupulous devotion—a devotion reinforced by many-sided learning and a fabulous memory —to his vocation as a teacher of anyone who wishes to learn. It is a source of deep pleasure and pride to me to attempt to put on record what I, and many others, feel about this great Oxford figure whose moral and intellectual character is an asset to his country and to the cause of justice and human equality everywhere.

It is from him, at least as much as from his writings, that many members of my generation at Oxford have learnt that political theory is a branch of moral philosophy, which starts from the discovery, or application, of moral notions in the sphere of political relations. I do not mean, as I think some Idealist philosophers may have believed, that all historical movements or conflicts between human beings are reducible to movements or conflicts of ideas or spiritual forces, nor even that they are effects (or aspects) of them. But I do mean (and I do not think that Professor Cole would disagree) that to understand such movements or conflicts is, above all, to understand the ideas or attitudes to life involved in them, which alone make such movements a part of human history, and not mere natural events. Political words and notions and acts are not intelligible save in the context of the issues that divide the men who use them. Consequently our own attitudes and activities are likely to remain obscure to us, unless we understand the dominant issues of our own world. The greatest of these is the open war that is being fought between two systems of ideas which return different and conflicting answers to what has long been the central question of politics—the question of obedience and coercion. 'Why should I (or anyone) obey anyone else?' 'Why should I not live as I like?' 'Must I obey?' 'If I disobey, may I be coerced? By whom, and to what degree, and in the name of what, and for the sake of what?'

Upon the answers to the question of the permissible limits of coercion opposed views are held in the world today, each claiming the allegiance of very large numbers of men. It seems to me, therefore, that any aspect of this issue is worthy of examination.

I

To coerce a man is to deprive him of freedom—freedom from what? Almost every moralist in human history has praised freedom. Like happiness and goodness, like nature and reality, the meaning of this term is so porous that there is little interpretation that it seems able to resist. I do not propose to discuss either the history or the more than two hundred senses of this protean word recorded by historians of ideas. I propose to examine no more than two of these senses—but those central ones, with a great deal of human history behind them, and, I dare say, still to come. The first of these political senses of freedom or liberty (I shall use both words to mean the same), which (following much precedent) I shall call the 'negative' sense, is involved in the answer to the question 'What is the area within which the subject—a person or group of persons—is or should be left to do or be what he is able to do or be, without interference by other persons?' The second, which I shall call the positive sense, is involved in the answer to the question 'What, or who, is the source of control or interference that can determine someone to do, or be, this rather than that?' The two questions are clearly different, even though the answers to them may overlap.

The notion of 'negative' freedom

I am normally said to be free to the degree to which no man or body of men interferes with my activity. Political liberty in this sense is simply the area within which a man can act unobstructed by others. If I am prevented by others from doing what I could otherwise do, I am to that degree unfree; and if this area is contracted by other men beyond a certain minimum, I can be described as being coerced, or, it may be, enslaved. Coercion is not, however, a term that covers every form of inability. If I say that I am unable to jump more than ten feet in the air, or cannot read because I am blind, or cannot understand the darker pages of Hegel, it would be eccentric to say that I am to that degree enslaved or coerced. Coercion implies the deliberate interference of other human beings within the area in which I could otherwise act. You lack political liberty or freedom only if you are prevented from attaining a goal by human beings.[1] Mere incapacity to attain a goal is not lack of political freedom.[2] This is brought out by the use of such modern expressions as 'economic freedom' and its counterpart, 'economic slavery'. It is argued, very plausibly, that if a man is too poor to afford something on which there is no legal ban—a loaf of bread, a journey round the world, recourse to the law courts—he is as little free to have it as he would be if it were forbidden him by law. If my poverty were a kind of disease, which prevented me from buying bread, or paying for the journey round the world or getting my case heard, as lameness prevents me from running, this inability would not naturally be described as a lack of freedom, least of all political

[1] I do not, of course, mean to imply the truth of the converse.

[2] Helvétius made this point very clearly: 'The free man is the man who is not in irons, nor imprisoned in a gaol, nor terrorized like a slave by the fear of punishment . . . it is not lack of freedom not to fly like an eagle or swim like a whale.'

freedom. It is only because I believe that my inability to get a given thing is due to the fact that other human beings have made arrangements whereby I am, whereas others are not, prevented from having enough money with which to pay for it, that I think myself a victim of coercion or slavery. In other words, this use of the term depends on a particular social and economic theory about the causes of my poverty or weakness. If my lack of material means is due to my lack of mental or physical capacity, then I begin to speak of being deprived of freedom (and not simply about poverty) only if I accept the theory.[1] If, in addition, I believe that I am being kept in want by a specific arrangement which I consider unjust or unfair, I speak of economic slavery or oppression. 'The nature of things does not madden us, only ill will does', said Rousseau. The criterion of oppression is the part that I believe to be played by other human beings, directly or indirectly, with or without the intention of doing so, in frustrating my wishes. By being free in this sense I mean not being interfered with by others. The wider the area of non-interference the wider my freedom.

This is what the classical English political philosophers meant when they used this word.[2] They disagreed about how wide the area could or should be. They supposed that it could not, as things were, be unlimited, because if it were, it would entail a state in which all men could boundlessly interfere with all other men; and this kind of 'natural' freedom would lead to social chaos in which men's minimum needs would not be satisfied; or else the liberties of the weak would be suppressed by the strong. Because they perceived that human purposes and activities do not automatically harmonize with one another, and because (whatever their official doctrines) they put high value on other goals, such as justice, or happiness, or culture, or security, or varying degrees of equality, they were prepared to curtail freedom in

---

[1] The Marxist conception of social laws is, of course, the best-known version of this theory, but it forms a large element in some Christian and utilitarian, and all socialist, doctrines.

[2] 'A free man', said Hobbes, 'is he that . . . is not hindered to do what he hath the will to do.' Law is always a 'fetter', even if it protects you from being bound in chains that are heavier than those of the law, say, some more repressive law or custom, or arbitrary despotism or chaos. Bentham says much the same.

the interests of other values and, indeed, of freedom itself. For, without this, it was impossible to create the kind of association that they thought desirable. Consequently, it is assumed by these thinkers that the area of men's free action must be limited by law. But equally it is assumed, especially by such libertarians as Locke and Mill in England, and Constant and Tocqueville in France, that there ought to exist a certain minimum area of personal freedom which must on no account be violated; for if it is overstepped, the individual will find himself in an area too narrow for even that minimum development of his natural faculties which alone makes it possible to pursue, and even to conceive, the various ends which men hold good or right or sacred. It follows that a frontier must be drawn between the area of private life and that of public authority. Where it is to be drawn is a matter of argument, indeed of haggling. Men are largely interdependent, and no man's activity is so completely private as never to obstruct the lives of others in any way. 'Freedom for the pike is death for the minnows'; the liberty of some must depend on the restraint of others. 'Freedom for an Oxford don', others have been known to add, 'is a very different thing from freedom for an Egyptian peasant.'

This proposition derives its force from something that is both true and important, but the phrase itself remains a piece of political claptrap. It is true that to offer political rights, or safeguards against intervention by the state, to men who are half-naked, illiterate, underfed, and diseased is to mock their condition; they need medical help or education before they can understand, or make use of, an increase in their freedom. What is freedom to those who cannot make use of it? Without adequate conditions for the use of freedom, what is the value of freedom? First things come first: there are situations, as a nineteenth-century Russian radical writer declared, in which boots are superior to the works of Shakespeare; individual freedom is not everyone's primary need. For freedom is not the mere absence of frustration of whatever kind; this would inflate the meaning of the word until it meant too much or too little. The Egyptian peasant needs clothes or medicine before, and more than, personal liberty, but the minimum freedom that he needs today, and the greater degree of freedom that he may need tomorrow, is not some species of freedom peculiar to him, but identical with that of professors, artists, and millionaires.

What troubles the consciences of Western liberals is not, I think, the belief that the freedom that men seek differs according to their social or economic conditions, but that the minority who possess it have gained it by exploiting, or, at least, averting their gaze from, the vast majority who do not. They believe, with good reason, that if individual liberty is an ultimate end for human beings, none should be deprived of it by others; least of all that some should enjoy it at the expense of others. Equality of liberty; not to treat others as I should not wish them to treat me; repayment of my debt to those who alone have made possible my liberty or prosperity or enlightenment; justice, in its simplest and most universal sense—these are the foundations of liberal morality. Liberty is not the only goal of men. I can, like the Russian critic Belinsky, say that if others are to be deprived of it —if my brothers are to remain in poverty, squalor, and chains— then I do not want it for myself, I reject it with both hands and infinitely prefer to share their fate. But nothing is gained by a confusion of terms. To avoid glaring inequality or widespread misery I am ready to sacrifice some, or all, of my freedom: I may do so willingly and freely: but it is freedom that I am giving up for the sake of justice or equality or the love of my fellow men. I should be guilt-stricken, and rightly so, if I were not, in some circumstances, ready to make this sacrifice. But a sacrifice is not an increase in what is being sacrificed, namely freedom, however great the moral need or the compensation for it. Everything is what it is: liberty is liberty, not equality or fairness or justice or culture, or human happiness or a quiet conscience. If the liberty of myself or my class or nation depends on the misery of a number of other human beings, the system which promotes this is unjust and immoral. But if I curtail or lose my freedom, in order to lessen the shame of such inequality, and do not thereby materially increase the individual liberty of others, an absolute loss of liberty occurs. This may be compensated for by a gain in justice or in happiness or in peace, but the loss remains, and it is a confusion of values to say that although my 'liberal', individual freedom may go by the board, some other kind of freedom—'social' or 'economic'—is increased. Yet it remains true that the freedom of some must at times be curtailed to secure the freedom of others. Upon what principle should this be done? If freedom is a sacred, untouchable value, there can be no such principle. One or other of these conflicting rules or principles must, at any rate in practice, yield: not always for reasons which can be clearly stated, let alone generalized into rules or universal maxims. Still, a practical compromise has to be found.

Philosophers with an optimistic view of human nature and a belief in the possibility of harmonizing human interests, such as Locke or Adam Smith and, in some moods, Mill, believed that social harmony and progress were compatible with reserving a large area for private life over which neither the state nor any other authority must be allowed to trespass. Hobbes, and those who agreed with him, especially conservative or reactionary thinkers, argued that if men were to be prevented from destroying one another and making social life a jungle or a wilderness, greater safeguards must be instituted to keep them in their places; he wished correspondingly to increase the area of centralized control and decrease that of the individual. But both sides agreed that some portion of human existence must remain independent of the sphere of social control. To invade that preserve, however small, would be despotism. The most eloquent of all defenders of freedom and privacy, Benjamin Constant, who had not forgotten the Jacobin dictatorship, declared that at the very least the liberty of religion, opinion, expression, property, must be guaranteed against arbitrary invasion. Jefferson, Burke, Paine, Mill, compiled different catalogues of individual liberties, but the argument for keeping authority at bay is always substantially the same. We must preserve a minimum area of personal freedom if we are not to 'degrade or deny our nature'. We cannot remain absolutely free, and must give up some of our liberty to preserve the rest. But total self-surrender is self-defeating. What then must the minimum be? That which a man cannot give up without offending against the essence of his human nature. What is this essence? What are the standards which it entails? This has been, and perhaps always will be, a matter of infinite debate. But whatever the principle in terms of which the area of non-interference is to be drawn, whether it is that of natural law or natural rights, or of utility or the pronouncements of a categorical imperative, or the sanctity of the social contract, or any other concept with which men have sought to clarify and justify their convictions, liberty in this sense means liberty *from*; absence of interference beyond the shifting, but always recognizable, frontier. 'The only freedom which deserves the name is that of pursuing our own good in our own way', said the most celebrated of its champions. If this is so, is compulsion ever justified? Mill had no doubt that it was. Since justice demands that all individuals be entitled to a minimum of freedom, all other individuals were of necessity to be restrained, if need be by force, from depriving anyone of it. Indeed, the whole function of law was the prevention of just such collisions: the state was reduced to what Lassalle contemptuously described as the functions of a night-watchman or traffic policeman.

What made the protection of individual liberty so sacred to Mill? In his famous essay he declares that, unless men are left to live as they wish 'in the path which merely concerns themselves', civilization cannot advance; the truth will not, for lack of a free market in ideas, come to light; there will be no scope for spontaneity, originality, genius, for mental energy, for moral courage. Society will be crushed by the weight of 'collective mediocrity'. Whatever is rich and diversified will be crushed by the weight of custom, by men's constant tendency to conformity, which breeds only 'withered capacities', 'pinched and hidebound', 'cramped and warped' human beings. 'Pagan self-assertion is as worthy as Christian self-denial.' 'All the errors which a man is likely to commit against advice and warning are far outweighed by the evil of allowing others to constrain him to what they deem is good.' The defence of liberty consists in the 'negative' goal of warding off interference. To threaten a man with persecution unless he submits to a life in which he exercises no choices of his goals; to block before him every door but one, no matter how noble the prospect upon which it opens, or how benevolent the motives of those who arrange this, is to sin against the truth that he is a man, a being with a life of his own to live. This is liberty as it has been conceived by liberals in the modern world from the days of Erasmus (some would say of Occam) to our own. Every plea for civil liberties and individual rights, every protest against exploitation and humiliation, against the encroachment of public authority, or the mass hypnosis of custom or organized propaganda, springs from this individualistic, and much disputed, conception of man.

Three facts about this position may be noted. In the first place Mill confuses two distinct notions. One is that all coercion is, in so far as it frustrates human desires, bad as such, although it may have to be applied to prevent other, greater evils; while non-interference, which is the opposite of coercion, is good as such, although it is not the only good. This is the 'negative' conception of liberty in its classical form. The other is that men should seek to discover the truth, or to develop a certain type of character of which Mill approved—critical, original, imaginative, independent, non-conforming to the point of eccentricity, and so on—and that truth can be found, and such character can be bred, only in conditions of freedom. Both these are liberal views, but they are not identical, and the connexion between them is, at best, empirical. No one would argue that truth or freedom of self-expression could flourish where dogma crushes all thought. But the evidence of history tends to show (as, indeed, was argued by James Stephen in his formidable attack on Mill in his *Liberty, Equality, Fraternity*) that integrity, love of truth, and fiery individualism grow at least as often in severely disciplined communities among, for example, the puritan Calvinists of Scotland or New England, or under military discipline, as in more tolerant or indifferent societies; and if this is so, Mill's argument for liberty as a necessary condition for the growth of human genius falls to the ground. If his two goals proved incompatible, Mill would be faced with a cruel dilemma, quite apart from the further difficulties created by the inconsistency of his doctrines with strict utilitarianism, even in his own humane version of it.[1]

---

[1] This is but another illustration of the natural tendency of all but a very few thinkers to believe that all the things they hold good must be intimately connected, or at least compatible, with one another. The history of thought, like the history of nations, is strewn with examples of inconsistent, or at least disparate, elements artificially yoked together in a despotic system, or held together by the danger of some common enemy. In due course the danger passes, and conflicts between the allies arise, which often disrupt the system, sometimes to the great benefit of mankind.

In the second place, the doctrine is comparatively modern. There seems to be scarcely any discussion of individual liberty as a conscious political ideal (as opposed to its actual existence) in the ancient world. Condorcet had already remarked that the notion of individual rights was absent from the legal conceptions of the Romans and Greeks; this seems to hold equally of the Jewish, Chinese, and all other ancient civilizations that have since come to light.[1] The domination of this ideal has been the exception rather than the rule, even in the recent history of the West. Nor has liberty in this sense often formed a rallying cry for the great masses of mankind. The desire not to be impinged upon, to be left to oneself, has been a mark of high civilization both on the part of individuals and communities. The sense of privacy itself, of the area of personal relationships as something sacred in its own right, derives from a conception of freedom which, for all its religious roots, is scarcely older, in its developed state, than the Renaissance or the Reformation.[2] Yet its decline would mark the death of a civilization, of an entire moral outlook.

The third characteristic of this notion of liberty is of greater importance. It is that liberty in this sense is not incompatible with some kinds of autocracy, or at any rate with the absence of self-government. Liberty in this sense is principally concerned with the area of control, not with its source. Just as a democracy may, in fact, deprive the individual citizen of a great many liberties which he might have in some other form of society, so it is perfectly conceivable that a liberal-minded despot would allow his subjects a large measure of personal freedom. The despot who leaves his subjects a wide area of liberty may be unjust, or encourage the wildest inequalities, care little for order, or virtue, or knowledge; but provided he does not curb their liberty, or at least curbs it less than many other régimes, he meets with Mill's specification.[3] Freedom in this sense is not, at any rate logically,

---

[1] See the valuable discussion of this in Michel Villey, *Leçons d'histoire de la philosophie du droit*, who traces the embryo of the notion of subjective rights to Occam.

[2] Christian (and Jewish or Moslem) belief in the absolute authority of divine or natural laws, or in the equality of all men in the sight of God, is very different from belief in freedom to live as one prefers.

[3] Indeed, it is arguable that in the Prussia of Frederick the Great or in the Austria of Josef II men of imagination, originality, and creative genius, and, indeed, minorities

connected with democracy or self-government. Self-government may, on the whole, provide a better guarantee of the preservation of civil liberties than other régimes, and has been defended as such by libertarians. But there is no necessary connexion between individual liberty and democratic rule. The answer to the question 'Who governs me?' is logically distinct from the question 'How far does government interfere with me?' It is in this difference that the great contrast between the two concepts of negative and positive liberty, in the end, consists.[1] For the 'positive' sense of liberty comes to light if we try to answer the question, not 'What am I free to do or be?', but 'By whom am I ruled?' or 'Who is to say what I am, and what I am not, to be or do?' The connexion between democracy and individual liberty

of all kinds, were less persecuted and felt the pressure, both of institutions and custom, less heavy upon them than in many an earlier or later democracy.

[1] 'Negative liberty' is something the extent of which, in a given case, it is difficult to estimate. It might, prima facie, seem to depend simply on the power to choose between at any rate two alternatives. Nevertheless, not all choices are equally free, or free at all. If in a totalitarian state I betray my friend under threat of torture, perhaps even if I act from fear of losing my job, I can reasonably say that I did not act freely. Nevertheless, I did, of course, make a choice, and could, at any rate in theory, have chosen to be killed or tortured or imprisoned. The mere existence of alternatives is not, therefore, enough to make my action free (although it may be voluntary) in the normal sense of the word. The extent of my freedom seems to depend on (a) how many possibilities are open to me (although the method of counting these can never be more than impressionistic. Possibilities of action are not discrete entities like apples, which can be exhaustively enumerated); (b) how easy or difficult each of these possibilities is to actualize; (c) how important in my plan of life, given my character and circumstances, these possibilities are when compared with each other; (d) how far they are closed and opened by deliberate human acts; (e) what value not merely the agent, but the general sentiment of the society in which he lives, puts on the various possibilities. All these magnitudes must be 'integrated', and a conclusion, necessarily never precise, or indisputable, drawn from this process. It may well be that there are many incommensurable kinds and degrees of freedom, and that they cannot be drawn up on any single scale of magnitude. Moreover, in the case of societies, we are faced by such (logically absurd) questions as 'Would arrangement X increase the liberty of Mr. A more than it would that of Messrs. B, C, and D between them, added together?' The same difficulties arise in applying utilitarian criteria. Nevertheless, provided we do not demand precise measurement, we can give valid reasons for saying that the average subject of the King of Sweden is, on the whole, a good deal freer today than the average citizen of Spain or Albania. Total patterns of life must be compared directly as wholes, although the method by which we make the comparison, and the truth of the conclusions, are difficult or impossible to demonstrate. But the vagueness of the concepts, and the multiplicity of the criteria involved, is an attribute of the subject-matter itself, not of our imperfect methods of measurement, or incapacity for precise thought.

is a good deal more tenuous than it seemed to many advocates of both. The desire to be governed by myself, or at any rate to participate in the process by which my life is to be controlled, may be as deep a wish as that of a free area for action, and perhaps historically older. But it is not a desire for the same thing. So different is it, indeed, as to have led in the end to the great clash of ideologies that dominates our world. For it is this—the 'positive' conception of liberty: not freedom from, but freedom to— to lead one prescribed form of life—which the adherents of the 'negative' notion represent as being, at times, no better than a specious disguise for brutal tyranny.

II

The notion of positive freedom

The 'positive' sense of the word 'liberty' derives from the wish on the part of the individual to be his own master. I wish my life and decisions to depend on myself, not on external forces of whatever kind. I wish to be the instrument of my own, not of other men's, acts of will. I wish to be a subject, not an object; to be moved by reasons, by conscious purposes, which are my own, not by causes which affect me, as it were, from outside. I wish to be somebody, not nobody; a doer—deciding, not being decided for, self-directed and not acted upon by external nature or by other men as if I were a thing, or an animal, or a slave incapable of playing a human role, that is, of conceiving goals and policies of my own and realizing them. This is at least part of what I mean when I say that I am rational, and that it is my reason that distinguishes me as a human being from the rest of the world. I wish, above all, to be conscious of myself as a thinking, willing, active being, bearing responsibility for my choices and able to explain them by references to my own ideas and purposes. I feel free to the degree that I believe this to be true, and enslaved to the degree that I am made to realize that it is not.

The freedom which consists in being one's own master, and the freedom which consists in not being prevented from choosing as I do by other men, may, on the face of it, seem concepts at no great logical distance from each other—no more than negative

and positive ways of saying much the same thing. Yet the 'positive' and 'negative' notions of freedom historically developed in
divergent directions not always by logically reputable steps,
until, in the end, they came into direct conflict with each other.

One way of making this clear is in terms of the independent
momentum which the, initially perhaps quite harmless, metaphor of self-mastery acquired. 'I am my own master'; 'I am slave
to no man'; but may I not (as Platonists or Hegelians tend to say)
be a slave to nature? Or to my own 'unbridled' passions? Are
these not so many species of the identical genus 'slave'—some
political or legal, others moral or spiritual? Have not men had
the experience of liberating themselves from spiritual slavery,
or slavery to nature, and do they not in the course of it become
aware, on the one hand, of a self which dominates, and, on the
other, of something in them which is brought to heel? This
dominant self is then variously identified with reason, with my
'higher nature', with the self which calculates and aims at what
will satisfy it in the long run, with my 'real', or 'ideal', or 'autonomous' self, or with my self 'at its best'; which is then contrasted with irrational impulse, uncontrolled desires, my 'lower'
nature, the pursuit of immediate pleasures, my 'empirical' or
'heteronomous' self, swept by every gust of desire and passion,
needing to be rigidly disciplined if it is ever to rise to the full
height of its 'real' nature. Presently the two selves may be represented as divided by an even larger gap: the real self may be conceived as something wider than the individual (as the term is
normally understood), as a social 'whole' of which the individual
is an element or aspect: a tribe, a race, a church, a state, the great
society of the living and the dead and the yet unborn. This entity
is then identified as being the 'true' self which, by imposing its
collective, or 'organic', single will upon its recalcitrant 'members', achieves its own, and therefore their, 'higher' freedom.
The perils of using organic metaphors to justify the coercion of
some men by others in order to raise them to a 'higher' level of
freedom have often been pointed out. But what gives such plausibility as it has to this kind of language is that we recognize that it
is possible, and at times justifiable, to coerce men in the name of
some goal (let us say, justice or public health) which they would,

if they were more enlightened, themselves pursue, but do not, because they are blind or ignorant or corrupt. This renders it easy for me to conceive of myself as coercing others for their own sake, in their, not my, interest. I am then claiming that I know what they truly need better than they know it themselves. What, at most, this entails is that they would not resist me if they were rational and as wise as I and understood their interests as I do. But I may go on to claim a good deal more than this. I may declare that they are actually aiming at what in their benighted state they consciously resist, because there exists within them an occult entity—their latent rational will, or their 'true' purpose—and that this entity, although it is belied by all that they overtly feel and do and say, is their 'real' self, of which the poor empirical self in space and time may know nothing or little; and that this inner spirit is the only self that deserves to have its wishes taken into account.[1] Once I take this view, I am in a position to ignore the actual wishes of men or societies, to bully, oppress, torture them in the name, and on behalf, of their 'real' selves, in the secure knowledge that whatever is the true goal of man (happiness, performance of duty, wisdom, a just society, self-fulfilment) must be identical with his freedom—the free choice of his 'true', albeit often submerged and inarticulate, self.

This paradox has been often exposed. It is one thing to say that I know what is good for X, while he himself does not; and even to ignore his wishes for its—and his—sake; and a very different one to say that he has *eo ipso* chosen it, not indeed consciously, not as he seems in everyday life, but in his role as a rational self which his empirical self may not know—the 'real' self which discerns the good, and cannot help choosing it once it is revealed. This monstrous impersonation, which consists in equating what X would choose if he were something he is not, or at least not yet, with what X actually seeks and chooses, is at the heart of all political

---

[1] 'The ideal of true freedom is the maximum of power for all the members of human society alike to make the best of themselves', said T. H. Green in 1881. Apart from the confusion of freedom with equality, this entails that if a man chose some immediate pleasure—which (in whose view?) would not enable him to make the best of himself (what self?)—what he was exercising was not 'true' freedom: and if deprived of it, would not lose anything that mattered. Green was a genuine liberal: but many a tyrant could use this formula to justify his worst acts of oppression.

theories of self-realization. It is one thing to say that I may be coerced for my own good which I am too blind to see: this may, on occasion, be for my benefit; indeed it may enlarge the scope of my liberty. It is another to say that if it is my good, then I am not being coerced, for I have willed it, whether I know this or not, and am free (or 'truly' free) even while my poor earthly body and foolish mind bitterly reject it, and struggle against those who seek however benevolently to impose it, with the greatest desperation.

This magical transformation, or sleight of hand (for which William James so justly mocked the Hegelians), can no doubt be perpetrated just as easily with the 'negative' concept of freedom, where the self that should not be interfered with is no longer the individual with his actual wishes and needs as they are normally conceived, but the 'real' man within, identified with the pursuit of some ideal purpose not dreamed of by his empirical self. And, as in the case of the 'positively' free self, this entity may be inflated into some super-personal entity—a state, a class, a nation, or the march of history itself, regarded as a more 'real' subject of attributes than the empirical self. But the 'positive' conception of freedom as self-mastery, with its suggestion of a man divided against himself, has, in fact, and as a matter of history, of doctrine and of practice, lent itself more easily to this splitting of personality into two: the transcendent, dominant controller, and the empirical bundle of desires and passions to be disciplined and brought to heel. It is this historical fact that has been influential. This demonstrates (if demonstration of so obvious a truth is needed) that conceptions of freedom directly derive from views of what constitutes a self, a person, a man. Enough manipulation with the definition of man, and freedom can be made to mean whatever the manipulator wishes. Recent history has made it only too clear that the issue is not merely academic.

The consequences of distinguishing between two selves will become even clearer if one considers the two major forms which the desire to be self-directed—directed by one's 'true' self—has historically taken: the first, that of self-abnegation in order to attain independence; the second, that of self-realization, or total self-identification with a specific principle or ideal in order to attain the selfsame end.

III

The retreat to the inner citadel

I am the possessor of reason and will; I conceive ends and I desire to pursue them; but if I am prevented from attaining them I no longer feel master of the situation. I may be prevented by the laws of nature, or by accidents, or the activities of men, or the effect, often undesigned, of human institutions. These forces may be too much for me. What am I to do to avoid being crushed by them? I must liberate myself from desires that I know I cannot realize. I wish to be master of my kingdom, but my frontiers are long and insecure, therefore I contract them in order to reduce or eliminate the vulnerable area. I begin by desiring happiness, or power, or knowledge, or the attainment of some specific object. But I cannot command them. I choose to avoid defeat and waste, and therefore decide to strive for nothing that I cannot be sure to obtain. I determine myself not to desire what is unattainable. The tyrant threatens me with the destruction of my property, with imprisonment, with the exile or death of those I love. But if I no longer feel attached to property, no longer care whether or not I am in prison, if I have killed within myself my natural affections, then he cannot bend me to his will, for all that is left of myself is no longer subject to empirical fears or desires. It is as if I had performed a strategic retreat into an inner citadel—my reason, my soul, my 'noumenal' self—which, do what they may, neither external blind force, nor human malice, can touch. I have withdrawn into myself; there, and there alone, I am secure. It is as if I were to say: 'I have a wound in my leg. There are two methods of freeing myself from pain. One is to heal the wound. But if the cure is too difficult or uncertain, there is another method. I can get rid of the wound by cutting off my leg. If I train myself to want nothing to which the possession of my leg is indispensable, I shall not feel the lack of it.' This is the traditional self-emancipation of ascetics and quietists, of stoics or Buddhist sages, men of various religions or of none, who have fled the world, and escaped the yoke of society or public opinion, by some process of deliberate self-transformation that enables them to care no longer for any of its values, to remain, isolated and independent, on its edges, no longer vulnerable to its weapons.[1] All political isolationism, all economic autarky, every form of autonomy, has in it some element of this attitude. I eliminate the obstacles in my path by abandoning the path; I retreat into my own sect, my own planned economy, my own deliberately insulated territory, where no voices from outside need be listened to, and no external forces can have effect. This is a form of the search for security ; but it has also been called the search for personal or national freedom or independence.

From this doctrine, as it applies to individuals, it is no very great distance to the conceptions of those who, like Kant, identify freedom not indeed with the elimination of desires, but with resistance to them, and control over them. I identify myself with the controller and escape the slavery of the controlled. I am free because, and in so far as, I am autonomous. I obey laws, but I have imposed them on, or found them in, my own uncoerced self. Freedom is obedience, but 'obedience to a law which we prescribe to ourselves', and no man can enslave himself. Heteronomy is dependence on outside factors, liability to be a plaything of the external world that I cannot myself fully control, and which *pro tanto* controls and 'enslaves' me. I am free only to the degree to which my person is 'fettered' by nothing that obeys forces over which I have no control; I cannot control the laws of nature; my free activity must therefore, *ex hypothesi*, be lifted above the empirical world of causality. This is not the place in which to discuss the validity of this ancient and famous doctrine; I only wish to remark that the related notions of freedom as resistance to (or escape from) unrealizable desire, and as independence of the sphere of causality, have played a central role in politics no less than in ethics.

For if the essence of men is that they are autonomous beings— authors of values, of ends in themselves, the ultimate authority of which consists precisely in the fact that they are willed freely— then nothing is worse than to treat them as if they were not autonomous, but natural objects, played on by causal influences,

---

[1] 'A wise man, though he be a slave, is at liberty, and from this it follows that though a fool rule, he is in slavery', said St. Ambrose. It might equally well have been said by Epictetus or Kant.

creatures at the mercy of external stimuli, whose choices can be manipulated by their rulers, whether by threats of force or offers of rewards. To treat men in this way is to treat them as if they were not self-determined. 'Nobody may compel me to be happy in his own way', said Kant. 'Paternalism is the greatest despotism imaginable.' This is so because it is to treat men as if they were not free, but human material for me, the benevolent reformer, to mould in accordance with my own, not their, freely adopted purpose. This is, of course, precisely the policy that the early utilitarians recommended. Helvétius (and Bentham) believed not in resisting, but in using, men's tendency to be slaves to their passions; they wished to dangle rewards and punishments before men—the acutest possible form of heteronomy—if by this means the 'slaves' might be made happier.[1] But to manipulate men, to propel them towards goals which you—the social reformer—see, but they may not, is to deny their human essence, to treat them as objects without wills of their own, and therefore to degrade them. That is why to lie to men, or to deceive them, that is, to use them as means for my, not their own, independently conceived ends, even if it is for their own benefit, is, in effect, to treat them as sub-human, to behave as if their ends are less ultimate and sacred than my own. In the name of what can I ever be justified in forcing men to do what they have not willed or consented to? Only in the name of some value higher than themselves. But if, as Kant held, all values are made so by the free acts of men, and called values only so far as they are this, there is no value higher than the individual. Therefore to do this is to coerce men in the name of something less ultimate than themselves—to bend them to my will, or to someone else's particular craving for (his or their) happiness or expediency or security or convenience. I am aiming at something desired (from whatever motive, no matter how noble) by me or my group, to which I am using other men as means. But this is a contradiction of what I know men to be, namely ends in themselves. All forms of

---

[1] 'Proletarian coercion, in all its forms, from executions to forced labour, is, paradoxical as it may sound, the method of moulding communist humanity out of the human material of the capitalist period.' These lines by the Bolshevik leader Nikolai Bukharin, in a work which appeared in 1920, especially the term 'human material', vividly convey this attitude.

tampering with human beings, getting at them, shaping them against their will to your own pattern, all thought control and conditioning,[1] is, therefore, a denial of that in men which makes them men and their values ultimate.

Kant's free individual is a transcendent being, beyond the realm of natural causality. But in its empirical form—in which the notion of man is that of ordinary life—this doctrine was the heart of liberal humanism, both moral and political, that was deeply influenced both by Kant and by Rousseau in the eighteenth century. In its *a priori* version it is a form of secularized Protestant individualism, in which the place of God is taken by the conception of the rational life, and the place of the individual soul which strains towards union with Him is replaced by the conception of the individual, endowed with reason, straining to be governed by reason and reason alone, and to depend upon nothing that might deflect or delude him by engaging his irrational nature. Autonomy, not heteronomy: to act and not to be acted upon. The notion of slavery to the passions is—for those who think in these terms—more than a metaphor. To rid myself of fear, or love, or the desire to conform is to liberate myself from the despotism of something which I cannot control. Sophocles, whom Plato reports as saying that old age alone has liberated him from the passion of love—the yoke of a cruel master—is reporting an experience as real as that of liberation from a human tyrant or slave owner. The psychological experience of observing myself yielding to some 'lower' impulse, acting from a motive that I dislike, or of doing something which at the very moment of doing I may detest, and reflecting later that I was 'not myself', or 'not in control of myself', when I did it, belongs to this way of thinking and speaking. I identify myself with my critical and rational moments. The consequences of my acts cannot matter, for they are not in my control; only my motives are. This is the creed of the solitary thinker who has defied the world and emancipated himself from the chains of

---

[1] Kant's psychology, and that of the Stoics and Christians too, assumed that some element in man—the 'inner fastness of his mind'—could be made secure against conditioning. The development of the techniques of hypnosis, 'brain washing', subliminal suggestion, and the like, has made this *a priori* assumption, at least as an empirical hypothesis, less plausible.

men and things. In this form, the doctrine may seem primarily an ethical creed, and scarcely political at all; nevertheless, its political implications are clear, and it enters into the tradition of liberal individualism at least as deeply as the 'negative' concept of freedom.

It is perhaps worth remarking that in its individualistic form the concept of the rational sage who has escaped into the inner fortress of his true self seems to arise when the external world has proved exceptionally arid, cruel, or unjust. 'He is truly free', said Rousseau, 'who desires what he can perform, and does what he desires.' In a world where a man seeking happiness or justice or freedom (in whatever sense) can do little, because he finds too many avenues of action blocked to him, the temptation to withdraw into himself may become irresistible. It may have been so in Greece, where the Stoic ideal cannot be wholly unconnected with the fall of the independent democracies before centralized Macedonian autocracy. It was so in Rome, for analogous reasons, after the end of the Republic.[1] It arose in Germany in the seventeenth century, during the period of the deepest national degradation of the German states that followed the Thirty Years War, when the character of public life, particularly in the small principalities, forced those who prized the dignity of human life, not for the first or last time, into a kind of inner emigration. The doctrine that maintains that what I cannot have I must teach myself not to desire; that a desire eliminated, or successfully resisted, is as good as a desire satisfied, is a sublime, but, it seems to me, unmistakable, form of the doctrine of sour grapes: what I cannot be sure of, I cannot truly want.

This makes it clear why the definition of negative liberty as the ability to do what one wishes—which is, in effect, the definition adopted by Mill—will not do. If I find that I am able to do little or nothing of what I wish, I need only contract or extinguish my wishes, and I am made free. If the tyrant (or 'hidden persuader') manages to condition his subjects (or customers) into

---

[1] It is not perhaps far-fetched to assume that the quietism of the Eastern sages was, similarly, a response to the despotism of the great autocracies, and flourished at periods when individuals were apt to be humiliated, or at any rate ignored or ruthlessly managed, by those possessed of the instruments of physical coercion.

losing their original wishes and embrace ('internalize') the form of life he has invented for them, he will, on this definition, have succeeded in liberating them. He will, no doubt, have made them *feel* free—as Epictetus feels freer than his master (and the proverbial good man is said to feel happy on the rack). But what he has created is the very antithesis of political freedom.

Ascetic self-denial may be a source of integrity or serenity and spiritual strength, but it is difficult to see how it can be called an enlargement of liberty. If I save myself from an adversary by retreating indoors and locking every entrance and exit, I may remain freer than if I had been captured by him, but am I freer than if I had defeated or captured him? If I go too far, contract myself into too small a space, I shall suffocate and die. The logical culmination of the process of destroying everything through which I can possibly be wounded is suicide. While I exist in the natural world, I can never be wholly secure. Total liberation in this sense (as Schopenhauer correctly perceived) is conferred only by death.[1]

I find myself in a world in which I meet with obstacles to my will. Those who are wedded to the 'negative' concept of freedom may perhaps be forgiven if they think that self-abnegation is not the only method of overcoming obstacles; that it is also possible to do so by removing them: in the case of non-human objects, by physical action; in the case of human resistance, by force or persuasion, as when I induce somebody to make room for me in his carriage, or conquer a country which threatens the interests of my own. Such acts may be unjust, they may involve violence, cruelty, the enslavement of others, but it can scarcely be denied that thereby the agent is able in the most literal sense to increase his own freedom. It is an irony of history that this truth is repudiated by some of those who practise it most forcibly, men

[1] It is worth remarking that those who demanded—and fought for—liberty for the individual or for the nation in France during this period of German quietism did not fall into this attitude. Might this not be precisely because, despite the despotism of the French monarchy and the arrogance and arbitrary behaviour of privileged groups in the French state, France was a proud and powerful nation, where the reality of political power was not beyond the grasp of men of talent, so that withdrawal from battle into some untroubled heaven above it, whence it could be surveyed dispassionately by the self-sufficient philosopher, was not the only way out? The same holds for England in the nineteenth century and well after it, and for the United States today.

who, even while they conquer power and freedom of action, reject the 'negative' concept of it in favour of its 'positive' counterpart. Their view rules over half our world; let us see upon what metaphysical foundation it rests.

IV

Self-realization

The only true method of attaining freedom, we are told, is by the use of critical reason, the understanding of what is necessary and what is contingent. If I am a schoolboy, all but the simplest truths of mathematics obtrude themselves as obstacles to the free functioning of my mind, as theorems whose necessity I do not understand; they are pronounced to be true by some external authority, and present themselves to me as foreign bodies which I am expected mechanically to absorb into my system. But when I understand the functions of the symbols, the axioms, the formation and transformation rules—the logic whereby the conclusions are obtained—and grasp that these things cannot be otherwise, because they appear to follow from the laws that govern the processes of my own reason,[1] then mathematical truths no longer obtrude themselves as external entities forced upon me which I must receive whether I want it or not, but as something which I now freely will in the course of the natural functioning of my own rational activity. For the mathematician, the proof of these theorems is part of the free exercise of his natural reasoning capacity. For the musician, after he has assimilated the pattern of the composer's score, and has made the composer's ends his own, the playing of the music is not obedience to external laws, a compulsion and a barrier to liberty, but a free, unimpeded exercise. The player is not bound to the score as an ox to the plough, or a factory worker to the machine. He has absorbed the score into his own system, has, by understanding it, identified it with himself, has changed it from an impediment to free activity into an element in that activity itself. What applies to music or mathematics must, we are told, in principle apply to

[1] Or, as some modern theorists maintain, because I have, or could have, invented them for myself, since the rules are man-made.

all other obstacles which present themselves as so many lumps of external stuff blocking free self-development. That is the programme of enlightened rationalism from Spinoza to the latest (at times unconscious) disciples of Hegel. *Sapere aude*. What you know, that of which you understand the necessity—the rational necessity—you cannot, while remaining rational, want to be otherwise. For to want something to be other than what it must be is, given the premises—the necessities that govern the world —to be *pro tanto* either ignorant or irrational. Passions, prejudices, fears, neuroses, spring from ignorance, and take the form of myths and illusions. To be ruled by myths, whether they spring from the vivid imaginations of unscrupulous charlatans who deceive us in order to exploit us, or from psychological or sociological causes, is a form of heteronomy, of being dominated by outside factors in a direction not necessarily willed by the agent. The scientific determinists of the eighteenth century supposed that the study of the sciences of nature, and the creation of sciences of society on the same model, would make the operation of such causes transparently clear, and thus enable individuals to recognize their own part in the working of a rational world, frustrating only when misunderstood. Knowledge liberates, as Epicurus taught long ago, by automatically eliminating irrational fears and desires.

Herder, Hegel, and Marx substituted their own vitalistic models of social life for the older, mechanical ones, but believed, no less than their opponents, that to understand the world is to be freed. They merely differed from them in stressing the part played by change and growth in what made human beings human. Social life could not be understood by an analogy drawn from mathematics or physics. One must also understand history, that is, the peculiar laws of continuous growth, whether by 'dialectical' conflict or otherwise, that govern individuals and groups, in their interplay with each other and with nature. Not to grasp this is, according to these thinkers, to fall into a particular kind of error, namely the belief that human nature is static, that its essential properties are the same everywhere and at all times, that it is governed by unvarying natural laws, whether they are conceived in theological or materialistic terms, which entails the fallacious corollary that a wise lawgiver can, in principle, create a perfectly harmonious society at any time by appropriate education and legislation, because rational men, in all ages and countries, must always demand the same unaltering satisfactions of the same unaltering basic needs. Hegel believed that his contemporaries (and indeed all his predecessors) misunderstood the nature of institutions because they did not understand the laws—the rationally intelligible laws, since they spring from the operation of reason—that create and alter institutions and transform human character and human action. Marx and his disciples maintained that the path of human beings was obstructed not only by natural forces, or the imperfections of their own character, but, even more, by the workings of their own social institutions, which they had originally created (not always consciously) for certain purposes, but whose functioning they systematically came to misconceive,[1] and which thereupon became obstacles in their creators' progress. He offered social and economic hypotheses to account for the inevitability of such misunderstanding, in particular of the illusion that such man-made arrangements were independent forces, as inescapable as the laws of nature. As instances of such pseudo-objective forces, he pointed to the laws of supply and demand, or of the institution of property, or of the eternal division of society into rich and poor, or owners and workers, as so many unaltering human categories. Not until we had reached a stage at which the spells of these illusions could be broken, that is, until enough men reached a social stage that alone enabled them to understand that these laws and institutions were themselves the work of human minds and hands, historically needed in their day, and later mistaken for inexorable, objective powers, could the old world be destroyed, and more adequate and liberating social machinery substituted.

We are enslaved by despots—institutions or beliefs or neuroses—which can be removed only by being analysed and understood. We are imprisoned by evil spirits which we have ourselves—albeit not consciously—created, and can exorcize them only by becoming conscious and acting appropriately: indeed, for Marx understanding *is* appropriate action. I am free if, and only if, I

---

[1] In practice even more than in theory.

plan my life in accordance with my own will; plans entail rules; a rule does not oppress me or enslave me if I impose it on myself consciously, or accept it freely, having understood it, whether it was invented by me or by others, provided that it is rational, that is to say, conforms to the necessities of things. To understand why things must be as they must be is to will them to be so. Knowledge liberates not by offering us more open possibilities amongst which we can make our choice, but by preserving us from the frustration of attempting the impossible. To want necessary laws to be other than they are is to be prey to an irrational desire—a desire that what must be X should also be not X. To go further, and believe these laws to be other than what they necessarily are, is to be insane. That is the metaphysical heart of rationalism. The notion of liberty contained in it is not the 'negative' conception of a field (ideally) without obstacles, a vacuum in which nothing obstructs me, but the notion of self-direction or self-control. I can do what I will with my own. I am a rational being; whatever I can demonstrate to myself as being necessary, as incapable of being otherwise in a rational society—that is, in a society directed by rational minds, towards goals such as a rational being would have—I cannot, being rational, wish to sweep out of my way. I assimilate it into my substance as I do the laws of logic, of mathematics, of physics, the rules of art, the principles that govern everything of which I understand, and therefore will, the rational purpose, by which I can never be thwarted, since I cannot want it to be other than it is.

This is the positive doctrine of liberation by reason. Socialized forms of it, widely disparate and opposed to each other as they are, are at the heart of many of the nationalist, communist, authoritarian, and totalitarian creeds of our day. It may, in the course of its evolution, have wandered far from its rationalist moorings. Nevertheless, it is this freedom that, in democracies and in dictatorships, is argued about, and fought for, in many parts of the earth today. Without attempting to trace the historical evolution of this idea, I should like to comment on some of its vicissitudes.

V

The Temple of Sarastro

Those who believed in freedom as rational self-direction were bound, sooner or later, to consider how this was to be applied not merely to a man's inner life, but to his relations with other members of his society. Even the most individualistic among them—and Rousseau, Kant, and Fichte certainly began as individualists—came at some point to ask themselves whether a rational life not only for the individual, but also for society, was possible, and if so, how it was to be achieved. I wish to be free to live as my rational will (my 'real self') commands, but so must others be. How am I to avoid collisions with their wills? Where is the frontier that lies between my (rationally determined) rights and the identical rights of others? For if I am rational, I cannot deny that what is right for me must, for the same reasons, be right for others who are rational like me. A rational (or free) state would be a state governed by such laws as all rational men would freely accept; that is to say, such laws as they would themselves have enacted had they been asked what, as rational beings, they demanded; hence the frontiers would be such as all rational men would consider to be the right frontiers for rational beings. But who, in fact, was to determine what these frontiers were? Thinkers of this type argued that if moral and political problems were genuine—as surely they were—they must in principle be soluble; that is to say, there must exist one and only one true solution to any problem. All truths could in principle be discovered by any rational thinker, and demonstrated so clearly that all other rational men could not but accept them; indeed, this was already to a large extent the case in the new natural sciences. On this assumption, the problem of political liberty was soluble by establishing a just order that would give to each man all the freedom to which a rational being was entitled. My claim to unfettered freedom can prima facie at times not be reconciled with your equally unqualified claim; but the rational solution of one problem cannot collide with the equally true solution of another, for two truths cannot logically be incompatible; therefore a just order must in principle be discoverable—an order of which the rules make possible correct solutions to all possible problems that could arise in it. This ideal, harmonious state of affairs was sometimes imagined as a Garden of Eden before the Fall of Man, from which we were expelled, but for which we were still filled with longing; or as a golden age still before us, in which men, having become rational, will no longer be 'other-directed', nor 'alienate' or frustrate one another. In existing societies justice and equality are ideals which still call for some measure of coercion, because the premature lifting of social controls might lead to the oppression of the weaker and the stupider by the stronger or abler or more energetic and unscrupulous. But it is only irrationality on the part of men (according to this doctrine) that leads them to wish to oppress or exploit or humiliate one another. Rational men will respect the principle of reason in each other, and lack all desire to fight or dominate one another. The desire to dominate is itself a symptom of irrationality, and can be explained and cured by rational methods. Spinoza offers one kind of explanation and remedy, Hegel another, Marx a third. Some of these theories may perhaps, to some degree, supplement each other, others are not combinable. But they all assume that in a society of perfectly rational beings the lust for domination over men will be absent or ineffective. The existence of, or craving for, oppression will be the first symptom that the true solution to the problems of social life has not been reached.

This can be put in another way. Freedom is self-mastery, the elimination of obstacles to my will, whatever these obstacles may be—the resistance of nature, of my ungoverned passions, of irrational institutions, of the opposing wills or behaviour of others. Nature I can, at least in principle, always mould by technical means, and shape to my will. But how am I to treat recalcitrant human beings? I must, if I can, impose my will on them too, 'mould' them to my pattern, cast parts for them in my play. But will this not mean that I alone am free, while they are slaves? They will be so if my plan has nothing to do with their wishes or values, only with my own. But if my plan is fully rational, it will allow for the full development of their 'true' natures, the realization of their capacities for rational decisions 'for making the best of themselves'—as a part of the realization of my own 'true' self. All true solutions to all genuine problems must be compatible: more than this, they must fit into a single whole: for this is what is meant by calling them all rational and the universe harmonious. Each man has his specific character, abilities, aspirations, ends. If I grasp both what these ends and natures are, and how they all relate to one another, I can, at least in principle, if I have the knowledge and the strength, satisfy them all, so long as the nature and the purposes in question are rational. Rationality is knowing things and people for what they are: I must not use stones to make violins, nor try to make born violin players play flutes. If the universe is governed by reason, then there will be no need for coercion; a correctly planned life for all will coincide with full freedom—the freedom of rational self-direction—for all. This will be so if, and only if, the plan is the true plan—the one unique pattern which alone fulfils the claims of reason. Its laws will be the rules which reason prescribes: they will only seem irksome to those whose reason is dormant, who do not understand the true 'needs' of their own 'real' selves. So long as each player recognizes and plays the part set him by reason—the faculty that understands his true nature and discerns his true ends—there can be no conflict. Each man will be a liberated, self-directed actor in the cosmic drama. Thus Spinoza tells us that 'children, although they are coerced, are not slaves', because 'they obey orders given in their own interests', and that 'The subject of a true commonwealth is no slave, because the common interests must include his own.' Similarly, Locke says 'Where there is no law there is no freedom', because rational laws are directions to a man's 'proper interests' or 'general good'; and adds that since such laws are what 'hedges us from bogs and precipices' they 'ill deserve the name of confinement', and speaks of desires to escape from such laws as being irrational, forms of 'licence', as 'brutish', and so on. Montesquieu, forgetting his liberal moments, speaks of political liberty as being not permission to do what we want, or even what the law allows, but only 'the power of doing what we ought to will', which Kant virtually repeats. Burke proclaims the individual's 'right' to be restrained in his own interest, because 'the presumed consent of every rational creature is in unison with the predisposed order of things'. The common assumption of these thinkers (and of many a schoolman before them and Jacobin and Communist after them) is that the rational ends of our 'true' natures must coincide, or be made to coincide, however violently our poor, ignorant, desire-ridden, passionate, empirical selves may cry out against this process. Freedom is not freedom to do what is irrational, or stupid, or wrong. To force empirical selves into the right pattern is no tyranny, but liberation.[1] Rousseau tells me that if I freely surrender all the parts of my life to society, I create an entity which, because it has been built by an equality of sacrifice of all its members, cannot wish to hurt any one of them; in such a society, we are informed, it can be nobody's interest to damage anyone else. 'In giving myself to all, I give myself to none', and get back as much as I lose, with enough new force to preserve my new gains. Kant tells us that when 'the individual has entirely abandoned his wild, lawless freedom, to find it again, unimpaired, in a state of dependence according to law', that alone is true freedom, 'for this dependence is the work of my own will acting as a lawgiver'. Liberty, so far from being incompatible with authority, becomes virtually identical with it. This is the thought and language of all the declarations of the rights of man in the eighteenth century, and of all those who look upon society as a design constructed according to the rational laws of the wise lawgiver, or of nature, or of history, or of the Supreme Being. Bentham, almost alone, doggedly went on repeating that the business of laws was not to liberate but to restrain: 'Every law is an infraction of liberty'—even if such 'infraction' leads to an increase of the sum of liberty.

If the underlying assumptions had been correct—if the method of solving social problems resembled the way in which solutions to the problems of the natural sciences are found, and if reason were what rationalists said that it was, all this would perhaps

[1] On this Bentham seems to me to have said the last word: 'Is not liberty to do evil, liberty? If not, what is it? Do we not say that it is necessary to take liberty from idiots and bad men, because they abuse it?' Compare with this a typical statement made by a Jacobin club of the same period: 'No man is free in doing evil. To prevent him is to set him free.' This is echoed in almost identical terms by British Idealists at the end of the following century.

follow. In the ideal case, liberty coincides with law: autonomy with authority. A law which forbids me to do what I could not, as a sane being, conceivably wish to do is not a restraint of my freedom. In the ideal society, composed of wholly responsible beings, rules, because I should scarcely be conscious of them, would gradually wither away. Only one social movement was bold enough to render this assumption quite explicit and accept its consequences—that of the Anarchists. But all forms of liberalism founded on a rationalist metaphysics are less or more watered-down versions of this creed.

In due course, the thinkers who bent their energies to the solution of the problem on these lines came to be faced with the question of how in practice men were to be made rational in this way. Clearly they must be educated. For the uneducated are irrational, heteronomous, and need to be coerced, if only to make life tolerable for the rational if they are to live in the same society and not be compelled to withdraw to a desert or some Olympian height. But the uneducated cannot be expected to understand or co-operate with the purposes of their educators. Education, says Fichte, must inevitably work in such a way that 'you will later recognize the reasons for what I am doing now'. Children cannot be expected to understand why they are compelled to go to school, nor the ignorant—that is, for the moment, the majority of man-kind—why they are made to obey the laws that will presently make them rational. 'Compulsion is also a kind of education.' You learn the great virtue of obedience to superior persons. If you cannot understand your own interests as a rational being, I cannot be expected to consult you, or abide by your wishes, in the course of making you rational. I must, in the end, force you to be protected against smallpox, even though you may not wish it. Even Mill is prepared to say that I may forcibly prevent a man from crossing a bridge if there is not time to warn him that it is about to collapse, for I know, or am justified in assuming, that he cannot wish to fall into the water. Fichte knows what the uneducated German of his time wishes to be or do better than he can possibly know them for himself. The sage knows you better than you know yourself, for you are the victim of your passions, a slave living a heteronomous life, purblind, unable to understand your true goals. You want to be a human being. It is the aim of the state to satisfy your wish. 'Compulsion is justified by education for future insight.' The reason within me, if it is to triumph, must eliminate and suppress my 'lower' instincts, my passions and desires, which render me a slave; similarly (the fatal transition from individual to social concepts is almost imperceptible) the higher elements in society—the better educated, the more rational, those who 'possess the highest insight of their time and people'—may exercise compulsion to rationalize the irrational section of society. For—so Hegel, Bradley, Bosanquet have often assured us—by obeying the rational man we obey ourselves: not indeed as we are, sunk in our ignorance and our passions, weak creatures afflicted by diseases that need a healer, wards who require a guardian, but as we could be if we were rational; as we could be even now, if only we would listen to the rational element which is, *ex hypothesi*, within every human being who deserves the name.

The philosophers of 'Objective Reason', from the tough, rigidly centralized, 'organic' state of Fichte, to the mild and humane liberalism of T. H. Green, certainly supposed themselves to be fulfilling, and not resisting, the rational demands which, however inchoate, were to be found in the breast of every sentient being. But I may reject such democratic optimism, and turning away from the teleological determinism of the Hegelians towards some more voluntarist philosophy, conceive the idea of imposing on my society—for its own betterment—a plan of my own, which in my rational wisdom I have elaborated; and which, unless I act on my own, perhaps against the permanent wishes of the vast majority of my fellow citizens, may never come to fruition at all. Or, abandoning the concept of reason altogether, I may conceive myself as an inspired artist, who moulds men into patterns in the light of his unique vision, as painters combine colours or composers sounds; humanity is the raw material upon which I impose my creative will; even though men suffer and die in the process, they are lifted by it to a height to which they could never have risen without my coercive—but creative—violation of their lives. This is the argument used by every dictator, inquisitor, and bully who seeks some moral, or even aesthetic, justification for his conduct. I must do for men (or with them) what they cannot do for themselves, and I cannot ask their permission or consent, because they are in no condition to know what is best for them; indeed, what they will permit and accept may mean a life of contemptible mediocrity, or perhaps even their ruin and suicide. Let me quote from the true progenitor of the heroic doctrine, Fichte, once again: 'No one has . . . rights against reason.' 'Man is afraid of subordinating his subjectivity to the laws of reason. He prefers tradition or arbitrariness.' Nevertheless, subordinated he must be.[1] Fichte puts forward the claims of what he called reason; Napoleon, or Carlyle, or romantic authoritarians may worship other values, and see in their establishment by force the only path to 'true' freedom.

The same attitude was pointedly expressed by Auguste Comte, who asked 'If we do not allow free thinking in chemistry or biology, why should we allow it in morals or politics?' Why indeed? If it makes sense to speak of political truths—assertions of social ends which all men, because they are men, must, once they are discovered, agree to be such; and if, as Comte believed, scientific method will in due course reveal them; then what case is there for freedom of opinion or action—at least as an end in itself, and not merely as a stimulating intellectual climate, either for individuals or for groups? Why should any conduct be tolerated that is not authorized by appropriate experts? Comte put bluntly what had been implicit in the rationalist theory of politics from its ancient Greek beginnings. There can, in principle, be only one correct way of life; the wise lead it spontaneously, that is why they are called wise. The unwise must be dragged towards it by all the social means in the power of the wise; for why should demonstrable error be suffered to survive and breed? The immature and untutored must be made to say to themselves: 'Only the truth liberates, and the only way in which I can learn the truth is by doing blindly today, what you, who know it, order me, or coerce me, to do, in the certain knowledge

[1] 'To compel men to adopt the right form of government, to impose Right on them by force, is not only the right, but the sacred duty of every man who has both the insight and the power to do so.'

that only thus will I arrive at your clear vision, and be free like you.'

We have wandered indeed from our liberal beginnings. This argument, employed by Fichte in his latest phase, and after him by other defenders of authority, from Victorian schoolmasters and colonial administrators to the latest nationalist or communist dictator, is precisely what the Stoic and Kantian morality protests against most bitterly in the name of the reason of the free individual following his own inner light. In this way the rationalist argument, with its assumption of the single true solution, has led by steps which, if not logically valid, are historically and psychologically intelligible, from an ethical doctrine of individual responsibility and individual self-perfection to an authoritarian state obedient to the directives of an *élite* of Platonic guardians.

What can have led to so strange a reversal—the transformation of Kant's severe individualism into something close to a pure totalitarian doctrine on the part of thinkers, some of whom claimed to be his disciples? This question is not of merely historical interest, for not a few contemporary liberals have gone through the same peculiar evolution. It is true that Kant insisted, following Rousseau, that a capacity for rational self-direction belonged to all men; that there could be no experts in moral matters, since morality was a matter not of specialized knowledge (as the utilitarians and *philosophes* had maintained), but of the correct use of a universal human faculty; and consequently that what made men free was not acting in certain self-improving ways, which they could be coerced to do, but knowing why they ought to do so, which nobody could do for, or on behalf of, anyone else. But even Kant, when he came to deal with political issues, conceded that no law, provided that it was such that I should, if I were asked, approve it as a rational being, could possibly deprive me of any portion of my rational freedom. With this the door was opened wide to the rule of experts. I cannot consult all men about all enactments all the time. The government cannot be a continuous plebiscite. Moreover, some men are not as well attuned to the voice of their own reason as others: some seem singularly deaf. If I am a legislator or a ruler, I must assume that if the law I impose is rational (and I can only consult my own reason) it will automatically be approved by all the members of my society so far as they are rational beings. For if they disapprove, they must, *pro tanto*, be irrational; then they will need to be repressed by reason: whether their own or mine cannot matter, for the pronouncements of reason must be the same in all minds. I issue my orders, and if you resist, take it upon myself to repress the irrational element in you which opposes reason. My task would be easier if you repressed it in yourself; I try to educate you to do so. But I am responsible for public welfare, I cannot wait until all men are wholly rational. Kant may protest that the essence of the subject's freedom is that he, and he alone, has given himself the order to obey. But this is a counsel of perfection. If you fail to discipline yourself, I must do so for you; and you cannot complain of lack of freedom, for the fact that Kant's rational judge has sent you to prison is evidence that you have not listened to your own inner reason, that, like a child, a savage, an idiot, you are not ripe for self-direction or permanently incapable of it.[1]

If this leads to despotism, albeit by the best or the wisest—

---

[1] Kant came nearest to asserting the 'negative' ideal of liberty when (in one of his political treatises) he declared that 'the greatest problem of the human race, to the solution of which it is compelled by nature, is the establishment of a civil society universally administering right according to law. It is only in a society which possesses the greatest liberty . . .—with . . . the most exact determination and guarantee of the limits of [the] liberty [of each individual] in order that it may co-exist with the liberty of others—that the highest purpose of nature, which is the development of all her capacities, can be attained in the case of mankind.' Apart from the teleological implications, this formulation does not at first appear very different from orthodox liberalism. The crucial point, however, is how to determine the criterion for 'the exact determination and guarantee of the limits' of individual liberty. Most modern liberals, at their most consistent, want a situation in which as many individuals as possible can realize as many of their ends as possible, without assessment of the value of these ends as such, save in so far as they may frustrate the purposes of others. They wish the frontiers between individuals or groups of men to be drawn solely with a view to preventing collisions between human purposes, all of which must be considered to be equally ultimate, uncriticizable ends in themselves. Kant, and the rationalists of his type, do not regard all ends as of equal value. For them the limits of liberty are determined by applying the rules of 'reason', which is much more than the mere generality of rules as such, and is a faculty that creates or reveals a purpose identical in, and for, all men. In the name of reason anything that is non-rational may be condemned, so that the various personal aims which their individual imagination and idiosyncrasies lead men to pursue—for example aesthetic and other non-rational kinds of self-fulfilment—may, at least in theory, be ruthlessly suppressed to make way for the demands of reason. The authority of reason and of the duties it lays

to Sarastro's temple in the *Magic Flute*—but still despotism, which turns out to be identical with freedom, can it be that there is something amiss in the premisses of the argument? that the basic assumptions are themselves somewhere at fault? Let me state them once more: first, that all men have one true purpose, and one only, that of rational self-direction; second, that the ends of all rational beings must of necessity fit into a single universal, harmonious pattern, which some men may be able to discern more clearly than others; third, that all conflict, and consequently all tragedy, is due solely to the clash of reason with the irrational or the insufficiently rational—the immature and undeveloped elements in life—whether individual or communal, and that such clashes are, in principle, avoidable, and for wholly rational beings impossible; finally, that when all men have been made rational, they will obey the rational laws of their own natures, which are one and the same in them all, and so be at once wholly law-abiding and wholly free. Can it be that Socrates and the creators of the central Western tradition in ethics and politics who followed him have been mistaken, for more than two millennia, that virtue is not knowledge, nor freedom identical with either? That despite the fact that it rules the lives of more men than ever before in its long history, not one of the basic assumptions of this famous view is demonstrable, or, perhaps, even true?

VI

The search for status

There is yet another historically important approach to this topic, which, by confounding liberty with her sisters, equality and fraternity, leads to similarly illiberal conclusions. Ever since the issue was raised towards the end of the eighteenth century, the question of what is meant by 'an individual' has been asked persistently, and with increasing effect. In so far as I live in

upon men is identified with individual freedom, on the assumption that only rational ends can be the 'true' objects of a 'free' man's 'real' nature.

I have never, I must own, understood what 'reason' means in this context; and here merely wish to point out that the *a priori* assumptions of this philosophical psychology are not compatible with empiricism: that is to say, with any doctrine founded on knowledge derived from experience of what men are and seek.

society, everything that I do inevitably affects, and is affected by, what others do. Even Mill's strenuous effort to mark the distinction between the spheres of private and social life breaks down under examination. Virtually all Mill's critics have pointed out that everything that I do may have results which will harm other human beings. Moreover, I am a social being in a deeper sense than that of interaction with others. For am I not what I am, to some degree, in virtue of what others think and feel me to be? When I ask myself what I am, and answer: an Englishman, a Chinese, a merchant, a man of no importance, a millionaire, a convict—I find upon analysis that to possess these attributes entails being recognized as belonging to a particular group or class by other persons in my society, and that this recognition is part of the meaning of most of the terms that denote some of my most personal and permanent characteristics. I am not disembodied reason. Nor am I Robinson Crusoe, alone upon his island. It is not only that my material life depends upon interaction with other men, or that I am what I am as a result of social forces, but that some, perhaps all, of my ideas about myself, in particular my sense of my own moral and social identity, are intelligible only in terms of the social network in which I am (the metaphor must not be pressed too far) an element. The lack of freedom about which men or groups complain amounts, as often as not, to the lack of proper recognition. I may be seeking not for what Mill would wish me to seek, namely security from coercion, arbitrary arrest, tyranny, deprivation of certain opportunities of action, or for room within which I am legally accountable to no one for my movements. Equally, I may not be seeking for a rational plan of social life, or the self-perfection of a dispassionate sage. What I may seek to avoid is simply being ignored, or patronized, or despised, or being taken too much for granted—in short, not being treated as an individual, having my uniqueness insufficiently recognized, being classed as a member of some featureless amalgam, a statistical unit without identifiable, specifically human features and purposes of my own. This is the degradation that I am fighting against—not equality of legal rights, nor liberty to do as I wish (although I may want these too), but for a condition in which I can feel that I am, because I am taken to be, a responsible agent, whose will is taken into consideration because I am entitled to it, even if I am attacked and persecuted for being what I am or choosing as I do. This is a hankering after status and recognition: 'The poorest he that is in England hath a life to live as the greatest he.' I desire to be understood and recognized, even if this means to be unpopular and disliked. And the only persons who can so recognize me, and thereby give me the sense of being someone, are the members of the society to which, historically, morally, economically, and perhaps ethnically, I feel that I belong.[1] My individual self is not something which I can detach from my relationship with others, or from those attributes of myself which consist in their attitude towards me. Consequently, when I demand to be liberated from, let us say, the status of political or social dependence, what I demand is an alteration of the attitude towards me of those whose opinions and behaviour help to determine my own image of myself. And what is true of the individual is true of groups, social, political, economic, religious, that is, of men conscious of needs and purposes which they have as members of such groups. What oppressed classes or nationalities, as a rule, demand is neither simply unhampered liberty of action for their members, nor, above everything, equality of social or economic opportunity, still less assignment of a place in a frictionless, organic state devised by the rational lawgiver. What they want, as often as not, is simply recognition (of their class or nation, or colour or race) as an independent source of human activity, as an entity with a will of its own, intending to act in accordance with it (whether it is good or legitimate, or not), and not to be ruled, educated, guided, with however light a hand, as being not quite fully

[1] This has an obvious affinity with Kant's doctrine of human freedom; but it is a socialized and empirical version of it, and therefore almost its opposite. Kant's free man needs no public recognition for his inner freedom. If he is treated as a means to some external purpose, that is a wrong act on the part of his exploiters, but his own 'noumenal' status is untouched, and he is fully free, and fully a man, however he may be treated. The need spoken of here is bound up wholly with the relation that I have with others; I am nothing if I am unrecognized. I cannot ignore the attitude of others with Byronic disdain, fully conscious of my own intrinsic worth and vocation, or escape into my inner life, for I am in my own eyes as others see me. I identify myself with the point of view of my milieu: I feel myself to be somebody or nobody in terms of my position and function in the social whole; this is the most 'heteronomous' condition imaginable.

human, and therefore not quite fully free. This gives a far wider than a purely rationalist sense to Kant's 'paternalism is the greatest despotism imaginable'. Paternalism is despotic, not because it is more oppressive than naked, brutal, unenlightened tyranny, nor merely because it ignores the transcendental reason embodied in me, but because it is an insult to my conception of myself as a human being, determined to make my own life in accordance with my own (not necessarily rational or benevolent) purposes, and, above all, entitled to be recognized as such by others. For if I am not so recognized, then I may fail to recognize, I may doubt, my own claim to be a fully independent human being. For what I am is, in large part, determined by what I feel and think; and what I feel and think is determined by the feeling and thought prevailing in the society to which I belong, of which, in Burke's sense, I form not an isolable atom, but an ingredient (to use a perilous but indispensable metaphor) in a social pattern. I may feel unfree in the sense of not being recognized as a self-governing individual human being; but I may feel it also as a member of an unrecognized or insufficiently respected group: then I wish for the emancipation of my entire class, or community, or nation, or race, or profession. So much can I desire this, that I may, in my bitter longing for status, prefer to be bullied and misgoverned by some member of my own race or social class, by whom I am, nevertheless, recognized as a man and a rival—that is as an equal —to being well and tolerantly treated by someone from some higher and remoter group, who does not recognize me for what I wish to feel myself to be. This is the heart of the great cry for recognition on the part of both individuals and groups, and in our own day, of professions and classes, nations and races. Although I may not get 'negative' liberty at the hands of the members of my own society, yet they are members of my own group; they understand me, as I understand them; and this understanding creates within me the sense of being somebody in the world. It is this desire for reciprocal recognition that leads the most authoritarian democracies to be, at times, consciously preferred by its members to the most enlightened oligarchies, or sometimes causes a member of some newly liberated Asian or African state to complain less today, when he is rudely treated by members of his own race or nation, than when he was governed by some cautious, just, gentle, well-meaning administrator from outside. Unless this phenomenon is grasped, the ideals and behaviour of entire peoples who, in Mill's sense of the word, suffer deprivation of elementary human rights, and who, with every appearance of sincerity, speak of enjoying more freedom than when they possessed a wider measure of these rights, becomes an unintelligible paradox.

Yet it is not with individual liberty, in either the 'negative' or in the 'positive' senses of the word, that this desire for status and recognition can easily be identified. It is something no less profoundly needed and passionately fought for by human beings— it is something akin to, but not itself, freedom; although it entails negative freedom for the entire group, it is more closely related to solidarity, fraternity, mutual understanding, need for association on equal terms, all of which are sometimes—but misleadingly—called social freedom. Social and political terms are necessarily vague. The attempt to make the vocabulary of politics too precise may render it useless. But it is no service to the truth to loosen usage beyond necessity. The essence of the notion of liberty, both in the 'positive' and the 'negative' senses, is the holding off of something or someone—of others who trespass on my field or assert their authority over me, or of obsessions, fears, neuroses, irrational forces—intruders and despots of one kind or another. The desire for recognition is a desire for something different: for union, closer understanding, integration of interests, a life of common dependence and common sacrifice. It is only the confusion of desire for liberty with this profound and universal craving for status and understanding, further confounded by being identified with the notion of social self-direction, where the self to be liberated is no longer the individual but the 'social whole', that makes it possible for men, while submitting to the authority of oligarchs or dictators, to claim that this in some sense liberates them.

Much has been written on the fallacy of regarding social groups as being literally persons or selves, whose control and discipline of their members is no more than self-discipline, voluntary self-control which leaves the individual agent free. But even on the 'organic' view, would it be natural or desirable to call the demand for recognition and status a demand for liberty in some third sense? It is true that the group from which recognition is sought must itself have a sufficient measure of 'negative' freedom—from control by any outside authority—otherwise recognition by it will not give the claimant the status he seeks. But is the struggle for higher status, the wish to escape from an inferior position, to be called a struggle for liberty? Is it mere pedantry to confine this word to the main senses discussed above, or are we, as I suspect, in danger of calling any improvement of his social situation favoured by a human being an increase of his liberty, and will this not render this term so vague and distended as to make it virtually useless? And yet we cannot simply dismiss this case as a mere confusion of the notion of freedom with that of status, or solidarity, or fraternity, or equality, or some combination of these. For the craving for status is, in certain respects, very close to the desire to be an independent agent.

We may refuse this goal the title of liberty; yet it would be a shallow view that assumed that analogies between individuals and groups, or organic metaphors, or several senses of the word liberty, are mere fallacies, due either to assertions of likeness between entities in respects in which they are unlike, or simple semantic confusion. What is wanted by those who are prepared to barter their own and others' liberty of individual action for the status of their group, and their own status within the group, is not simply a surrender of liberty for the sake of security, of some assured place in a harmonious hierarchy in which all men and all classes know their place, and are prepared to exchange the painful privilege of choosing—'the burden of freedom'—for the peace and comfort and relative mindlessness of an authoritarian or totalitarian structure. No doubt, there are such men and such desires, and no doubt such surrenders of individual liberty can occur, and, indeed, have often occurred. But it is a profound misunderstanding of the temper of our times to assume that this is what makes nationalism or Marxism attractive to nations which have been ruled by alien masters, or to classes whose lives were directed by other classes in a semi-feudal, or some other hierarchically organized, régime. What they seek is more akin to what

Mill called 'pagan self-assertion', but in a collective, socialized form. Indeed, much of what he says about his own reasons for desiring liberty—the value that he puts on boldness and non-conformity, on the assertion of the individual's own values in the face of the prevailing opinion, on strong and self-reliant personalities free from the leading strings of the official law-givers and instructors of society—has little enough to do with his conception of freedom as non-interference, but a great deal with the desire of men not to have their personalities set at too low a value, assumed to be incapable of autonomous, original, 'authentic' behaviour, even if such behaviour is to be met with opprobrium, or social restrictions, or inhibitive legislation. This wish to assert the 'personality' of my class, or group or nation, is connected both with the answer to the question 'What is to be the area of authority?' (for the group must not be interfered with by outside masters), and, even more closely, with the answer to the question 'Who is to govern us?'—govern well or badly, liberally or oppressively—but above all 'who?' And such answers as: 'by representatives elected by my own and others' untrammelled choice', or 'all of us gathered together in regular assemblies', or 'the best', or 'the wisest', or 'the nation as embodied in these or those persons or institutions', or 'the divine leader', are answers that are logically, and at times also politically and socially, independent of what extent of 'negative' liberty I demand for my own or my group's activities. Provided the answer to 'Who shall govern me?' is somebody or something which I can represent as 'my own', as something which belongs to me, or to whom I belong, I can, by using words which convey fraternity and solidarity, as well as some part of the connotation of the 'positive' sense of the word freedom (which it is difficult to specify more precisely), describe it as a hybrid form of freedom; at any rate as an ideal which is perhaps more prominent than any other in the world today, yet one which no existing term seems precisely to fit. Those who purchase it at the price of their 'negative', Millian freedom certainly claim to be 'liberated' by this means, in this confused, but ardently felt, sense. 'Whose service is perfect freedom' can in this way be secularized, and the state, or the nation, or the race, or an assembly, or a dictator, or my family or milieu, or I myself, can be substituted for the Deity, without thereby rendering the word 'freedom' wholly meaningless.[1]

No doubt every interpretation of the word liberty, however unusual, must include a minimum of what I have called 'negative' liberty. There must be an area within which I am not frustrated. No society literally suppresses all the liberties of its members; a being who is prevented by others from doing anything at all on his own is not a moral agent at all, and could not either legally or morally be regarded as a human being, even if a physiologist or a biologist, or even a psychologist, felt inclined to classify him as a man. But the fathers of liberalism—Mill and Constant—want more than this minimum: they demand a maximum degree of non-interference compatible with the minimum demands of social life. It seems unlikely that this extreme demand for liberty has ever been made by any but a small minority of highly civilized and self-conscious human beings. The bulk of humanity has certainly at most times been prepared to sacrifice this to other goals: security, status, prosperity, power, virtue, rewards in the next world; or justice, equality, fraternity, and many other values which appear wholly, or in part, incompatible with the attainment of the greatest degree of individual liberty, and certainly do not need it as a pre-condition for their own realization. It is not a demand for *Lebensraum* for each individual that has stimulated the rebellions and wars of liberation for which men were ready to die in the past, or, indeed, in the present. Men who have fought for freedom have commonly fought for the right to be governed by themselves or their representatives—sternly governed, if need be, like the Spartans, with little individual liberty, but in a manner which allowed them to participate, or

---

[1] This argument should be distinguished from the traditional approach of some of the disciples of Burke or Hegel who say that, since I am made what I am by society or history, to escape from them is impossible and to attempt it irrational. No doubt I cannot leap out of my skin, or breathe outside my proper element; it is a mere tautology to say that I am what I am, and cannot want to be liberated from my essential characteristics, some of which are social. But it does not follow that all my attributes are intrinsic and inalienable, and that I cannot seek to alter my status within the 'social network', or 'cosmic web', which determines my nature; if this were the case, no meaning could be attached to such words as 'choice' or 'decision' or 'activity'. If they are to mean anything, attempts to protect myself against authority, or even to escape from my 'station and its duties', cannot be excluded as automatically irrational or suicidal.

at any rate to believe that they were participating, in the legislation and administration of their collective lives. And men who have made revolutions have, as often as not, meant by liberty no more than the conquest of power and authority by a given sect of believers in a doctrine, or by a class, or by some other social group, old or new. Their victories certainly frustrated those whom they ousted, and sometimes repressed, enslaved, or exterminated vast numbers of human beings. Yet such revolutionaries have usually felt it necessary to argue that, despite this, they represented the party of liberty, or 'true' liberty, by claiming universality for their ideal, which the 'real selves' of even those who resisted them were also alleged to be seeking, although they were held to have lost the way to the goal, or to have mistaken the goal itself owing to some moral or spiritual blindness. All this has little to do with Mill's notion of liberty as limited only by the danger of doing harm to others. It is the non-recognition of this psychological and political fact (which lurks behind the apparent ambiguity of the term 'liberty') that has, perhaps, blinded some contemporary liberals to the world in which they live. Their plea is clear, their cause is just. But they do not allow for the variety of basic human needs. Nor yet for the ingenuity with which men can prove to their own satisfaction that the road to one ideal also leads to its contrary.

VII

Liberty and sovereignty

The French Revolution, like all great revolutions, was, at least in its Jacobin form, just such an eruption of the desire for 'positive' freedom of collective self-direction on the part of a large body of Frenchmen who felt liberated as a nation, even though the result was, for a good many of them, a severe restriction of individual freedoms. Rousseau had spoken exultantly of the fact that the laws of liberty might prove to be more austere than the yoke of tyranny. Tyranny is service to human masters. The law cannot be a tyrant. Rousseau does not mean by liberty the 'negative' freedom of the individual not to be interfered with within a defined area, but the possession by all, and not merely by some, of the fully qualified members of a society of a share in the public power which is entitled to interfere with every aspect of every citizen's life. The liberals of the first half of the nineteenth century correctly foresaw that liberty in this 'positive' sense could easily destroy too many of the 'negative' liberties that they held sacred. They pointed out that the sovereignty of the people could easily destroy that of individuals. Mill explained, patiently and unanswerably, that government by the people was not, in his sense, necessarily freedom at all. For those who govern are not necessarily the same 'people' as those who are governed, and democratic self-government is not the government 'of each by himself' but, at best, of 'each by the rest'. Mill and his disciples spoke of the tyranny of the majority and of the tyranny of 'the prevailing feeling and opinion', and saw no great difference between that and any other kind of tyranny which encroaches upon men's activities beyond the sacred frontiers of private life.

No one saw the conflict between the two types of liberty better, or expressed it more clearly, than Benjamin Constant. He pointed out that the transference by a successful rising of the un-limited authority, commonly called sovereignty, from one set of hands to another does not increase liberty, but merely shifts the burden of slavery. He reasonably asked why a man should deeply care whether he is crushed by a popular government or by a monarch, or even by a set of oppressive laws. He saw that the main problem for those who desire 'negative', individual free-dom is not who wields this authority, but how much authority should be placed in any set of hands. For unlimited authority in anybody's grasp was bound, he believed, sooner or later, to destroy somebody. He maintained that usually men protested against this or that set of governors as oppressive, when the real cause of oppression lay in the mere fact of the accumulation of power itself, wherever it might happen to be, since liberty was endangered by the mere existence of absolute authority as such. 'It is not the arm that is unjust', he wrote, 'but the weapon that is too heavy—some weights are too heavy for the human hand.' Democracy may disarm a given oligarchy, a given privileged individual or set of individuals, but it can still crush individuals as mercilessly as any previous ruler. In an essay comparing the liberty of the moderns with that of the ancients he said that an equal right to oppress—or interfere—is not equivalent to liberty. Nor does universal consent to loss of liberty somehow miraculously preserve it merely by being universal, or by being consent. If I consent to be oppressed, or acquiesce in my condition with detachment or irony, am I the less oppressed? If I sell myself into slavery, am I the less a slave? If I commit suicide, am I the less dead because I have taken my own life freely? 'Popular government is a spasmodic tyranny, monarchy a more efficiently centralized despotism.' Constant saw in Rousseau the most dangerous enemy of individual liberty, because he had declared that 'by giving myself to all I give myself to none'. Constant could not see why, even though the sovereign is 'everybody', it should not oppress one of the 'members' of its indivisible self, if it so decided. I may, of course, prefer to be deprived of my liberties by an assembly, or a family, or a class, in which I am a minority. It may give me an opportunity one day of persuading the others to do for me that to which I feel I am entitled. But to be deprived of my liberty at the hands of my family or friends or fellow citizens is to be deprived of it just as effectively. Hobbes was at any rate more candid: he did not pretend that a sovereign does not enslave: he justified this slavery, but at least did not have the effrontery to call it freedom.

Throughout the nineteenth century liberal thinkers maintained that if liberty involved a limit upon the powers of any man to force me to do what I did not, or might not, wish to do, then, whatever the ideal in the name of which I was coerced, I was not free; that the doctrine of absolute sovereignty was a tyrannical doctrine in itself. If I wish to preserve my liberty, it is not enough to say that it must not be violated unless someone or other—the absolute ruler, or the popular assembly, or the King in Parliament, or the judges, or some combination of authorities, or the laws themselves—for the laws may be oppressive—authorizes its violation. I must establish a society in which there must be some frontiers of freedom which nobody should be permitted to cross. Different names or natures may be given to the rules that determine these frontiers: they may be called natural rights, or the word of God, or Natural Law, or the demands of utility or of the 'permanent interests of man'; I may believe them to be valid *a priori*, or assert them to be my own ultimate ends, or the ends of my society or culture. What these rules or commandments will have in common is that they are accepted so widely, and are grounded so deeply in the actual nature of men as they have developed through history, as to be, by now, an essential part of what we mean by being a normal human being. Genuine belief in the inviolability of a minimum extent of individual liberty entails some such absolute stand. For it is clear that it has little to hope for from the rule of majorities; democracy as such is logically uncommitted to it, and historically has at times failed to protect it, while remaining faithful to its own principles. Few governments, it has been observed, have found much difficulty in causing their subjects to generate any will that the government wanted. 'The triumph of despotism is to force the slaves to declare themselves free.' It may need no force; the slaves may proclaim their freedom quite sincerely: but they are none the less slaves. Perhaps the chief value for liberals of political—'positive' —rights, of participating in the government, is as a means for protecting what they hold to be an ultimate value, namely individual—'negative'—liberty.

But if democracies can, without ceasing to be democratic, suppress freedom, at least as liberals have used the word, what would make a society truly free? For Constant, Mill, Tocqueville, and the liberal tradition to which they belong, no society is free unless it is governed by at any rate two interrelated principles: first, that no power, but only rights, can be regarded as absolute, so that all men, whatever power governs them, have an absolute right to refuse to behave inhumanly; and, second, that there are frontiers, not artificially drawn, within which men should be inviolable, these frontiers being defined in terms of rules so long and widely accepted that their observance has entered into the very conception of what it is to be a normal human being, and, therefore, also of what it is to act inhumanly or insanely; rules of which it would be absurd to say, for example, that they could be abrogated by some formal procedure on the part of some court or sovereign body. When I speak of a man as being normal, a part of what I mean is that he could not break these rules easily, without a qualm of revulsion. It is such rules as these that are broken when a man is declared guilty without trial, or punished under a retroactive law; when children are ordered to denounce their parents, friends to betray one another, soldiers to use methods of barbarism; when men are tortured or murdered, or minorities are massacred because they irritate a majority or a tyrant. Such acts, even if they are made legal by the sovereign, cause horror even in these days, and this springs from the recognition of the moral validity—irrespective of the laws—of some absolute barriers to the imposition of one man's will on another.[1] The freedom of a society, or a class or a group, in this sense of freedom, is measured by the strength of these barriers, and the number and importance of the paths which they keep open for their members—if not for all, for at any rate a great number of them.[2]

This is almost at the opposite pole from the purposes of those who believe in liberty in the 'positive'—self-directive—sense. The former want to curb authority as such. The latter want it placed in their own hands. That is a cardinal issue. These are not two different interpretations of a single concept, but two profoundly divergent and irreconcilable attitudes to the ends of life. It is as well to recognize this, even if in practice it is often necessary to strike a compromise between them. For each of them makes absolute claims. These claims cannot both be fully satisfied. But it is a profound lack of social and moral understanding not to recognize that the satisfaction that each of them seeks is an ultimate value which, both historically and morally, has an equal right to be classed among the deepest interests of mankind.

[1] But see Introduction, p. x.

[2] In Great Britain such legal power is, of course, constitutionally vested in the absolute sovereign—the King in Parliament. What makes this country comparatively free, therefore, is the fact that this theoretically omnipotent entity is restrained by custom or opinion from behaving as such. It is clear that what matters is not the form of these restraints on power—whether they are legal, or moral, or constitutional—but their effectiveness.

VIII

The One and the Many

One belief, more than any other, is responsible for the slaughter of individuals on the altars of the great historical ideals—justice or progress or the happiness of future generations, or the sacred mission or emancipation of a nation or race or class, or even liberty itself, which demands the sacrifice of individuals for the freedom of society. This is the belief that somewhere, in the past or in the future, in divine revelation or in the mind of an individual thinker, in the pronouncements of history or science, or in the simple heart of an uncorrupted good man, there is a final solution. This ancient faith rests on the conviction that all the positive values in which men have believed must, in the end, be compatible, and perhaps even entail one another. 'Nature binds truth, happiness, and virtue together as by an indissoluble chain', said one of the best men who ever lived, and spoke in similar terms of liberty, equality, and justice.[1] But is this true? It is a commonplace that neither political equality nor efficient organization nor social justice is compatible with more than a modicum of individual liberty, and certainly not with un-restricted *laissez-faire*; that justice and generosity, public and private loyalties, the demands of genius and the claims of society, can conflict violently with each other. And it is no great way from that to the generalization that not all good things are compatible, still less all the ideals of mankind. But somewhere, we shall be told, and in some way, it must be possible for all these values to live together, for unless this is so, the universe is not a cosmos, not a harmony; unless this is so, conflicts of values may be an intrinsic, irremovable element in human life. To admit that the fulfilment

[1] Condorcet, from whose *Esquisse* these words are quoted, declares that the task of social science is to show 'by what bonds Nature has united the progress of enlightenment with that of liberty, virtue, and respect for the natural rights of man; how these ideals, which alone are truly good, yet so often separated from each other that they are even believed to be incompatible, should, on the contrary, become inseparable, as soon as enlightenment has reached a certain level simultaneously among a large number of nations'. He goes on to say that: 'Men still preserve the errors of their childhood, of their country, and of their age long after having recognized all the truths needed for destroying them.' Ironically enough, his belief in the need and possibility of uniting all good things may well be precisely the kind of error he himself so well described.

of some of our ideals may in principle make the fulfilment of others impossible is to say that the notion of total human fulfilment is a formal contradiction, a metaphysical chimaera. For every rationalist metaphysician, from Plato to the last disciples of Hegel or Marx, this abandonment of the notion of a final harmony in which all riddles are solved, all contradictions reconciled, is a piece of crude empiricism, abdication before brute facts, intolerable bankruptcy of reason before things as they are, failure to explain and to justify, to reduce everything to a system, which 'reason' indignantly rejects. But if we are not armed with an *a priori* guarantee of the proposition that a total harmony of true values is somewhere to be found—perhaps in some ideal realm the characteristics of which we can, in our finite state, not so much as conceive—we must fall back on the ordinary resources of empirical observation and ordinary human knowledge. And these certainly give us no warrant for supposing (or even understanding what would be meant by saying) that all good things, or all bad things for that matter, are reconcilable with each other. The world that we encounter in ordinary experience is one in which we are faced with choices between ends equally ultimate, and claims equally absolute, the realization of some of which must inevitably involve the sacrifice of others. Indeed, it is because this is their situation that men place such immense value upon the freedom to choose; for if they had assurance that in some perfect state, realizable by men on earth, no ends pursued by them would ever be in conflict, the necessity and agony of choice would disappear, and with it the central importance of the freedom to choose. Any method of bringing this final state nearer would then seem fully justified, no matter how much freedom were sacrificed to forward its advance. It is, I have no doubt, some such dogmatic certainty that has been responsible for the deep, serene, unshakeable conviction in the minds of some of the most merciless tyrants and persecutors in history that what they did was fully justified by its purpose. I do not say that the ideal of self-perfection—whether for individuals or nations or churches or classes—is to be condemned in itself, or that the language which was used in its defence was in all cases the result of a confused or fraudulent use of words, or of moral or intellectual perversity. Indeed, I have tried to show that it is the notion of freedom in its 'positive' sense that is at the heart of the demands for national or social self-direction which animate the most powerful and morally just public movements of our time, and that not to recognize this is to misunderstand the most vital facts and ideas of our age. But equally it seems to me that the belief that some single formula can in principle be found whereby all the diverse ends of men can be harmoniously realized is demonstrably false. If, as I believe, the ends of men are many, and not all of them are in principle compatible with each other, then the possibility of conflict—and of tragedy—can never wholly be eliminated from human life, either personal or social. The necessity of choosing between absolute claims is then an inescapable characteristic of the human condition. This gives its value to freedom as Acton had conceived of it—as an end in itself, and not as a temporary need, arising out of our confused notions and irrational and disordered lives, a predicament which a panacea could one day put right.

I do not wish to say that individual freedom is, even in the most liberal societies, the sole, or even the dominant, criterion of social action. We compel children to be educated, and we forbid public executions. These are certainly curbs to freedom. We justify them on the ground that ignorance, or a barbarian upbringing, or cruel pleasures and excitements are worse for us than the amount of restraint needed to repress them. This judgment in turn depends on how we determine good and evil, that is to say, on our moral, religious, intellectual, economic, and aesthetic values; which are, in their turn, bound up with our conception of man, and of the basic demands of his nature. In other words, our solution of such problems is based on our vision, by which we are consciously or unconsciously guided, of what constitutes a fulfilled human life, as contrasted with Mill's 'cramped and warped', 'pinched and hidebound' natures. To protest against the laws governing censorship or personal morals as intolerable infringements of personal liberty presupposes a belief that the activities which such laws forbid are fundamental needs of men as men, in a good (or, indeed, any) society. To defend such laws is to hold that these needs are not essential, or that they cannot be satisfied without sacrificing other values which come higher—satisfy deeper needs—than individual freedom, determined by some standard that is not merely subjective, a standard for which some objective status—empirical or *a priori*—is claimed.

The extent of a man's, or a people's, liberty to choose to live as they desire must be weighed against the claims of many other values, of which equality, or justice, or happiness, or security, or public order are perhaps the most obvious examples. For this reason, it cannot be unlimited. We are rightly reminded by R. H. Tawney that the liberty of the strong, whether their strength is physical or economic, must be restrained. This maxim claims respect, not as a consequence of some *a priori* rule, whereby the respect for the liberty of one man logically entails respect for the liberty of others like him; but simply because respect for the principles of justice, or shame at gross inequality of treatment, is as basic in men as the desire for liberty. That we cannot have everything is a necessary, not a contingent, truth. Burke's plea for the constant need to compensate, to reconcile, to balance; Mill's plea for novel 'experiments in living' with their permanent possibility of error, the knowledge that it is not merely in practice but in principle impossible to reach clear-cut and certain answers, even in an ideal world of wholly good and rational men and wholly clear ideas—may madden those who seek for final solutions and single, all-embracing systems, guaranteed to be eternal. Nevertheless, it is a conclusion that cannot be escaped by those who, with Kant, have learnt the truth that out of the crooked timber of humanity no straight thing was ever made.

There is little need to stress the fact that monism, and faith in a single criterion, has always proved a deep source of satisfaction both to the intellect and to the emotions. Whether the standard of judgment derives from the vision of some future perfection, as in the minds of the *philosophes* in the eighteenth century and their technocratic successors in our own day, or is rooted in the past—*la terre et les morts*—as maintained by German historicists or French theocrats, or neo-Conservatives in English-speaking countries, it is bound, provided it is inflexible enough, to encounter some unforeseen and unforeseeable human development, which it will not fit; and will then be used to justify the *a priori* barbarities of Procrustes—the vivisection of actual human societies into some fixed pattern dictated by our fallible understanding of a largely imaginary past or a wholly imaginary future. To preserve our absolute categories or ideals at the expense of human lives offends equally against the principles of science and of history; it is an attitude found in equal measure on the right and left wings in our days, and is not reconcilable with the principles accepted by those who respect the facts.

Pluralism, with the measure of 'negative' liberty that it entails, seems to me a truer and more humane ideal than the goals of those who seek in the great, disciplined, authoritarian structures the ideal of 'positive' self-mastery by classes, or peoples, or the whole of mankind. It is truer, because it does, at least, recognize the fact that human goals are many, not all of them commensurable, and in perpetual rivalry with one another. To assume that all values can be graded on one scale, so that it is a mere matter of inspection to determine the highest, seems to me to falsify our knowledge that men are free agents, to represent moral decision as an operation which a slide-rule could, in principle, perform. To say that in some ultimate, all-reconciling, yet realizable synthesis, duty *is* interest, or individual freedom *is* pure democracy or an authoritarian state, is to throw a metaphysical blanket over either self-deceit or deliberate hypocrisy. It is more humane because it does not (as the system builders do) deprive men, in the name of some remote, or incoherent, ideal, of much that they have found to be indispensable to their life as unpredictably self-transforming human beings.[1] In the end, men choose between ultimate values; they choose as they do, because their life and thought are determined by fundamental moral categories and concepts that are, at any rate over large stretches of time and space, a part of their being and thought

---

[1] On this also Bentham seems to me to have spoken well: 'Individual interests are the only real interests . . . can it be conceived that there are men so absurd as to . . . prefer the man who is not to him who is; to torment the living, under pretence of promoting the happiness of them who are not born, and who may never be born?' This is one of the infrequent occasions when Burke agrees with Bentham; for this passage is at the heart of the empirical, as against the metaphysical, view of politics.

and sense of their own identity; part of what makes them human.

It may be that the ideal of freedom to choose ends without claiming eternal validity for them, and the pluralism of values connected with this, is only the late fruit of our declining capitalist civilization: an ideal which remote ages and primitive societies have not recognized, and one which posterity will regard with curiosity, even sympathy, but little comprehension. This may be so; but no sceptical conclusions seem to me to follow. Principles are not less sacred because their duration cannot be guaranteed. Indeed, the very desire for guarantees that our values are eternal and secure in some objective heaven is perhaps only a craving for the certainties of childhood or the absolute values of our primitive past. 'To realise the relative validity of one's convictions', said an admirable writer of our time, 'and yet stand for them unflinchingly, is what distinguishes a civilised man from a barbarian.' To demand more than this is perhaps a deep and incurable metaphysical need; but to allow it to determine one's practice is a symptom of an equally deep, and more dangerous, moral and political immaturity.

JOHN STUART MILL AND THE ENDS OF LIFE[1]

'. . . the importance, to man and society . . . of giving full freedom
to human nature to expand itself in innumerable and conflicting
directions.'   J. S. MILL, *Autobiography*

I MUST begin by thanking you for the honour that you have
done me, in inviting me to address you on the subject to which
the Robert Waley Cohen Memorial Lectures are dedicated—
tolerance. In a world in which human rights were never trampled
on, and men did not persecute each other for what they believed
or what they were, this Council would have no reason for existence. This, however, is not our world. We are a good deal
remoter from this desirable condition than some of our more
civilized ancestors, and, in this respect, unfortunately conform
only too well to the common pattern of human experience. The
periods and societies in which civil liberties were respected, and
variety of opinion and faith tolerated, have been very few and
far between—oases in the desert of human uniformity, intolerance, and oppression. Among the great Victorian preachers,
Carlyle and Marx have turned out to be better prophets than
Macaulay and the Whigs, but not necessarily better friends to
mankind; sceptical, to put it at its lowest, of the principles which
this Council exists to promote. Their greatest champion, the
man who formulated these principles most clearly and thereby
founded modern liberalism, was, as everyone knows, the author
of the *Essay on Liberty*, John Stuart Mill. This book—this great
short book, as Sir Richard Livingstone has justly called it in his
own lecture in this series—was published one hundred years ago.
The subject was then in the forefront of discussion. The year
1859 saw the death of the two best-known champions of individual liberty in Europe, Macaulay and Tocqueville. It marked

[1] This Robert Waley Cohen Memorial Lecture, delivered at The Conference Hall,
County Hall, London, on 2 December 1959, was first published by The Council of
Christians and Jews, Kingsway Chambers, 162a Strand, London, W.C. 2, in the same
year.

the centenary of the birth of Friedrich Schiller, who was acclaimed as the poet of the free and creative personality fighting against great odds. The individual was seen by some as the victim of, by others as rising to his apotheosis in, the new and triumphant forces of nationalism and industrialism which exalted the power and the glory of great disciplined human masses that were transforming the world in factories or battlefields or political assemblies. The predicament of the individual versus the State or the nation or the industrial organization or the social or political group was becoming an acute personal and public problem. In the same year there appeared Darwin's *On the Origin of Species*, probably the most influential work of science of its century, which at once did much to destroy the ancient accumulation of dogma and prejudice, and, in its misapplication to psychology, ethics, and politics, was used to justify violent imperialism and naked competition. Almost simultaneously with it there appeared an essay, written by an obscure economist expounding a doctrine which has had a decisive influence on mankind. The author was Karl Marx, the book was the *Critique of Political Economy*, the preface to which contained the clearest statement of the materialist interpretation of history—the heart of all that goes under the name of Marxism today. But the impact made upon political thought by Mill's treatise was more immediate, and perhaps no less permanent. It superseded earlier formulations of the case for individualism and toleration, from Milton and Locke to Montesquieu and Voltaire, and, despite its outdated psychology and lack of logical cogency, it remains the classic statement of the case for individual liberty. We are sometimes told that a man's behaviour is a more genuine expression of his beliefs than his words. In Mill's case there is no conflict. His life embodied his beliefs. His single-minded devotion to the cause of toleration and reason was unique even among the dedicated lives of the nineteenth century. The centenary of his profession of faith should not, therefore, be allowed to pass without a word before this Council.

I

Everyone knows the story of John Stuart Mill's extraordinary education. His father, James Mill, was the last of the great *raisonneurs* of the eighteenth century, and remained completely unaffected by the new romantic currents of the time in which he lived. Like his teacher Bentham and the French philosophical materialists, he saw man as a natural object and considered that a systematic study of the human species—conducted on lines similar to those of zoology or botany or physics—could and should be established on firm empirical foundations. He believed himself to have grasped the principles of the new science of man, and was firmly convinced that any man educated in the light of it, brought up as a rational being by other rational beings, would thereby be preserved from ignorance and weakness, the two great sources of unreason in thought and action, which was alone responsible for the miseries and vices of mankind. He brought up his son, John Stuart, in isolation from other—less rationally educated—children; his own brothers and sisters were virtually his only companions. The boy knew Greek by the age of five, algebra and Latin by the age of nine. He was fed on a carefully distilled intellectual diet, prepared by his father, compounded of natural science and the classical literatures. No religion, no metaphysics, little poetry—nothing that Bentham had stigmatized as the accumulation of human idiocy and error—were permitted to reach him. Music, perhaps because it was supposed that it could not easily misrepresent the real world, was the only art in which he could indulge himself freely. The experiment was, in a sense, an appalling success. John Mill, by the time he reached the age of twelve, possessed the learning of an exceptionally erudite man of thirty. In his own sober, clear, literal-minded, painfully honest account of himself, he says that his emotions were starved while his mind was violently over-developed. His father had no doubt of the value of his experiment. He had succeeded in producing an excellently informed and perfectly rational being. The truth of Bentham's views on education had been thoroughly vindicated.

The results of such treatment will astonish no one in our psychologically less naïve age. In his early manhood John Mill went through his first agonizing crisis. He felt lack of purpose, a paralysis of the will and terrible despair. With his well trained and, indeed, ineradicable habit of reducing emotional dissatisfaction to a clearly formulated problem, he asked himself a simple question: supposing that the noble Benthamite ideal of universal happiness which he had been taught to believe, and to the best of his ability did believe, were realized, would this, in fact, fulfil all his desires? He admitted to himself, to his horror, that it would not. What, then, was the true end of life? He saw no purpose in existence: everything in his world now seemed dry and bleak. He tried to analyse his condition. Was he perhaps totally devoid of feeling—was he a monster with a large part of normal human nature atrophied? He felt that he had no motives for continuing to live, and wished for death. One day, as he was reading a pathetic story in the memoirs of the now almost forgotten French writer Marmontel, he was suddenly moved to tears. This convinced him that he was capable of emotion, and with this his recovery began. It took the form of a revolt, slow, concealed, reluctant, but profound and irresistible, against the view of life inculcated by his father and the Benthamites. He read the poetry of Wordsworth, he read and met Coleridge; his view of the nature of man, his history and his destiny, was transformed. John Mill was not by temperament rebellious. He loved and deeply admired his father, and was convinced of the validity of his main philosophical tenets. He stood with Bentham against dogmatism, transcendentalism, obscurantism, all that resisted the march of reason, analysis, and empirical science. To these beliefs he held firmly all his life. Nevertheless his conception of man, and therefore of much else, suffered a great change. He became not so much an open heretic from the original utilitarian movement, as a disciple who quietly left the fold, preserving what he thought true or valuable, but feeling bound by none of the rules and principles of the movement. He continued to profess that happiness was the sole end of human existence, but his conception of what contributed to it changed into something very different from that of his mentors, for what he came to value most was neither rationality nor contentment, but diversity, versatility, fullness of life—the unaccountable leap of individual genius, the spontaneity and uniqueness of a man, a group, a civilization. What he hated and feared was narrowness, uniformity, the crippling effect of persecution, the crushing of individuals by the weight of authority or of custom or of public opinion; he set himself against the worship of order or tidiness, or even peace, if they were bought at the price of obliterating the variety and colour of untamed human beings with unextinguished passions and untrammelled imaginations. This was, perhaps, a natural enough compensation for his own drilled, emotionally shrivelled, warped, childhood and adolescence.

By the time he was seventeen he was mentally fully formed. John Mill's intellectual equipment was probably unique in that or any other age. He was clear-headed, candid, highly articulate, intensely serious, and without any trace of fear, vanity, or humour. During the next ten years he wrote articles and reviews, with all the weight of the official heir presumptive of the whole utilitarian movement upon his shoulders; and although his articles made him a great name, and he grew to be a formidable publicist and a source of pride to his mentors and allies, yet the note of his writings is not theirs. He praised what his father had praised— rationality, empirical method, democracy, equality, and he attacked what the utilitarians attacked—religion, belief in intuitive and undemonstrable truths and their dogmatic consequences, which, in their view and in his, led to the abandonment of reason, hierarchical societies, vested interests, intolerance of free criticism, prejudice, reaction, injustice, despotism, misery. Yet the emphasis had shifted. James Mill and Bentham had wanted literally nothing but pleasure obtained by whatever means were the most effective. If someone had offered them a medicine which could scientifically be shown to put those who took it into a state of permanent contentment, their premises would have bound them to accept this as the panacea for all that they thought evil. Provided that the largest possible number of men receive lasting happiness, or even freedom from pain, it should not matter how this is achieved. Bentham and Mill believed in education and legislation as the roads to happiness. But if a shorter way had been discovered, in the form of pills to swallow, techniques of subliminal suggestion, or other means of conditioning human beings in which our century has made such strides, then, being men of fanatical consistency, they might well have accepted this as a better, because more effective and perhaps less costly, alternative than the means that they had advocated. John Stuart Mill, as he made plain both by his life and by his writings, would have rejected with both hands any such solution. He would have condemned it as degrading the nature of man. For him man differs from animals primarily neither as the possessor of reason, nor as an inventor of tools and methods, but as a being capable of choice, one who is most himself in choosing and not being chosen for; the rider and not the horse; the seeker of ends, and not merely of means, ends that he pursues, each in his own fashion: with the corollary that the more various these fashions, the richer the lives of men become; the larger the field of interplay between individuals, the greater the opportunities of the new and the unexpected; the more numerous the possibilities for altering his own character in some fresh or unexplored direction, the more paths open before each individual, and the wider will be his freedom of action and thought.

In the last analysis, all appearances to the contrary, this is what Mill seems to me to have cared about most of all. He is officially committed to the exclusive pursuit of happiness. He believes deeply in justice, but his voice is most his own when he describes the glories of individual freedom, or denounces whatever seeks to curtail or extinguish it. Bentham, too, unlike his French predecessors who trusted in moral and scientific experts, had laid it down that each man is the best judge of his own happiness. Nevertheless, this principle would remain valid for Bentham even after every living man had swallowed the happiness-inducing pill and society was thereby lifted or reduced to a condition of unbroken and uniform bliss. For Bentham individualism is a psychological datum; for Mill it is an ideal. Mill likes dissent, independence, solitary thinkers, those who defy the establishment. In an article written at the age of seventeen (demanding toleration for a now almost forgotten atheist named Carlyle), he strikes a note which sounds and resounds in his writings throughout the rest of his life: 'Christians, whose reformers perished in the dungeon or at the stake as heretics, as apostates, as blasphemers—Christians, whose religion breathes charity, liberty and mercy in every line . . . that they, having gained the power of which they were the victims, should employ it in the self same way . . . in vindictive persecution . . . is most monstrous.'[1] He remained the champion of heretics, apostates, and blasphemers, of liberty and mercy, for the rest of his life.

His acts were in harmony with his professions. The public policies with which Mill's name was associated as a journalist, a reformer, and a politician, were seldom connected with the typically utilitarian projects advocated by Bentham and successfully realized by many of his disciples: great industrial, financial, educational schemes, reforms of public health or the organization of labour or leisure. The issues to which Mill was dedicated, whether in his published views or his actions, were concerned with something different: the extension of individual freedom, especially freedom of speech: seldom with anything else. When Mill declared that war was better than oppression, or that a revolution that would kill all men with an income of more than £500 per annum might improve things greatly, or that the Emperor Napoleon III of France was the vilest man alive; when he expressed delight at Palmerston's fall over the Bill that sought to make conspiracy against foreign despots a criminal offence in England; when he denounced the Southern States in the American Civil War, or made himself violently unpopular by speaking in the House of Commons in defence of Fenian assassins (and thereby probably saving their lives), or for the rights of women, or of workers, or of colonial peoples, and thereby made himself the most passionate and best-known champion in England of the insulted and the oppressed, it is difficult to suppose that it was not liberty and justice (at whatever cost) but utility (which counts the cost) that were uppermost in his mind. His articles and his political support saved Durham and his Report, when both were in danger of being defeated by the combination of right- and left-wing adversaries, and thereby did much to ensure self-government in the British Commonwealth. He helped to destroy the reputation of Governor Eyre who had perpetrated brutalities

[1] From a tribute to John Stuart Mill by James Bain, quoted in the full and interesting *Life of John Stuart Mill* by Michael St. John Packe, p. 54.

in Jamaica. He saved the right of public meeting and of free speech in Hyde Park, against a Government that wished to destroy it. He wrote and spoke for proportional representation because this alone, in his view, would allow minorities (not necessarily virtuous or rational ones) to make their voices heard. When, to the surprise of radicals, he opposed the dissolution of the East India Company for which he, like his father before him, had worked so devotedly, he did this because he feared the dead hand of the Government more than the paternalist and not inhumane rule of the Company's officials. On the other hand he did not oppose State intervention as such; he welcomed it in education or labour legislation because he thought that without it the weakest would be enslaved and crushed; and because it would increase the range of choices for the great majority of men, even if it restrained some. What is common to all these causes is not any direct connexion they might have with the 'greater happiness' principle but the fact that they turn on the issue of human rights —that is to say, of liberty and toleration.

I do not, of course, mean to suggest that there was no such connexion in Mill's own mind. He often seems to advocate freedom on the ground that without it the truth cannot be discovered —we cannot perform those experiments either in thought or 'in living' which alone reveal to us new, unthought-of ways of maximizing pleasure and minimizing pain—the only ultimate source of value. Freedom, then, is valuable as a means, not as an end. But when we ask what Mill meant either by pleasure or by happiness, the answer is far from clear. Whatever happiness may be, it is, according to Mill, not what Bentham took it to be: for his conception of human nature is pronounced too narrow and altogether inadequate; he has no imaginative grasp of history or society or individual psychology; he does not understand either what holds, or what should hold, society together—common ideals, loyalties, national character; he is not aware of honour, dignity, self-culture, or the love of beauty, order, power, action; he understands only the 'business' aspects of life. Are these goals, which Mill rightly regards as central, so many means to a single universal goal—happiness? Or are they species of it? Mill never clearly tells us. He says that happiness—or utility—is of no use as a criterion of conduct—destroying at one blow the proudest claim, and indeed the central doctrine, of the Benthamite system. 'We think', he says in his essay on Bentham (published only after his father's death), 'utility or happiness much too complex or indefinite an end to be sought except through the medium of various secondary ends, concerning which there may be, and often is, agreement among persons who differ in the ultimate standard.' This is simple and definite enough in Bentham; but Mill rejects his formula because it rests on a false view of human nature. It is 'complex and indefinite' in Mill because he packs into it the many diverse (and, perhaps, not always compatible) ends which men in fact pursue for their own sake, and which Bentham had either ignored or falsely classified under the head of pleasure: love, hatred, desire for justice, for action, for freedom, for power, for beauty, for knowledge, for self-sacrifice. In J. S. Mill's writings happiness comes to mean something very like 'realization of one's wishes', whatever they may be. This stretches its meaning to the point of vacuity. The letter remains; but the spirit —the old, tough-minded Benthamite view for which happiness, if it was not a clear and concrete criterion of action, was nothing at all, as worthless as the 'transcendental' intuitionist moonshine it was meant to replace—the true utilitarian spirit—has fled. Mill does indeed add that 'when two or more of the secondary principles conflict, direct appeal to some first principle becomes necessary'; this principle is utility; but he gives no indication how this notion, drained of its old, materialistic but intelligible content, is to be applied. It is this tendency of Mill's to escape into what Bentham called 'vague generality' that leads one to ask what, in fact, was Mill's real scale of values as shown in his writings and actions. If his life and the causes he advocated are any evidence, then it seems clear that in public life the highest values for him—whether or not he calls them 'secondary ends'— were individual liberty, variety, and justice. If challenged about variety Mill would have defended it on the ground that without a sufficient degree of it many, at present wholly unforeseeable, forms of human happiness (or satisfaction, or fulfilment, or higher levels of life—however the degrees of these were to be determined and compared) would be left unknown, untried, unrealized; among them happier lives than any yet experienced. This is his thesis and he chooses to call it utilitarianism. But if anyone were to argue that a given, actual or attainable, social arrangement yielded enough happiness—that given the virtually impassable limitations of the nature of men and their environment (e.g. the very high improbability of men's becoming immortal or growing as tall as Everest) it were better to concentrate on the best that we have, since change would, in all empirical likelihood, lead to lowering of general happiness, and should therefore be avoided, we may be sure that Mill would have rejected this argument out of hand. He was committed to the answer that we can never tell (until we have tried) where greater truth or happiness (or any other form of experience) may lie. Finality is therefore in principle impossible: all solutions must be tentative and provisional. This is the voice of a disciple of both Saint-Simon and Constant or Humboldt. It runs directly counter to traditional—that is, eighteenth-century—utilitarianism, which rested on the view that there exists an unalterable nature of things, and answers to social, as to other, problems, can, at least in principle, be scientifically discovered once and for all. It is this perhaps, that, despite his fear of ignorant and irrational democracy and consequent craving for government by the enlightened and the expert (and insistence, early and late in his life, on the importance of objects of common, even uncritical, worship) checked his Saint-Simonism, turned him against Comte, and preserved him from the elitist tendency of his Fabian disciples.

There was a spontaneous and uncalculating idealism in his mind and his actions that was wholly alien to the dispassionate and penetrating irony of Bentham, or the vain and stubborn rationalism of James Mill. He tells us that his father's educational methods had turned him into a desiccated calculating machine, not too far removed from the popular image of the inhuman utilitarian philosopher; his very awareness of this makes one wonder whether it can ever have been wholly true. Despite the solemn bald head, the black clothes, the grave expression, the measured phrases, the total lack of humour, Mill's life is an unceasing revolt against his father's outlook and ideals, the greater for being subterranean and unacknowledged.

Mill had scarcely any prophetic gift. Unlike his contemporaries, Marx, Burckhardt, Tocqueville, he had no vision of what the twentieth century would bring, neither of the political and social consequences of industrialization, nor of the discovery of the strength of irrational and unconscious factors in human behaviour, nor of the terrifying techniques to which this knowledge has led and is leading. The transformation of society which has resulted—the rise of dominant secular ideologies and the wars between them, the awakening of Africa and Asia, the peculiar combination of nationalism and socialism in our day—these were outside Mill's horizon. But if he was not sensitive to the contours of the future, he was acutely aware of the destructive factors at work in his own world. He detested and feared standardization. He perceived that in the name of philanthropy, democracy, and equality a society was being created in which human objectives were artificially made narrower and smaller and the majority of men were being converted, to use his admired friend Tocqueville's phrase, into mere 'industrious sheep', in which, in his own words, 'collective mediocrity' was gradually strangling originality and individual gifts. He was against what have been called 'organization men', a class of persons to whom Bentham could have had in principle no rational objection. He knew, feared, and hated timidity, mildness, natural conformity, lack of interest in human issues. This was common ground between him and his friend, his suspicious and disloyal friend, Thomas Carlyle. Above all he was on his guard against those who, for the sake of being left in peace to cultivate their gardens, were ready to sell their fundamental human right to self-government in the public spheres of life; these characteristics of our lives today he would have recognized with horror. He took human solidarity for granted, perhaps altogether too much for granted. He did not fear the isolation of individuals or groups, the factors that make for the alienation and disintegration of individuals and societies. He was preoccupied with the opposite evils of socialization and uniformity.[1] He longed for the widest

[1] He did not seem to look on socialism, which under the influence of Mrs. Taylor he advocated in the *Political Economy* and later, as a danger to individual liberty in the way in which democracy, for example, might be so. This is not the place to examine the

variety of human life and character. He saw that this could not be obtained without protecting individuals from each other, and, above all, from the terrible weight of social pressure; this led to his insistent and persistent demands for toleration.

Toleration, Professor Butterfield has told us in his own lecture in this series, implies a certain disrespect. I tolerate your absurd beliefs and your foolish acts, though I know them to be absurd and foolish. Mill would, I think, have agreed. He believed that to hold an opinion deeply is to throw our feelings into it. He once declared[1] that when we deeply care, we must dislike those who hold the opposite views. He preferred this to cold temperaments and opinions. He asked us not necessarily to respect the views of others—very far from it—only to try to understand and tolerate them; only tolerate; disapprove, think ill of, if need be mock or despise, but tolerate; for without conviction, without some anti-pathetic feeling, there was, he thought, no deep conviction; and without deep conviction there were no ends of life, and then the awful abyss on the edge of which he had himself once stood would yawn before us. But without tolerance the conditions for rational criticism, rational condemnation, are destroyed. He therefore pleads for reason and toleration at all costs. To understand is not necessarily to forgive. We may argue, attack, reject, condemn with passion and hatred. But we may not suppress or stifle: for that is to destroy the bad and the good, and is tantamount to col-lective moral and intellectual suicide. Sceptical respect for the opinions of our opponents seems to him preferable to indifference or cynicism. But even these attitudes are less harmful than intolerance, or an imposed orthodoxy which kills rational dis-cussion. This is Mill's faith. It obtained its classical formulation in the tract on Liberty, which he began writing in 1855 in colla-boration with his wife, who, after his father, was the dominant figure in his life. Until his dying day he believed her to be endowed with a genius vastly superior to his own. He published

very peculiar relationship of Mill's socialist to his individualist convictions. Despite his socialist professions, none of the socialist leaders of his time—neither Louis Blanc nor Proudhon nor Lassalle nor Herzen—not to speak of Marx—appears to have regarded him even as a fellow traveller. He was to them the very embodiment of a mild reformist liberal or *bourgeois* radical. Only the Fabians claimed him as an ancestor.

[1] *Autobiography*, pp. 42–43 (World's Classics edition).

the essay after her death in 1859 without those improvements which he was sure that her unique gifts would have brought to it. It is this event that I venture to invite you to celebrate today.

II

I shall not impose upon your patience by giving you an abstract of Mill's argument. I should like to remind you only of those salient ideas to which Mill attached the greatest importance—beliefs which his opponents attacked in his lifetime, and attack even more vehemently today. These propositions are still far from self-evident; time has not turned them to platitudes; they are not even now undisputed assumptions of a civilized outlook. Let me attempt to consider them briefly:

Men want to curtail the liberties of other men, either (a) because they wish to impose their power on others; or (b) because they want conformity—they do not wish to think differently from others, or others to think differently from themselves; or, finally, (c) because they believe that to the question of how one should live there can be (as with any genuine question) one true answer and one only; this answer is discoverable by means of reason, or intuition, or direct revelation, or a form of life or 'unity of theory and practice'; its authority is identifiable with one of these avenues to final knowledge; all deviation from it is error which imperils human salvation; this justifies legislation against, or even extirpation of, those who lead away from the truth, whatever their character or intentions. Mill dismisses the first two motives as being irrational, since they stake out no intellectually argued claim, and are therefore incapable of being answered by rational argument. The only motive which he is prepared to take seriously is the last, namely, that if the true ends of life can be discovered, those who oppose these truths are spreading pernicious falsehood, and must be repressed. To this he replies that men are not infallible; that the supposedly pernicious view might turn out to be true after all; that those who killed Socrates and Christ sincerely believed them to be purveyors of wicked falsehoods, and were themselves men as worthy of respect as any to be found today; that Marcus Aurelius, 'the gentlest and most amiable of rulers', known as the most enlightened man of his time and one of the noblest, nevertheless authorized the persecution of Christianity as a moral and social danger, and that no argument ever used by any other persecutor had not been equally open to him. We cannot suppose that persecution never kills the truth. 'It is a piece of idle sentimentality', Mill observes, 'that truth, merely as truth, has any inherent power denied to error, of prevailing against the dungeon and the stake.'[1] Persecution is historically only too effective. 'To speak only of religious opinions: a reformation broke out at least twenty times before Luther, and was put down. Arnold of Brescia was put down. Fra Dolcino was put down. Savonarola was put down. The Albigeois were put down. The Vaudois were put down. The Lollards were put down. The Hussites were put down.... In Spain, Italy, Flanders, the Austrian Empire, Protestantism was rooted out; and most likely would have been so in England had Queen Mary lived or Queen Elizabeth died. ... No reasonable person can doubt that Christianity might have been extirpated in the Roman Empire.'[1] And if it be said against this that, just because we have erred in the past, it is mere cowardice to refrain from striking down evil when we see it in the present in case we may be mistaken again; or, to put it in another way, that, even if we are not infallible, yet, if we are to live at all, we must make decisions and act, and must do so on nothing better than probability, according to our lights, with constant risk of error; for all living involves risk, and what alternative have we? Mill answers that 'There is the greatest difference between presuming an opinion to be true, because with every opportunity for contesting it, it has not been refuted, and assuming its truth for the purpose of not permitting its refutation.'[1] You can indeed stop 'bad men from perverting society with false or pernicious views',[1] but only if you give men liberty to deny that what you yourself call bad, or pernicious, or perverted, or false, is such; otherwise your conviction is founded on mere dogma and is not rational, and cannot be analysed or altered in the light of any new facts and ideas. Without infallibility how can truth emerge save in discussion? there is no *a priori* road towards it; a new experience, a new argument, can in principle

[1] *On Liberty*, p. 37 (World's Classics edition).

always alter our views, no matter how strongly held. To shut doors is to blind yourself to the truth deliberately, to condemn yourself to incorrigible error.

Mill had a strong and subtle brain and his arguments are never negligible. But it is, in this case, plain that his conclusion only follows from premisses which he does not make explicit. He was an empiricist; that is, he believed that no truths are—or could be—rationally established, except on the evidence of observation. New observations could in principle always upset a conclusion founded on earlier ones. He believed this rule to be true of the laws of physics, even of the laws of logic and mathematics; how much more, therefore, in 'ideological' fields where no scientific certainty prevailed—in ethics, politics, religion, history, the entire field of human affairs, where only probability reigns; here, unless full liberty of opinion and argument is permitted, nothing can ever be rationally established. But those who disagree with him, and believe in intuited truths, in principle not corrigible by experience, will disregard this argument. Mill can write them off as obscurantists, dogmatists, irrationalists. Yet something more is needed than mere contemptuous dismissal if their views, more powerful today perhaps than even in Mill's own century, are to be rationally contested. Again, it may well be that without full freedom of discussion the truth cannot emerge. But this may be only a necessary, not a sufficient, condition of its discovery; the truth may, for all our efforts, remain at the bottom of a well, and in the meantime the worse cause may win, and do enormous damage to mankind. Is it so clear that we must permit opinions advocating, say, race hatred to be uttered freely, because Milton has said that 'though all the winds of doctrine are let loose upon the earth . . . whoever knew truth put to the worse in a free and open encounter?' because 'the truth must always prevail in a fair fight with falsehood'? These are brave and optimistic judgments, but how good is the empirical evidence for them today? Are demagogues and liars, scoundrels and blind fanatics, always, in liberal societies, stopped in time, or refuted in the end? How high a price is it right to pay for the great boon of freedom of discussion? A very high one, no doubt; but is it limitless? And if not, who shall say what sacrifice is, or is not, too great? Mill goes on to say that an opinion believed to be false may yet be partially true; for there is no absolute truth, only different roads towards it; the suppression of an apparent falsehood may also suppress what is true in it, to the loss of mankind. This argument, again, will not tell with those who believe that absolute truth is discoverable once and for all, whether by metaphysical or theological argument, or by some direct insight, or by leading a certain kind of life, or, as Mill's own mentors believed, by scientific or empirical methods.

His argument is plausible only on the assumption which, whether he knew it or not, Mill all too obviously made, that human knowledge was in principle never complete, and always fallible; that there was no single, universally visible, truth; that each man, each nation, each civilization might take its own road towards its own goal, not necessarily harmonious with those of others; that men are altered, and the truths in which they believe are altered, by new experiences and their own actions—what he calls 'experiments in living'; that consequently the conviction, common to Aristotelians and a good many Christian scholastics and atheistical materialists alike, that there exists a basic knowable human nature, one and the same, at all times, in all places, in all men—a static, unchanging substance underneath the altering appearances, with permanent needs, dictated by a single, discoverable goal, or pattern of goals, the same for all mankind—is mistaken; and so, too, is the notion that is bound up with it, of a single true doctrine carrying salvation to all men everywhere, contained in natural law, or the revelation of a sacred book, or the insight of a man of genius, or the natural wisdom of ordinary men, or the calculations made by an elite of utilitarian scientists set up to govern mankind.

Mill—bravely for a professed utilitarian—observes that the human (that is the social) sciences are too confused and uncertain to be properly called sciences at all—there are in them no valid generalizations, no laws, and therefore no predictions or rules of action can properly be deduced from them. He honoured the memory of his father, whose whole philosophy was based on the opposite assumption; he respected Auguste Comte, and subsidized Herbert Spencer, both of whom claimed to have laid the foundations for just such a science of society. Yet his own half-articulate assumption contradicts this. Mill believes that man is spontaneous, that he has freedom of choice, that he moulds his own character, that as a result of the interplay of men with nature and with other men something novel continually arises, and that this novelty is precisely what is most characteristic and most human in men. Because Mill's entire view of human nature turns out to rest not on the notion of the repetition of an identical pattern, but on his perception of human lives as subject to perpetual incompleteness, self-transformation, and novelty, his words are today alive and relevant to our own problems; whereas the works of James Mill, and of Buckle and Comte and Spencer, remain huge half-forgotten hulks in the river of nineteenth-century thought. He does not demand or predict ideal conditions for the final solution of human problems or for obtaining universal agreement on all crucial issues. He assumes that finality is impossible, and implies that it is undesirable too. He does not demonstrate this. Rigour in argument is not among his accomplishments. Yet it is this belief, which undermines the foundations on which Helvétius, Bentham, and James Mill built their doctrines—a system never formally repudiated by him—that gives his case both its plausibility and its humanity.

His remaining arguments are weaker still. He says that unless it is contested, truth is liable to degenerate into dogma or prejudice; men would no longer feel it as a living truth; opposition is needed to keep it alive. 'Both teachers and learners go to sleep at their post, as soon as there is no enemy in the field', overcome as they are by 'the deep slumber of a decided opinion'.[1] So deeply did Mill believe this, that he declared that if there were no genuine dissenters, we had an obligation to invent arguments against ourselves, in order to keep ourselves in a state of intellectual fitness. This resembles nothing so much as Hegel's argument for war as keeping human society from stagnation. Yet if the truth about human affairs were in principle demonstrable, as it is, say, in arithmetic, the invention of false propositions in order to be knocked down would scarcely be needed to preserve our understanding of it. What Mill seems really to be asking for is diversity

[1] *Liberty*, p. 53.

of opinion for its own sake. He speaks of the need for 'fair play to all sides of the truth'[1]—a phrase that a man would scarcely employ if he believed in simple, complete truths as the earlier utilitarians did; and he makes use of bad arguments to conceal this scepticism, perhaps even from himself. 'In an imperfect state of the human mind', he says, 'the interests of the truth require a diversity of opinions.'[2] Or again, 'Do we really accept the logic of the persecutors [and say] we may persecute others because we are right, and they may not persecute us because they are wrong?'[3] Catholics, Protestants, Jews, Moslems have all justified persecution by this argument in their day; and on their premisses there may be nothing logically amiss with it. It is these premisses that Mill rejects, and rejects not, it seems to me, as a result of a chain of reasoning, but because he believes—even if he never, so far as I know, admits this explicitly—that there are no final truths not corrigible by experience, at any rate in what is now called the ideological sphere—that of value judgments and of general outlook and attitude to life. Yet within this framework of ideas and values, despite all the stress on the value of 'experiments in living' and what they may reveal, Mill is ready to stake a very great deal on the truth of his convictions about what he thinks to be the deepest and most permanent interests of men. Although his reasons are drawn from experience and not *a priori* knowledge, the propositions themselves are very like those defended on metaphysical grounds by the traditional upholders of the doctrine of natural rights. Mill believes in liberty, that is, the rigid limitation of the right to coerce, because he is sure that men cannot develop and flourish and become fully human unless they are left free from interference by other men within a certain minimum area of their lives, which he regards as—or wishes to make—inviolable. This is his view of what men are, and therefore of their basic moral and intellectual needs, and he formulates his conclusions in the celebrated maxims according to which 'The individual is not accountable to society for his actions, in so far as these concern the interests of no person but himself',[4] and that 'The only reason for which power can be rightfully exercised over any member of a civilised community against his

---

[1] *Liberty*, p. 50.   [2] *Liberty*, p. 63.   [3] *Liberty*, p. 106.   [4] *Liberty*, p. 115.

will is to prevent harm to others. His own good, either physical or moral, is not a sufficient warrant. He cannot rightfully be compelled to do or to forbear . . . because in the opinion of others to do so would not be wise or even right.'[1] This is Mill's profession of faith, and the ultimate basis of political liberalism, and therefore the proper target of attack—both on psychological and moral (and social) grounds—by its opponents during Mill's lifetime and after. Carlyle reacted with characteristic fury in a letter to his brother Alexander: 'As if it were a sin to control or coerce into better methods human swine in any way. . . . Ach Gott in Himmel!'[2]

Milder and more rational critics have not failed to point out that the limits of private and public domain are difficult to demarcate, that anything a man does could, in principle, frustrate others; that no man is an island; that the social and the individual aspects of human beings often cannot, in practice, be disentangled. Mill was told that when men look upon forms of worship in which other men persist as being not merely 'abominable' in themselves, but as an offence to them or to their God, they may be irrational and bigoted, but they are not necessarily lying; and that when he asks rhetorically why Moslems should not forbid the eating of pork to everyone, since they are genuinely disgusted by it, the answer, on utilitarian premisses, is by no means self-evident. It might be argued that there is no *a priori* reason for supposing that most men would not be happier—if that is the goal—in a wholly socialized world where private life and personal freedom are reduced to vanishing point, than in Mill's individualist order; and that whether this is so or not is a matter for experimental verification. Mill constantly protests against the fact that social and legal rules are too often determined merely by 'the likings and dislikings of society', and correctly points out that these are often irrational or are founded on ignorance. But if damage to others is what concerns him most (as he professes), then the fact that their resistance to this or that belief is instinctive, or intuitive, or founded on no rational ground, does not make it the less painful, and, to that extent,

[1] *Liberty*, p. 15.
[2] *New Letters of Thomas Carlyle* (ed. A. Carlyle), vol. ii, p. 196.

damaging to them. Why should rational men be entitled to the satisfaction of their ends more than the irrational? Why not the irrational, if the greatest happiness of the greatest number (and the greatest number are seldom rational) is the sole justified purpose of action? Only a competent social psychologist can tell what will make a given society happiest. If happiness is the sole criterion, then human sacrifice, or the burning of witches, at times when such practices had strong public feeling behind them, did doubtless, in their day, contribute to the happiness of the majority. If there is no other moral criterion, then the question whether the slaughter of innocent old women (together with the ignorance and prejudice which made this acceptable) or the advance in knowledge and rationality (which ended such abominations but robbed men of comforting illusions)—which of these yielded a higher balance of happiness is only a matter of actuarial calculation. Mill paid no attention to such considerations: nothing could go more violently against all that he felt and believed. At the centre of Mill's thought and feeling lies, not his utilitarianism, nor the concern about enlightenment, nor about dividing the private from the public domain—for he himself at times concedes that the State may invade the private domain, in order to promote education, hygiene, or social security or justice —but his passionate belief that men are made human by their capacity for choice—choice of evil and good equally. Fallibility, the right to err, as a corollary of the capacity for self-improvement; distrust of symmetry and finality as enemies of freedom—these are the principles which Mill never abandons. He is acutely aware of the many-sidedness of the truth and of the irreducible complexity of life, which rules out the very possibility of any simple solution, or the idea of a final answer to any concrete problem. Greatly daring, and without looking back at the stern intellectual puritanism in which he was brought up, he preaches the necessity of understanding and gaining illumination from doctrines that are incompatible with one another—say those of Coleridge and Bentham; he explained in his autobiography the need to understand and learn from both.[1]

---

[1] And in the essays on *Coleridge* and *Bentham*.

III

Kant once remarked that 'out of the crooked timber of humanity no straight thing was ever made'. Mill believed this deeply. This, and his almost Hegelian distrust of simple models and of cut-and-dried formulae to cover complex, contradictory, and changing situations, made him a very hesitant and uncertain adherent of organized parties and programmes. Despite his father's advocacy, despite Mrs. Taylor's passionate faith in the ultimate solution of all social evils by some great institutional change (in her case that of socialism), he could not rest in the notion of a clearly discernible final goal, because he saw that men differed and evolved, not merely as a result of natural causes, but also because of what they themselves did to alter their own characters, at times in unintended ways. This alone makes their conduct unpredictable, and renders laws or theories, whether inspired by analogies with mechanics or with biology, nevertheless incapable of embracing the complexity and qualitative properties of even an individual character, let alone of a group of men. Hence the imposition of any such construction upon a living society is bound, in his favourite words of warning, to dwarf, maim, cramp, wither the human faculties.

His greatest break with his father was brought about by this conviction: by his belief (which he never explicitly admitted) that particular predicaments required each its own specific treatment; that the application of correct judgment, in curing a social malady, mattered at least as much as knowledge of the laws of anatomy or pharmacology. He was a British empiricist and not a French rationalist, or a German metaphysician, sensitive to day-to-day play of circumstances, differences of 'climate', as well as to the individual nature of each case, as Helvétius or Saint-Simon or Fichte, concerned as they were with the *grandes lignes* of development, were not. Hence his unceasing anxiety, as great as Tocqueville's and greater than Montesquieu's, to preserve variety, to keep doors open to change, to resist the dangers of social pressure, and above all his hatred of the human pack in full cry against a victim, his desire to protect dissidents and heretics as such. The whole burden of his charge against the 'progressives' (he means utilitarians and perhaps socialists) is that, as a rule, they do no more than try to alter social opinion in order to make it more favourable to this or that scheme or reform, instead of assailing the monstrous principle itself which says that social opinion 'should be a law for individuals'.[1]

Mill's overmastering desire for variety and individuality for their own sake emerges in many shapes. He notes that 'Mankind are greater gainers by suffering each other to live as seems good to themselves, than by compelling each to live as seems good to the rest'[2]—a truism which, he declares, 'stands opposed to the general tendency of existing opinion and practice'. At other times he speaks in sharper terms. He remarks that 'it is the habit of our time to desire nothing strongly. Its ideal of character is to be without any marked character; to maim by compression, like a Chinese lady's foot, every part of human nature which stands out prominently, and tends to make the person markedly dissimilar in outline to commonplace humanity.'[3] And again 'The greatness of England is now all collective; individually small, we only appear capable of anything great by combining; and with this our moral and religious philanthropists are perfectly content. But it was men of another stamp that made England what it has been; and men of another stamp will be needed to prevent its decline.'[3] The tone of this, if not the content, would have shocked Bentham; so indeed would this bitter echo of Tocqueville: 'Comparatively speaking, they now read the same things, listen to the same things, see the same things, go to the same places, have their hopes and fears directed to the same objects, have the same rights and liberties and the same means of asserting them. . . . All the political changes of the age promote it, since they all tend to raise the low and lower the high. Every extension of education promoted it, because education brought people under common influences. Improvement in the means of communication promotes it. . . . Increase of commerce and manufacture promotes it. . . . The ascendancy of public opinion . . . forms so great a mass of influence hostile to individuality[4] [that] in this age the mere example of non-conformity,

---

[1] *Liberty*, p. 13.   [2] *Liberty*, p. 18.   [3] *Liberty*, p. 86.
[4] *Liberty*, pp. 90–91.

the mere refusal to bend the knee to custom, is itself a service.'[1]
We have come to such a pass that mere differences, resistance for
its own sake, protest as such, is now enough. Conformity, and the
intolerance which is its offensive and defensive arm, are for Mill
always detestable, and peculiarly horrifying in an age which
thinks itself enlightened; in which, nevertheless, a man can be
sent to prison for twenty-one months for atheism; jurymen are
rejected and foreigners denied justice because they hold no recognized religious beliefs; no public money is given for Hindu or
Moslem schools because an 'imbecile display'[2] is made by an
Under-Secretary, who declares that toleration is desirable only
among Christians but not for unbelievers. It is no better when
workers employ 'moral police'[3] to prevent some members of their
trade union being paid higher wages earned by superior skill or
industry than the wages paid to those who lack these attributes.
Such conduct is even more loathsome when it interferes with
private relations between individuals. He declared that 'what any
person might freely do with respect to sexual relations' should be
deemed to be an unimportant and purely private matter which
concerns no one but themselves; that to have held any human
being responsible to other people, and to the world, for the fact
itself (apart from such of its consequences as the birth of children,
which clearly created duties which should be socially enforced)
would one day be thought one of the superstitions and barbar-
isms of the infancy of the human race. The same seemed to him
to apply to the enforcement of temperance or Sabbath observance, or any of the matters on which 'intrusively pious members
of society should be told to mind their own business'.[4] No doubt
the gossip to which Mill was exposed during his relationship with
Mrs. Taylor before his marriage to her—the relationship which
Carlyle mocked at as platonic—made him peculiarly sensitive to
this form of social persecution. But it is of a piece with his deepest
and most permanent convictions.

Mill's suspicion of democracy as the only just, and yet potentially the most oppressive, form of government, springs from
the same roots. He wondered uneasily whether centralization of

[1] *Liberty*, p. 83.   [2] *Liberty*, p. 40.
[3] *Liberty*, p. 108.   [4] *Liberty*, p. 107.

authority and the inevitable dependence of each on all and 'surveillance of each by all' would not end by grinding all down into
'a tame uniformity of thought, dealings and actions', and pro-
duce 'automatons in human form' and 'liberticide'. Tocqueville
had written pessimistically about the moral and intellectual
effects of democracy in America. Mill agreed. He said that even
if such power did not destroy, it prevented existence; it com-
pressed, enervated, extinguished, and stupefied a people; and
turned them into a flock of 'timid and industrious animals of
whom the government is a shepherd'. Yet the only cure for this,
as Tocqueville himself maintained (it may be a little half-
heartedly), is more democracy,[1] which can alone educate a sufficient number of individuals to independence, resistance, and
strength. Men's disposition to impose their own views on others
is so strong that, in Mill's view, only want of power restricts it;
this power is growing; hence unless further barriers are erected
it will increase, leading to a proliferation of 'conformers, time
servers, hypocrites, created by silencing opinion',[2] and finally
to a society where timidity has killed independent thought, and
men confine themselves to safe subjects. Yet if we make the
barriers too high, and do not interfere with opinion at all, will
this not end, as Burke or the Hegelians have warned, in the dissolution of the social texture, atomization of society—anarchy?
To this Mill replies that 'the inconvenience arising from conduct
which neither violates specific duty to the public, nor hurts any
assignable individual, is one which society can afford to bear for
the sake of the greater good of human freedom'.[3] This is tantamount to saying that if society, despite the need for social co-
hesion, has itself failed to educate its citizens to be civilized men,
it has no right to punish them for irritating others, or being
misfits, or not conforming to some standard which the majority
accepts. A smooth and harmonious society could perhaps be
created, at any rate for a time, but it would be purchased at too
high a price. Plato saw correctly that if a frictionless society is to
emerge the poets must be driven out; what horrifies those who

---

[1] Which in any case he regarded as inevitable and, perhaps, to a vision wider than his
own time-bound one, ultimately more just and more generous.

[2] Packe, op. cit., p. 203.   [3] *Liberty*, p. 101.

revolt against this policy is not so much the expulsion of the fantasy-mongering poets as such, but the underlying desire for an end to variety, movement, individuality of any kind; a craving for a fixed pattern of life and thought, timeless, changeless, and uniform. Without the right of protest, and the capacity for it, there is for Mill no justice, there are no ends worth pursuing. 'If all mankind minus one were of one opinion, and only one person were of a contrary opinion, mankind would be no more justified in silencing that one person than he, if he had the power, would be justified in silencing mankind.'[1]

In his lecture in this series, to which I have already referred, Sir Richard Livingstone, whose sympathy with Mill is not in doubt, charges him with attributing too much rationality to human beings: the ideal of untrammelled freedom may be the right of those who have reached the maturity of their faculties, but of how many men today, or at most times, is this true? Surely Mill asks far too much and is far too optimistic? There is certainly an important sense in which Sir Richard is right: Mill was no prophet. Many social developments caused him grief, but he had no inkling of the mounting strength of the irrational forces that have moulded the history of the twentieth century. Burckhardt and Marx, Pareto and Freud, were more sensitive to the deeper currents of their own times, and saw a good deal more deeply into the springs of individual and social behaviour. But I know of no evidence that Mill overestimated the enlightenment of his own age, or that he supposed that the majority of men of his own time were mature or rational or likely soon to become so. What he did see before him was the spectacle of some men, civilized by any standards, who were kept down, or discriminated against, or persecuted by prejudice, stupidity, 'collective mediocrity'; he saw such men deprived of what he regarded as their most essential rights, and he protested. He believed that all human progress, all human greatness and virtue and freedom, depended chiefly on the preservation of such men and the clearing of paths before them. But he did not[2] want them appointed Platonic

[1] *Liberty*, p. 23.
[2] This is the line which divides him from Saint-Simon and Comte, and from H. G. Wells and the technocrats.

Guardians. He thought that others like them could be educated, and, when they were educated, would be entitled to make choices, and that these choices must not, within certain limits, be blocked or directed by others. He did not merely advocate education and forget the freedom to which it would entitle the educated (as Communists have), or press for total freedom of choice, and forget that without adequate education it would lead to chaos and, as a reaction to it, a new slavery (as anarchists do). He demanded both. But he did not think that this process would be rapid, or easy, or universal; he was on the whole a pessimistic man, and consequently at once defended and distrusted democracy, for which he has been duly attacked, and is still sharply criticized. Sir Richard has observed that Mill was acutely conscious of the circumstances of his age, and saw no further than that. This seems to me a just comment. The disease of Victorian England was claustrophobia—there was a sense of suffocation, and the best and most gifted men of the period, Mill and Carlyle, Nietzsche and Ibsen, men both of the left and of the right—demanded more air and more light. The mass neurosis of our age is agoraphobia; men are terrified of disintegration and of too little direction : they ask, like Hobbes's masterless men in a state of nature, for walls to keep out the raging ocean, for order, security, organization, clear and recognizable authority, and are alarmed by the prospect of too much freedom, which leaves them lost in a vast, friendless vacuum, a desert without paths or landmarks or goals. Our situation is different from that of the nineteenth century, and so are our problems: the area of irrationality is seen to be vaster and more complex than any that Mill had dreamed of. Mill's psychology has become antiquated and grows more so with every discovery that is made. He is justly criticized for paying too much attention to purely spiritual obstacles to the fruitful use of freedom—lack of moral and intellectual light; and too little (although nothing like as little as his detractors have maintained) to poverty, disease, and their causes, and to the common sources and the interaction of both, and for concentrating too narrowly on freedom of thought and expression. All this is true. Yet what solutions have we found, with all our new technological and psychological knowledge and great new powers, save the ancient prescription advocated by the creators of humanism—Erasmus and Spinoza, Locke and Montesquieu, Lessing and Diderot—reason, education, self-knowledge, responsibility—above all, self-knowledge? What other hope is there for men, or has there ever been?

IV

Mill's ideal is not original. It is an attempt to fuse rationalism and romanticism: the aim of Goethe and Wilhelm Humboldt; a rich, spontaneous, many-sided, fearless, free, and yet rational, self-directed character. Mill notes that Europeans owe much to 'plurality of paths'. From sheer differences and disagreements sprang toleration, variety, humanity. In a sudden outburst of anti-egalitarian feeling, he praises the Middle Ages because men were then more individual and more responsible: men died for ideas, and women were equal to men. 'The poor Middle Ages, its Papacy, its chivalry, its feudality, under what hands did they perish? Under that of the attorney, and fraudulent bankrupt, the false coiner.'[1] This is the language not of a philosophical radical, but of Burke, or Carlyle, or Chesterton. In his passion for the colour and the texture of life Mill has forgotten his list of martyrs, he has forgotten the teachings of his father, of Bentham, or Condorcet. He remembers only Coleridge, only the horrors of a levelling, middle-class society—the grey, conformist, congregation that worships the wicked principle that 'it is the absolute social right of every individual that every other individual should act in every respect exactly as he ought',[2] or, worse still, 'that it is one man's duty that another should be religious', for 'God not only abominates the acts of the misbeliever, but will not hold us guiltless if we leave them unmolested'.[3] These are the shibboleths of Victorian England, and if that is its conception of social justice, it were better dead. In a similar, earlier moment of acute indignation with the self-righteous defences of the exploitation of the poor, Mill had expressed his enthusiasm for revolution and slaughter, since justice was more precious than life. He was twenty-five years old when he wrote

[1] Packe, op. cit., pp. 294–5.   [2] *Liberty*, p. 110.   [3] *Liberty*, p. 112.

that. A quarter of a century later, he declared that a civilization which had not the inner strength to resist barbarism had better succumb.[1] This may not be the voice of Kant, but it is not that of utilitarianism; rather that of Rousseau or Mazzini.

But Mill seldom continues in this tone. His solution is not revolutionary. If human life is to be made tolerable, information must be centralized and power disseminated. If everyone knows as much as possible, and has not too much power, then we may yet avoid a state which 'dwarfs its men', in which 'there is the absolute rule of the head of the executive over a congregation of isolated individuals, all equals but all slaves'.[2] With small men 'no great things can be accomplished'.[2] There is a terrible danger in creeds and forms of life which 'compress', 'stunt', 'dwarf' men. The acute consciousness in our day of the dehumanizing effect of mass culture; of the destruction of genuine purposes, both individual and communal, by the treatment of men as irrational creatures to be deluded and manipulated by the media of mass advertising, and mass communication—and so 'alienated' from the basic purposes of human beings by being left exposed to the play of the forces of nature interacting with human ignorance, vice, stupidity, tradition, and above all self-deception and institutional blindness—all this was as deeply and painfully felt by Mill as by Ruskin or William Morris. In this matter he differs from them only in his clearer awareness of the dilemma created by the simultaneous needs for individual self-expression and for human community. It is on this theme that the tract on Liberty was composed. 'It is to be feared', Mill added gloomily, 'that the teachings' of his essay 'will retain their value for a long time.'

It was, I think, Bertrand Russell—Mill's godson—who remarked somewhere that the deepest convictions of philosophers are seldom contained in their formal arguments: fundamental beliefs, comprehensive views of life, are like citadels which must be guarded against the enemy. Philosophers expend their intellectual power in arguments against actual and possible objections to their doctrines, and although the reasons they find, and the logic that they use, may be complex, ingenious, and

---

[1] *Liberty*, p. 118.   [2] *Liberty*, p. 141.

formidable, they are defensive weapons; the inner fortress itself
—the vision of life for the sake of which the war is being waged—
will, as a rule, turn out to be relatively simple and unsophisticated.
Mill's defence of his position in the tract on Liberty is not, as has
often been pointed out, of the highest intellectual quality: most
of his arguments can be turned against him; certainly none is
conclusive, or such as would convince a determined or unsympathetic opponent. From the days of James Stephen, whose
powerful attack on Mill's position appeared in the year of Mill's
death, to the conservatives and socialists and authoritarians and
totalitarians of our day, the critics of Mill have, on the whole,
exceeded the number of his defenders. Nevertheless, the inner
citadel—the central thesis—has stood the test. It may need
elaboration or qualification, but it is still the clearest, most
candid, persuasive, and moving exposition of the point of view
of those who desire an open and tolerant society. The reason
for this is not merely the honesty of Mill's mind, or the moral
and intellectual charm of his prose, but the fact that he is
saying something true and important about some of the most
fundamental characteristics and aspirations of human beings.
Mill is not merely uttering a string of clear propositions (each of
which, viewed by itself, is of doubtful plausibility) connected by
such logical links as he can supply. He perceived something profound and essential about the destructive effect of man's most
successful efforts at self-improvement in modern society; about
the unintended consequences of modern democracy, and the
fallaciousness and practical dangers of the theories by which
some of the worst of these consequences were (and still are)
defended. That is why, despite the weakness of the argument, the
loose ends, the dated examples, the touch of the finishing gover-
ness that Disraeli so maliciously noted, despite the total lack of
that boldness of conception which only men of original genius
possess, his essay educated his generation, and is controversial
still. Mill's central propositions are not truisms, they are not
at all self-evident. They are statements of a position which has
been resisted and rejected by the modern descendants of his
most notable contemporaries, Marx, Carlyle, Dostoevsky, Newman, Comte, and they are still assailed because they are still

contemporary. The *Essay on Liberty* deals with specific social issues in terms of examples drawn from genuine and disturbing issues of its day, and its principles and conclusions are alive in part because they spring from acute moral crises in a man's life, and thereafter from a life spent in working for concrete causes and taking genuine—and therefore at times dangerous—decisions. Mill looked at the questions that puzzled him directly, and not through spectacles provided by any orthodoxy. His revolt against his father's education, his bold avowal of the values of Coleridge and the Romantics was the liberating act that dashed these spectacles to the ground. From these half-truths, too, he liberated himself in turn, and became a thinker in his own right. For this reason, while Spencer and Comte, Taine and Buckle—even Carlyle and Ruskin—figures who loomed very large in their generation—are fast receding into (or have been swallowed by) the shadows of the past, Mill himself remains real.

One of the symptoms of this kind of three-dimensional, rounded, authentic quality is that we feel sure that we can tell where he would have stood on the issues of our own day. Can anyone doubt what position he would have taken on the Dreyfus case, or the Boer War, or Fascism, or Communism? Or, for that matter, on Munich, or Suez, or Budapest, or Apartheid, or colonialism, or the Wolfenden report? Can we be so certain with regard to other eminent Victorian moralists? Carlyle or Ruskin or Dickens? or even Kingsley or Wilberforce or Newman? Surely that alone is some evidence of the permanence of the issues with which Mill dealt and the degree of his insight into them.

V

Mill is usually represented as a just and high-souled Victorian schoolmaster, honourable, sensitive, humane, but 'sober, censorious and sad'; something of a goose, something of a prig, a good and noble man, but bleak, sententious, and desiccated; a waxwork among other waxworks in an age now dead and gone and stiff with such effigies. His autobiography—one of the most moving accounts of a human life—modifies this impression. Mill was certainly an intellectual, and was well aware, and not at all ashamed, of this fact. He knew that his main interest lay in general ideas in a society largely distrustful of them: 'the English', he wrote to his friend d'Eichthal, 'invariably mistrust the most evident truths if he who propounds them is suspected of having general ideas.' He was excited by ideas and wanted them to be as interesting as possible. He admired the French for respecting intellectuals as the English did not. He noted that there was a good deal of talk in England about the march of intellect at home, but he remained sceptical. He wondered whether 'our march of intellect be not rather a march towards doing without intellect, and supplying our deficiency in giants by the united effort of the constantly increasing multitude of dwarfs'. The word 'dwarfs', and the fear of smallness, pervades all his writings.

Because he believed in the importance of ideas, he was prepared to change his own if others could convince him of their inadequacy, or when a new vision was revealed to him, as it was by Coleridge or Saint-Simon, or, as he believed, by the transcendent genius of Mrs. Taylor. He liked criticism for its own sake. He detested adulation, even praise of his own work. He attacked dogmatism in others and was genuinely free from it himself. Despite the efforts of his father and his mentors, he retained an unusually open mind, and his 'still and cold appearance' and 'the head that reasons as a great steam engine works'[1] were united (to quote his friend Stirling) with a 'warm, upright and really lofty soul' and a touching and pure-hearted readiness to learn from anyone, at any time. He lacked vanity and cared little for his reputation, and therefore did not cling to consistency for its own sake, nor to his own personal dignity, if a human issue was at stake. He was loyal to movements, to causes, and to parties, but could not be prevailed upon to support them at the price of saying what he did not think to be true. A characteristic instance of this is his attitude to religion. His father brought him up in the strictest and narrowest atheist dogma. He rebelled against it. He embraced no recognized faith, but he did not dismiss religion, as the French encyclopaedists or the Benthamites had done, as a tissue of childish fantasies and emotions, comforting illusions, mystical gibberish and deliberate lies. He held that the existence

[1] Packe, op. cit., p. 222.

of God was possible, indeed probable, but unproven, but that if God was good he could not be omnipotent, since he permitted evil to exist. He would not hear of a being at once wholly good and omnipotent whose nature defied the canons of human logic, since he rejected belief in mysteries as mere attempts to evade agonizing issues. If he did not understand (this must have happened often), he did not pretend to understand. Although he was prepared to fight for the rights of others to hold a faith detached from logic, he rejected it himself. He revered Christ as the best man who ever lived, and regarded theism as a noble, though to him unintelligible, set of beliefs. He regarded immortality as possible, but rated its probability very low. He was, in fact, a Victorian agnostic who was uncomfortable with atheism and regarded religion as something that was exclusively the individual's own affair. When he was invited to stand for Parliament, to which he was duly elected, he declared that he was prepared to answer any questions that the electors of Westminster might choose to put to him, save those on his religious views. This was not cowardice—his behaviour throughout the election was so candid and imprudently fearless, that someone remarked that on Mill's platform God Almighty Himself could not expect to be elected. His reason was that a man had an indefeasible right to keep his private life to himself and to fight for this right, if need be. When, at a later date, his stepdaughter Helen Taylor and others upbraided him for not aligning himself more firmly with the atheists, and accused him of temporizing and shilly-shallying, he remained unshaken. His doubts were his own property: no one was entitled to extort a confession of faith from him, unless it could be shown that his silence harmed others; since this could not be shown, he saw no reason for publicly committing himself. Like Acton after him, he regarded liberty and religious toleration as the indispensable protection of all true religion, and the distinction made by the Church between spiritual and temporal realms as one of the great achievements of Christianity, inasmuch as it had made possible freedom of opinion. This last he valued beyond all things, and he defended Bradlaugh passionately, although, and because, he did not agree with his opinions.

He was the teacher of a generation, of a nation, but still no more than a teacher, not a creator or an innovator. He is known for no lasting discovery or invention. He made scarcely any significant advance in logic or philosophy or economics or political thought. Yet his range, and his capacity for applying ideas to fields in which they would bear fruit was unexampled. He was not original, yet he transformed the structure of the human knowledge of his age.

Because he had an exceptionally honest, open, and civilized mind, which found natural expression in lucid and admirable prose; because he combined an unswerving pursuit of the truth with the belief that its house had many mansions, so that even 'one-eyed men like Bentham might see what men with normal vision would not';[1] because, despite his inhibited emotions and his over-developed intellect, despite his humourless, cerebral, solemn character, his conception of man was deeper, and his vision of history and life wider and less simple than that of his utilitarian predecessors or liberal followers, he has emerged as a major political thinker in our own day. He broke with the pseudo-scientific model, inherited from the classical world and the age of reason, of a determined human nature, endowed at all times, everywhere, with the same unaltering needs, emotions, motives, responding differently only to differences of situation and stimulus, or evolving according to some unaltering pattern. For this he substituted (not altogether consciously) the image of man as creative, incapable of self-completion, and therefore never wholly predictable: fallible, a complex combination of opposites, some reconcilable, others incapable of being resolved or harmonized; unable to cease from his search for truth, happiness, novelty, freedom, but with no guarantee, theological or logical or scientific, of being able to attain them: a free, imperfect being, capable of determining his own destiny in circumstances favourable to the development of his reason and his gifts. He was tormented by the problem of free will, and found no better solution for it than anyone else, although at times he thought he had solved it. He believed that it is neither rational thought, nor domination

[1] He goes on: 'Almost all rich veins of original and striking speculation have been opened by systematic half-thinkers.' *Essay on Bentham.*

over nature, but freedom to choose and to experiment that distinguishes men from the rest of nature; of all his ideas it is this view that has ensured his lasting fame.[1] By freedom he meant a condition in which men were not prevented from choosing both the object and the manner of their worship. For him only a society in which this condition was realized could be called fully human. No man deserves commemoration by this Council more than Mill, for it was created to serve an ideal which he regarded as more precious than life itself.

[1] It will be seen from the general tenor of this essay that I am not in agreement with those who wish to represent Mill as favouring some kind of hegemony of right-minded intellectuals. I do not see how this can be regarded as Mill's considered conclusion; not merely in view of the considerations that I have urged, but of his own warnings against Comtian despotism, which contemplated precisely such a hierarchy. At the same time, he was, in common with a good many other liberals in the nineteenth century both in England and elsewhere, not merely hostile to the influence of uncriticized traditionalism, or the sheer power of inertia, but apprehensive of the rule of the uneducated democratic majority, consequently he tried to insert into his system some guarantees against the vices of uncontrolled democracy, plainly hoping that, at any rate while ignorance and irrationality were still widespread (he was not over-optimistic about the rate of the growth of education), authority would tend to be exercised by the more rational, just, and well-informed persons in the community. It is, however, one thing to say that Mill was nervous of majorities as such, and another to accuse him of authoritarian tendencies, of favouring the rule of a rational élite, whatever the Fabians may or may not have derived from him. He was not responsible for the views of his disciples, particularly of those whom he himself had not chosen and never knew. Mill was the last man to be guilty of advocating what Bakunin, in the course of an attack on Marx, described as *la pédanto-cratie*, the government by professors, which he regarded as one of the most oppressive of all forms of despotism.

APPENDIX

(see page 17, note 1)

THIS is not an entirely accurate description of what occurred at the second Congress in 1903. (I owe this information to Mr. Chimen Abramsky's expert knowledge.) According to the official account of the proceedings, Plekhanov made the statement not in answer to a question, but in support of a thesis expressed by a delegate whose name was Mandelberg but who had adopted the *nom de guerre* of Posadovsky. Posadovsky is reported as saying: 'The statements made here for and against the amendments seem to me not mere differences about details, but to amount to a serious disagreement. There is no doubt that we do not agree about the following fundamental question: must we subordinate our future policies to this or that fundamental democratic principle or principles, recognizing them as absolute values; or must all democratic principles be subordinated exclusively to the exigencies of our party? I am quite definitely in favour of the latter. There are absolutely no democratic principles which we ought not to subordinate to the needs of our party.' (Cries of 'And the sanctity of the person?') 'Yes, that too! As a revolutionary party, seeking its final goal—the social revolution—we must be guided exclusively by considerations of what will help us to achieve this goal most rapidly. We must look on democratic principles solely from the point of view of the needs of our party; if this or that claim does not suit us, we shall not allow it. Hence I am against the amendments that have been offered, because one day they may have the effect of curtailing our freedom of action.' Plekhanov merely dotted the i's and crossed the t's of this unequivocal declaration, the first of its kind, so far as I know, in the history of European democracy.

INDEX

OXFORD

MORE OXFORD PAPERBACKS

This book is just one of nearly 1000 Oxford Paperbacks currently in print. If you would like details of other Oxford Paperbacks, including titles in the World's Classics, Oxford Reference, Oxford Books, OPUS, Past Masters, Oxford Authors, and Oxford Shakespeare series, please write to:

UK and Europe: Oxford Paperbacks Publicity Manager, Arts and Reference Publicity Department, Oxford University Press, Walton Street, Oxford OX2 6DP.

Customers in UK and Europe will find Oxford Paperbacks available in all good bookshops. But in case of difficulty please send orders to the Cash-with-Order Department, Oxford University Press Distribution Services, Saxon Way West, Corby, Northants NN18 9ES. Tel: 01536 741519; Fax: 01536 746337. Please send a cheque for the total cost of the books, plus £1.75 postage and packing for orders under £20; £2.75 for orders over £20. Customers outside the UK should add 10% of the cost of the books for postage and packing.

USA: Oxford Paperbacks Marketing Manager, Oxford University Press, Inc., 200 Madison Avenue, New York, N.Y. 10016.

Canada: Trade Department, Oxford University Press, 70 Wynford Drive, Don Mills, Ontario M3C 1J9.

Australia: Trade Marketing Manager, Oxford University Press, G.P.O. Box 2784Y, Melbourne 3001, Victoria.

South Africa: Oxford University Press, P.O. Box 1141, Cape Town 8000.

OPUS

A HISTORICAL INTRODUCTION TO THE PHILOSOPHY OF SCIENCE

John Losee

This challenging introduction, designed for readers without an extensive knowledge of formal logic or of the history of science, looks at the long-argued questions raised by philosophers and scientists about the proper evaluation of scientific interpretations. It offers an historical exposition of differing views on issues such as the merits of competing theories; the interdependence of observation and theory; and the nature of scientific progress. The author looks at explanations given by Plato, Aristotle, and Pythagoras, and through to Bacon and Descartes, to Nagel, Kuhn, and Laudan.

This edition incorporates an extended discussion of contemporary developments and changes within the history of science, and examines recent controversies and the search for a non-prescriptive philosophy of science.

'a challenging interdisciplinary work'
New Scientist

WORLD'S ⚙ CLASSICS
OXFORD

PHYSICS

ARISTOTLE

Translated by Robin Waterfield
Edited with an introduction by David Bostock

This book begins with an analysis of change, which introduces us to Aristotle's central concepts of matter and form, before moving on to an account of explanation in the sciences and a defence of teleological explanation.

Aristotle then turns to detailed, important, and often ingenious discussions of notions such as infinity, place, void, time, and continuity. He ends with an argument designed to show that the changes we experience in the world demand as their cause a single unchanging cause of all change, namely God.

This is the first complete translation of Physics into English since 1930. It presents Aristotle's thought accurately, while at the same time simplifying and expanding the often crabbed and elliptical style of the original, so that it is very much easier to read. A lucid introduction and extensive notes explain the general structure of each section of the book and shed light on particular problems.

OXFORD

RETHINKING LIFE AND DEATH
THE COLLAPSE OF OUR TRADITIONAL ETHICS

Peter Singer

A victim of the Hillsborough Disaster in 1989, Anthony Bland lay in hospital in a coma being fed liquid food by a pump, via a tube passing through his nose and into his stomach. On 4 February 1993 Britain's highest court ruled that doctors attending him could lawfully act to end his life.

Our traditional ways of thinking about life and death are collapsing. In a world of respirators and embryos stored for years in liquid nitrogen, we can no longer take the sanctity of human life as the cornerstone of our ethical outlook.

In this controversial book Peter Singer argues that we cannot deal with the crucial issues of death, abortion, euthanasia and the rights of nonhuman animals unless we sweep away the old ethic and build something new in its place.

Singer outlines a new set of commandments, based on compassion and commonsense, for the decisions everyone must make about life and death.

OPUS

TWENTIETH-CENTURY FRENCH PHILOSOPHY

Eric Matthews

This book gives a chronological survey of the works of the major French philosophers of the twentieth century.

Eric Matthews offers various explanations for the enduring importance of philosophy in French intellectual life and traces the developments which French philosophy has taken in the twentieth century from its roots in the thought of Descartes, with examinations of key figures such as Bergson, Sartre, Marcel, Merleau-Ponty, Foucault, and Derrida, and the recent French Feminists.

'*Twentieth-Century French Philosophy* is a clear, yet critical introduction to contemporary French Philosophy. . . . The undergraduate or other reader who comes to the area for the first time will gain a definite sense of an intellectual movement with its own questions and answers and its own rigour . . . not least of the book's virtues is its clarity.'
Garrett Barden
Author of *After Principles*

Oxford
Paperback
Reference

THE OXFORD DICTIONARY OF PHILOSOPHY

Edited by Simon Blackburn

* 2,500 entries covering the entire span of the subject including the most recent terms and concepts

* Biographical entries for nearly 500 philosophers

* Chronology of philosophical events

From Aristotle to Zen, this is the most comprehensive, authoritative, and up to date dictionary of philosophy available. Ideal for students or a general readership, it provides lively and accessible coverage of not only the Western philosophical tradition but also important themes from Chinese, Indian, Islamic, and Jewish philosophy. The paperback includes a new Chronology.

'an excellent source book and can be strongly recommended . . . there are generous and informative entries on the great philosophers . . . Overall the entries are written in an informed and judicious manner.'
Times Higher Education Supplement

PAST
MASTERS

RUSSELL

A. C. Grayling

Bertrand Russell (1872–1970) is one of the most famous and important philosophers of the twentieth century. In this account of his life and work A. C. Grayling introduces both his technical contributions to logic and philosophy, and his wide-ranging views on education, politics, war, and sexual morality. Russell is credited with being one of the prime movers of Analytic Philosophy, and with having played a part in the revolution in social attitudes witnessed throughout the twentieth-century world. This introduction gives a clear survey of Russell's achievements across their whole range.

KEYNES

Robert Skidelsky

John Maynard Keynes is a central thinker of the twentieth century. This is the only available short introduction to his life and work.

Keynes's doctrines continue to inspire strong feelings in admirers and detractors alike. This short, engaging study of his life and thought explores the many positive and negative stereotypes and also examines the quality of Keynes's mind, his cultural and social milieu, his ethical and practical philosophy, and his monetary thought. Recent scholarship has significantly altered the treatment and assessment of Keynes's contribution to twentieth-century economic thinking, and the current state of the debate initiated by the Keynesian revolution is discussed in a final chapter on its legacy.